Hunting Down Saddam

Also by Robin Moore

The Hunt for Bin Laden: Task Force Dagger

The Green Berets

The French Connection

Hunting Down Saddam

The Inside Story of the Search and Capture

ROBIN MOORE

St. Martin's Press ❧ New York

Title page photograph by AP/Wide World Photos

www.stmartins.com

ISBN 0-312-32916-4

EAN 978-0312-32916-7

First Edition: March 2004

10   9   8   7   6   5   4   3   2   1

CONTENTS

Just after midnight on an early December morning at Baghdad International Airport, my colleague Peter Lofgren and I were waiting patiently onboard a C-130 Hercules cargo aircraft, destined for Kuwait. Without notice, a military chaplain appeared out of the darkness near the ramp of the aircraft, and announced that the plane would be carrying three of our soldiers who had been KIA (Killed in Action). Instantly, there was staunch silence among the fifty or so passengers, the majority in uniform. Following the chaplain's announcement, a provisional honor guard carried onboard the first fallen comrade and rendered honors. Without direction, we rose in unison and snapped to attention, holding a salute as each casket was loaded onto the aircraft.

Stirring and emotional events like these tend to be far removed from the American public. These were America's sons, daughters, fathers, mothers, brothers, and sisters, who placed their lives in jeopardy to uphold the right of freedom.

As a former Special Forces soldier (Command Sergeant Major (D), Ret.), veteran of Operations URGENT FURY, DESERT STORM, and several Special Category Missions, I was honored to be asked to write the foreword to Robin Moore's *Hunting Down Saddam,* a book that brings to light the triumphs and tragedies behind Operation IRAQI FREEDOM and the hunt for Saddam Hussein. Moore is a Special Forces brother, an icon, and esteemed expert on the past and present lineage of Special Forces.

Robin Moore's illustrious career spans four decades as an author and supporter of Special Forces and the U.S. military, and cannot be measured in words or deeds—there are far too many. Moore is the only civilian to have received special permission to attend, and thus pass, the Special Forces Qualification Course and Airborne School. He was subsequently deployed to Vietnam with the 5th SFG (A) to Vietnam in 1964. He used his experiences to bring to the world an inside glimpse into the life of the Green Beret, in his book *The Green Berets*.

I was fortunate to make Robin Moore's acquaintance in 1981 while attending the Special Forces Qualification Course in Fort Bragg, North Carolina. As was true of most other soldiers in my position, Robin Moore and *The Green Berets* meant something to me personally. I remain very proud of Robin's devotion to our country and countrymen who are fighting and supporting the U.S. Global War on Terror (GWOT).

I was with Robin in Iraq in October and November 2003. I was there in my role as Area Security Manager for KBR (Kellogg, Brown & Root), stationed in Tikrit at Camp Speicher/Camp Ironhorse, alongside the U.S. Army's 4th Infantry Division. Robin was there to write this book. For his most recent bestseller, *The Hunt for Bin Laden,* Moore had spent nearly a month living next to the men of the 5th Special Forces Group (A) in Afghanistan. For *Hunting Down Saddam,* Moore did it again. Celebrating his seventy-eighth birthday in Baghdad, and suffering from Parkinson's disease, Moore still had the internal strength and fortitude to obtain firsthand accounts of battlefield experiences of our brave young men and women in uniform. In *Hunting Down Saddam,* he brings to the page his brilliance, authority, and determination in illustrating and capturing significant battles and the daily challenges of the soldiers and leaders of the 3rd, 5th, and 10th Special Forces Groups Airborne, as well as those of the 101st Airborne Assault Division "Screaming Eagles" and the 4th Infantry Division "Regulars," culminating with the capture of Saddam.

The content and characters in *Hunting Down Saddam* are a part of my life. Moore writes of the Green Berets with whom I used to fight, and he writes of the private contractors and reconstruction efforts in Iraq that I am involved with. Moore writes about Major General (MG) Ray Odierno, for whom I served as Force Protection Officer in Operation ALLIED FORCE, in Albania. And he writes of Odierno's 4th ID, who were behind the raid that captured Saddam, and who initially detained him a few hundred meters from my worksite in the Tikrit Palace compound. Incidentally, Robin Moore had spent time here during his trip to Iraq. He was given a tour of the Palace Compound, none of us knowing that Saddam himself would be brought there as a prisoner just seven weeks later.

In typical Robin Moore style, he unflinchingly examines the daring and emotional accounts of our fellow countrymen who are risking their lives as the U.S. military machine accomplishes its first objective of the war, regime change, and progresses toward the arduous objective: building a secure and free Iraq—free from lawlessness, terrorism, and oppression.

War is an exercise in the uncontrollable and unpredictable. War is volatile, unattractive, and disconcerting, at the same time explosive and gripping. Moore chronicles the dimensions of Operation IRAQI FREEDOM and the Global War on Terror, redefines the fundamentals of the unconventional warfare (UW) mission of Special Forces, and underscores the modern-day urban battlefield tactics of light and heavy U.S. Army Divisions. This book is a must-read for those seeking to understand the art of unconventional warfare, one of the premier trademarks of past and present-day Special Forces. Employing modern weaponry, tactics, techniques, and procedures, the outnumbered Green Berets overcame the odds on the battlefield, using nondoctrinal strategies to defeat and outwit the enemy. Although the best technology and weaponry are prolifically applied, the Special Forces credo of brotherhood continues to be the underlying strength that forges the cohesiveness of this special breed of men.

Unpredictably, the challenge to Coalition forces was exponentially increased after President Bush declared the cessation of major combat activity. At home, the American public tuned in and began to express euphoria. All the signs were present, the stock market was up and news broke that our men and women would be coming home soon.

Challenged daily with implausible and hearsay intelligence, the light and heavy forces of the U.S. Army's 101st Airborne Assault Division, led by MG David Petraeus, and the 4th Infantry Division, led by MG Ray Odierno, continued to attack at the heart of the insurgency, initially in a reactionary posture, reacting to the hit-and-run tactics of the Iraqi Fedayeen, Former Regime Loyalists, Al Qaeda, the al-Zarqawi Network as well as Ansar al-Islam, the Syrian Fedayeen, and other outside terrorist groups. Employing hit-and-run tactics, a strategy of guerrilla warfare, these insurgent forces appeared to be gaining an edge on an irregular and undefined battlefield. Attacks were occurring within minutes of each other within a three-hundred-kilometer area; an Area Network, a criterion of UW was now firmly established. Who was leading it? Saddam? Was and is it his remaining generals? How could the Coalition break the back of the insurgency? What level of involvement do outside forces have? Deaths were mounting and the Coalition needed a monumental event to break the will of the insurgency.

The U.S. war machine began to reinsert and employ hard-hitting and aggressive tactics, fueled and achieved through credible and real-time intelligence, and designed to punish those supporting the insurgency. In July of 2003, a series of informants seeking reward money came forth and began providing indeterminate information on the whereabouts of Saddam's sons. The U.S. Army intelligence collection efforts capitalized on this information and began linking the pieces of the puzzle. With what proved to be actionable intelligence, a brigade from the "Screaming Eagles" of the 101st Airborne Assault Division, led by Colonel (COL) Joe Anderson, and the ultrasecret Task Force 20, conducted a successful raid "to capture or kill" Uday and Qusay. This event would achieve a major milestone toward cracking the insurgency's command and control network and span of control in the northern region.

Hunting Down Saddam details the moments prior, during, and after significant victories such as the raid on Uday and Qusay Hussein, the taking of the city of Kirkuk, and, of course, the capture of Saddam himself. But Moore doesn't just simply give us his interpretation of the events; he includes firsthand accounts from soldiers themselves, from an embedded reporter, from a general, a commander, and others. Moore spent time interviewing and visiting the Special Forces (3rd, 5th, and 10th Groups), the 101st Airborne, the 82nd Airborne, the 4th Infantry Division, the security arm of Kellogg, Brown & Root, news stations, and embedded reporters. So many of these groups were eager to share their thoughts and insight into the war effort, providing personal recollections, letters to friends and family, diaries, military reports, after-action journals, and more. For example, Dana Lewis, embedded reporter for NBC and later FOX News, supplied Robin Moore with invaluable personal recollections and an ongoing report of the efforts of the 101st, with which he was stationed.

In an equally significant contribution, Lieutenant Colonel (LTC) Steve Russell, Commander of the "Regulars," 4th Infantry Division, shares the good, the bad, and the horrors of war through a series of personal dispatches. His account of the daily rigors of fighting the counterinsurgency war is an emotional roller-coaster ride, filled with motivating moments of victory and solemn moments of grief and loss. On December 13, 2003, at approximately 2030 hours, after eight months of hunting down Saddam, LTC Russell's cohorts in the 4th ID, led by COL Hickey and working with Task Force 121, finally nab High Value Target #1!

Robin Moore delivers the inside story of the long search for and eventual capture of Saddam Hussein. Transitioning on dangerous supply routes, flying over vulnerable Iraqi airspace, and even experiencing Iraqi insurgency indirect-fire attacks, Moore got the report firsthand, and from our nation's finest men and women. Moore em-

braces his devotion to his country and his craft in bringing the true
story of patriotism to the people of America and beyond.

> *"Let every nation know, whether it wishes us well or ill, that we shall pay any price, bear any burden, meet any hardship, support any friend, oppose any foe to assure the survival and the success of Liberty."*
>
> —John F. Kennedy

ACKNOWLEDGMENTS

With the capture of Saddam Hussein on December 13, 2003, my publisher, St. Martin's Press, and I agreed that this book had to be published much earlier than originally scheduled. This forced my writing partner and me to work nonstop to meet our new deadlines. Consequently, it is not by lack of deeds or valor that many of the units and soldiers who have fought bravely in Iraq are not mentioned specifically in this book. Others, particularly in certain areas of Special Operations, have remained anonymous by their own choosing. Moreover, some dates and place-names have been changed due to Special Operations Security. Nevertheless, we have tried to convey not the entire picture of the war in Iraq, but the parts of it that related to the search and capture of Saddam Hussein, his sons, the fall of Hussein's regime, and a personal portrait of the units that participated in these events.

I want to be sure that my project coordinator and writing partner be duly recognized as the force behind much of the hard work that goes into creating a finished, accurate, and most importantly, engaging and interesting account, which has become the book you are about to read. Chris Thompson was my coauthor and project coordinator on *The Hunt for Bin Laden,* and I could not have trusted anyone else to coordinate the mammoth effort in bringing *Hunting Down Saddam* to fruition.

While I was in Iraq in October and November, visiting bases and interviewing troops, Chris was preparing the material I had previously gathered from earlier in the war. Over the summer I had visited various military posts in the United States, interviewing soldiers returning from Iraq. I was able to get essential material and firsthand accounts from soldiers at Fort Carson, Colorado, home of the 10th Special Forces Group (Airborne); Fort Bragg, North Carolina, home of the 3rd Special Forces Group (Airborne) and the John F. Kennedy (JFK) Special Warfare Center; and Fort Campbell, Kentucky, home of the 5th Special Forces Group (Airborne).

From these visits, copious notes, maps, photos, and audiotapes were gathered. Chris had the daunting task of writing, transcribing, and verifying the accounts of the war's beginning. When I returned from Iraq in November, the final pieces of the book were fitting together. Or so we thought. Less than a month later, Saddam was found cowering in his "spider hole." The discovery changed our deadline drastically, and the book had its dramatic ending.

But now we had the enormous task of transcribing the new set of interviews that were conducted after the capture of Saddam Hussein. Fortunately, Joyce Thomas took over much of the transcribing, and Chris's assistant, E. M. Dubois, helped work on last-minute details and the all-important task of stress management during the manuscript's final days.

I must acknowledge the assistance I received from my good friend Russell Cummings, a former Green Beret himself, who accompanied me to Iraq and was by my side through sandstorms, helicopter trips across enemy territory, insurgent attacks on the compounds we were staying in, and late-night missions. He was able to keep me connected through the computer, no matter if we were staying the night in one of Saddam's palaces, a converted shipping container, or a makeshift hotel room. Russ was both a medic and a trained sniper in the Special Forces; I couldn't have asked for a better companion. His talents did not go unnoticed in Iraq, as he was offered a job with KBR (Kellogg, Brown & Root). Russ is now back in Iraq, working security for KBR.

I am also indebted to my extraordinarily competent literary agent, Sorche Fairbank. This was our fifth—and best—project together. She is an agent who pays attention to fine detail and has won the confidence of many publishers.

Over forty years ago, in my West Indies hangout, I met a lovely English girl of sixteen. I happened to be thirty-five-years old at the time. She was a great companion and a fine water-skier. Her name was Helen Kirkman. Except for a meeting in South Africa, Helen's life remained a mystery to me until last year, when fate brought us together once again. She arrived in the United States forty-two years after we first met and immediately became a major part of my life and a great friend to my Green Beret friends around the country. Before I toured the nation promoting my last book, *The Hunt for Bin Laden,* Helen used her contacts in the business world to help find a British publisher (Pan Macmillan) for the book. Helen's support continued and *Saddam* became the product of our mutual efforts in the literary field.

"It takes a village" has been used in describing efforts as diverse as raising a child, branding a product, fighting a fire, and even throwing a tailgate party. I'd like to add producing this book to the mix. The list of people to whom I became indebted for their assistance could not be written in its entirety, for the list is quite extensive. Nevertheless, I will attempt to name some of them.

I would like to thank St. Martin's Press—especially, Sally Richardson and George Witte for believing in the importance of this book. Diane Higgins, my wonderful editor and guiding hand, deserves much credit and thanks, as does Nichole Argyres, who saw to it that deadlines were met without compromising quality. Thanks, also, to the staff who rallied at St. Martin's to make this book happen, working long evenings and over holiday weekends. My gratitude to Amelie Littell, David Stanford Burr, Jeffrey Capshew, Karen Gillis, Eric Gladstone, Susan Joseph, John Murphy, Joseph Rinaldi, Heather Saunders, and James Sinclair. This is my third book effort with Diane and crew. The ongoing energy and dedication of the staff of St. Martin's Press is worthy of much praise and admiration.

Many thanks are due to FOX Television News, whose fourth-floor headquarters at the Sheraton Hotel where I was staying became an oasis for us while in Baghdad. On my seventy-eighth birthday, the people of FOX News threw a party for me, complete with a bottle of scotch, which slipped down my throat like nectar of the gods. Their own Dana Lewis, whose diary of action with the Screaming Eagles forms an intrinsic part of *Hunting Down Saddam,* deserves great mention for both his contributions and his last-minute, exclusive details regarding Saddam's capture. Dana rode all the way into Baghdad with the 101st Airborne Division; his candid accounts reflect the many faces of war and the emotions that accompany them.

The eighth floor of the Sheraton was home to KBR, whose assistance was invaluable. KBR hosted me in different areas of Iraq and saw to it that I had safe transport during my various interviews. John Jones, Mark Vargas, and the rest of the KBR crew in Iraq, I cannot thank you enough.

Mark Vargas deserves extra mention. A retired Special Forces Command Sergeant Major (CSM), Mark had a unique civilian and military vantage point during Operation IRAQI FREEDOM. As KBR's security manager in Tikrit, he worked side by side with the 4th Infantry Division in what is thought of as the most volatile region in Iraq. He also worked with Iraqi contractors and Iraqi trainees for the new police and security forces. I've known and known of Mark for more than twenty years, and couldn't have chosen a better person to write the foreword to *Hunting Down Saddam.* And I might add, a fortuitous choice it was, as the group of soldiers he worked with on a daily basis were the ones who found and captured Saddam, the only proper ending for this book.

Thanks to MG David Petraeus, commander of the 101st Airborne Division (Air Assault), who gave me an interesting briefing on Mosul and the problems he and his troops were experiencing at the time. He provided an overview of the actions of his group, from the time they crossed over into Iraq from Kuwait until the time they took over Mosul from the Green Berets who had liberated the city.

And thanks to COL "Smokin' Joe" Anderson, commander of the Strike Brigade of the 101st. He deserves great recognition for his part in the demise of Saddam's sons and for his contributions and expertise regarding this historic U.S. Army division.

Heartfelt thanks to LTC Steve Russell and the men of the 1-22 Infantry, 4th ID. When I was leaving FOB Ironhorse in Tikrit, LTC Russell pressed a disc in my hand. He had kept copies of detailed letters he'd sent home, chronicling the war through his and his soldiers' eyes. His letters were an extraordinarily personal glimpse into the war. Understanding the immense value of his words, LTC Russell granted permission to include his letters in the book.

Thanks to Colonel Bob Morris, without whom I would not have been able to make the trip into Iraq, nor have obtained important information on Operation RED DAWN in time. When I learned the Special Forces couldn't sponsor my trip to Iraq on account of my having Parkinson's disease, my longtime friend COL Morris was the man I turned to. Within twenty-four hours, he had arranged full accreditation, visas, and charter airline reservations, and his Partner's International Organization hosted me. Moreover, he quickly arranged my interviews with the 101st Airborne, the 82nd Airborne, and the 4th ID in Iraq. After the capture of Saddam, COL Morris stepped in once again and helped to arrange interviews with the soldiers from the 4th ID, whose accounts of Operation RED DAWN are a vital part of this book. Thanks also go to Captain Allen Roper in Iraq for organizing the Operation RED DAWN telephone interviews, and personally transcribing some.

I would also like to thank Andrew McAleer, a longtime friend, top-notch lawyer, and fellow author who gave up his weekend to notarize documents for my accreditation, without which I would have been stuck.

There are many men in the Special Forces community who also deserve mention and thanks for their invaluable aid—everything from first-rate information to their advice and support during the writing phase. In no particular order, I thank Major (MAJ) Steve Stone (Special Forces, Retired) and the Brothers at the Chapter 38 Team House—their communications network and countless assistance were invaluable. Colonel Michael S. Repass, commander of the 10th Group—an old friend who arranged interviews with members of the 10th Group and 3rd Group stationed there. MAJ Doug Hall—the 10th Group PAO (Public Affairs Officer) who graciously hosted me at Fort Carson, Colorado, and served as a reader and fact checker on an earlier draft of the book. Likewise MAJ Howard, 10th Group, who also provided the excellent briefing on the Special Forces efforts at the beginning of the war. Captain Sean Williams, MAJ Howard's aide at Fort Carson, was a great help while I was there in June 2003. And Sergeant Major (SGM) Tim Strong, who provided much of the layout of the Special Forces mission in northern Iraq. Thanks go as well to LTC Christopher Haas, 5th Group, who described in detail the endeavors of his Special Forces soldiers—from the moment they crossed the berm until the time they converted from warriors to nation builders.

Gratitude is also in order for LTC Angus Taverner, Media Operations Officer for the Ministry of Defence, for his assistance regarding Her Majesty's forces, Lynn and Rachel Thompson, Brigadier General (BG) David P. Burford, Peter Lofgren, Sergeant Major (Retired) William Boggs, Gean Duran (for the "Ace in the Hole"), Sini McKeon, Major General Ken Bowra, and "Wild Bill" Garrison, and all of the PAOs in Iraq who provided escort duty and sightseeing services while I was in the war zone. All of you helped in many important ways to make this book project a reality—from start to finish.

Last, but certainly not least, I must thank my surgeon Dr. Michael Reinhorn and the doctors and staff at Emerson Hospital in Concord, Massachusetts, who saved my life in mid-January, just as we finished the last page of this book. I'd been in a bit of pain for several days, but passed it off as "book indigestion." I was determined we'd meet our deadline. But by that Sunday morning, I was doubled over. After a series of X rays in the emergency room, I was told I had an intestinal blockage and could return home to take a large dose of castor oil. Two hours later there was frantic pounding at my door. A doctor friend, Charlie Maliss, shouted that I must get to the hospital, NOW! My white blood cell count reflected a critical stage of infection. The new diagnosis was a badly infected gall bladder. When my friend Paul Tessier, MD (Special Forces, Retired), heard the news, he immediately drove to the hospital from Maine to be at my side, where he stayed until my discharge. For his wise counsel and steady humor, I am much appreciative. My daughter Margo also dropped everything, including her own sick child, to be with me.

Gallons of antibiotics and the removal of one gangrenous gall bladder later, I am grateful to be able to thank them all.

Prologue

A Special Forces funeral always brings me to tears, and this was no exception. I was at Fort Campbell, Kentucky, with the 5th Special Forces Group (Airborne), who had been deployed in Iraq since they left Afghanistan in May of 2002, and who were the first to go into Iraq before the war was officially declared.

We were here to honor and pay our respects to two Special Forces soldiers who had been killed in a predawn firefight in the Iraqi town of Ramadi, about seventy miles from Baghdad. Seven others from the 3rd Battalion, 5th Special Forces Group were wounded in the raid.

The Special Forces motto, *De Oppresso Liber,* or "To Liberate the Oppressed," was embodied in the deeds of these two fine soldiers who gave the ultimate sacrifice: freeing people from tyranny and oppression—first from the Taliban, and now from Saddam Hussein, and at the expense of their own lives.

Sergeant Major Kenneth W. Barriger was asked to take the roll call of the team of Green Berets to which the fallen soldiers belonged.

As he read off their names one by one, the men attending the funeral of their lost friends replied: "Here, Sergeant Major."

Finally, the sergeant major called the name of Sergeant First Class William Bennett, but there was no reply from the team.

Once again, Sergeant Major Barriger called out "Sergeant First Class Bill Bennett."

Again—no answer.

After a long silence, the sergeant major called out the name of another member of the team.

"Master Sergeant Kevin Morehead."

Once more, a long silence filled the Fort Campbell chapel.

With the answer of a twenty-one-gun salute, the two Green Beret sergeants were accounted for as Killed in Action.

Master Sergeant Kevin Morehead and Sergeant First Class Bill Bennett were two of the first Special Forces men in Afghanistan after the terrorist attacks of September 11. They had been in Afghanistan with Captain Mark Nutsch's team (ODA 595), and went on from there as part of the first Special Forces on the scene of the new war in Iraq.

I had crossed paths with both men while writing *The Hunt for Bin Laden: Task Force Dagger*. Both I and Chris Thompson, my coauthor and project coordinator on the Bin Laden book, had met with their wives only months ago. Bill Bennett was a talented Special Forces Medical Sergeant, in the Army since 1986 and active in numerous overseas deployments and combat operations, including the Gulf War. Kevin Morehead was one of a few Special Forces soldiers who had buried a piece of the World Trade Center in an Afghan battlefield. He was killed two days before his thirty-fourth birthday, and less than two weeks before he was to return home.

Saddam

Saddam Hussein was born on April 28, 1937, in the village of Owja on the outskirts of Tikrit, Iraq, a city northwest of Baghdad. As a young boy, Saddam was raised mainly by his maternal uncle, in the town of ad Dawr, a mud-brick village on the banks of the Tigris River. Saddam Hussein's parents had been simple farmers, but his uncle, an officer in the Iraqi Army, gave him a glimpse of a life other than that of a humble peasant. He greatly influenced the young Saddam and instilled in him a deep passion for politics and the military.

Tikrit had always been Saddam's base of power; his birthplace held a special meaning for him, and was also part of his full name, as is the custom in Iraq: Saddam Hussein (Husayn) al-Tikriti. This connection to place was a part of his very identity. In his teenage years, Saddam moved to Baghdad, where he joined the Arab Socialist Ba'ath Party when he was nineteen years old. The Ba'ath Party was new then, and sought to overthrow the nation's prime minister, Abdul Karim Qassim.

As he entered his twenties, Saddam was ambitious and daring. He knew he did not want a life as a poor peasant or farmer, and the only way he saw out of that was through force. In 1959, when he was twenty-two, Saddam was involved in a brash coup attempt—an attempt to assassinate Prime Minister Qassim. The assassination attempt failed. Saddam was shot in the leg by the prime minister's bodyguard, but fled with his life. Showing a judicious knack for escaping, he fled to Syria.

On February 25, 1960, Iraqi courts sentenced Saddam to death, in absentia, for his part in the failed assassination attempt.

Saddam left Syria shortly after his arrival and journeyed to Egypt, where he studied at Cairo's College of Law. Three years later, his comrades in the Ba'ath Socialist Party were successful, and overthrew Qassim, in what is known as the Ramadan Revolution. Saddam was thrilled, and returned to Iraq, where he was soon elected to a leadership position in the Ba'ath Party. At this point, Saddam was just in his mid-twenties.

A very short time later, in the fall of 1963, Colonel Abd-al-Salam Muhammad Arif, Qassim's partner and co-leader in the coup that brought him to power in 1958, staged a successful coup against the Ba'athists, once again putting Saddam on the run. Colonel Abd-al-Salam Muhammad Arif began rounding up and cracking down on the remaining Ba'athists.

Saddam was not so lucky this time. Arif's men caught up with Saddam several months later, and he was thrown in prison, remaining there for two years. Saddam, determined to survive, escaped from prison. Soon after Saddam's escape, Arif died in a helicopter crash, and was succeeded by his older brother. Arif's brother took over for a very brief reign.

In July of 1968, Saddam and his fellow Ba'athists organized and carried out a successful and bloodless coup, ousting the Arif Regime. Saddam's cousin, General Ahmed Hasan al-Bakr, became the new president of Iraq.

Al-Bakr named his cousin Saddam vice president as well as head of the secret police, or the SSS (Special Security Service), hence controlling internal security and intelligence. Saddam's megalomaniacal vision of power began to manifest itself as he embarked upon an agenda to clean house in the new regime. In his role as head of the SSS, Saddam solidified his role as top enforcer, purging all non-Ba'athist traces of the former regime. He was ruthless. Dozens of Iraqi officials with questionable loyalties were sent into "retirement," imprisoned, or eliminated—the lucky ones were deported or forced to flee the country. Saddam wanted no more coups while he and his family were in power.

As vice president, Saddam wasted no time in trying to remove all possible competition and threat. In 1968, the thirty-year reign of terror began against the Shi'ia "Marsh Arabs" in the south and the Kurdish population in the north. Saddam wanted minorities suppressed by any means necessary—all under the umbrella of what Saddam called his "Arabization" Project, an agenda with all too familiar echoes of Nazi Germany.

Hundreds of thousands of non-Ba'athist citizens and Iraqis of non-Arab descent were arrested, deported, or killed. Entire Shi'ia Muslim and Kurdish villages were burned to the ground in a scorched earth strategy, though not before anything of value was carted away and split up between Saddam's most trusted personnel as a "reward" for their loyalty. Families, entire generations, were wiped out. Those targeted who were not murdered by Saddam's secret police or quick enough to flee were tortured and imprisoned.

Oil was, and is, Iraq's number one commodity by a significant margin. Since the fall of the Ottoman Empire in 1918, foreign oil companies maintained a constant presence in Iraq. Saddam wanted them out. In 1972, he led an effort to nationalize all of the foreign oil companies, thereby consolidating Iraq's wealth into a monopoly for the Ba'athists.

In July of 1979, al-Bakr resigned, and Saddam Hussein became the new president of Iraq. By now, the SSS (also known as the SSO) had been beefed up by Saddam, expanded and designed to be led by those whom Saddam was confident he could trust. To ensure that security, there once again was a wave of purging and murdering those in his ranks whose loyalty was not 100 percent ascertained. Saddam went on to ban the opposing political party, the Da'wa Party. Membership in its ranks was a capital crime, punishable by death.

The Shatt al-Arab waterway lies near the border of Iran and Iraq. It is here that the Tigris and Euphrates Rivers meet, at a place called al Qurnal. From al Qurnal, the river flows into the Persian Gulf; the Iranians claimed it was on their land, while Iraq felt it was on theirs. In September 1980, scarcely over a year after being named president, Saddam declared war against their big neighbor to the east. The Iraqi Army, surprisingly strong from oil wealth, routed the Iranians, forcing them back from the waterway. But Iran, a country over three times bigger in land mass and population, was not to be so easily defeated. Although the Iranian Army was not as sophisticated and organized as Iraq's, Iran had a steady supply of zealous warriors and eager martyrs.

By 1984, the war was only half over, and it wasn't going so well for Iraq. The Iranians had turned the tables on the war, and were invading Iraqi soil. Basra, Iraq's largest southern city, and less than fifteen miles from the Iranian border, was hit hard. The seesawing war continued, while the threat to Saddam compounded with new waves of Kurdish insurgencies in the north. Feeling collapse nigh, Saddam chose to deploy chemical warfare in the form of poison gas against the Iranian invaders, as well as against the Kurdish opposition. The results were a success for Saddam, and they were horrific. In one Kurdish village alone, Halabaja, an estimated five thousand people were killed, and more than twice that injured. An untold total number of Iranians and Kurds perished in Saddam's chemical attacks. By the end of the Iran-Iraq War in 1988, the casualties were estimated to be between 1 and 1.5 million people.

Two years later, Saddam sealed his fate with the world community when he invaded Kuwait on August 2, 1990. Saddam used many reasons to justify his action, but was steadfast on his claim that Kuwait was the 19th province of Iraq. Powers from the United States and the United Nations tried reasoning with him, but to no avail.

The invasion of Kuwait posed a number of threats that got the attention of the United States—not the least of which was the threat to Saudi Arabia, and in turn, the United States led a coalition force against the invading Iraqis. On January 17, 1991, the Persian Gulf War began with a massive air campaign. Five weeks later, the ground war started, and within seventy-two hours, Kuwait was liberated. Tens of thousands of Iraqi troops were killed, wounded, or taken prisoner.

Iraq signed a cease-fire agreement on March 3, 1991, the conditions of which included Saddam destroying all of his WMDs (Weapons of Mass Destruction, such as the poison gas he used in the 1980s on the Kurds and the Iranians). It called for a cease to his ruthless persecution of ethnic minority groups, and the return of any captured prisoners, all of which Saddam agreed to. Nevertheless, Saddam was not a man of his word, and he quickly crushed a Kurdish insurrection in the north and a Shi'ia rebellion in the south.

The massacre of the two groups put the world leaders on notice once again. This time the United Nations imposed the Northern and Southern No-Fly Zones across the north and south of Iraq so that Saddam would be unable to murder his own minority groups. Operations SOUTHERN WATCH and NORTHERN WATCH were put into place by the United States and the United Nations to police the adherence to the no-fly zones.

For not living up to a single promise on the cease-fire agreement, the UN imposed economic and military sanctions on Iraq. As the situation for his people got worse and worse, the more lavish and opulent Saddam and his inner circle became. For twelve years, Saddam did not budge. These sanctions severely punished the Iraqi people, yet Saddam would rather starve his own population than give in to the world's demands for justice.

On November 8, 2002, UN Security Council Resolution 1441 was passed, which stated that for twelve years, Saddam had been in "material breach" of every agreement that had been made at the end of the Persian Gulf War. Saddam had twelve years to live up to his end of the bargain, and failed to do so, on every single count.

In the years between the end of the Persian Gulf War and the start of Operation IRAQI FREEDOM, Saddam's Iraq was hit with three sets of major air strikes. Still, Saddam held fast as his people continued to starve and buckle under the weight of his oppression. With the Global War on Terror (GWOT) underway in the wake of 9/11, President George W. Bush decided that something more had to be done. Saddam not only laughed in the face of the world's demands and continued the slaughter of his own people, he also harbored terrorist cells such as Ansar al-Islam, and there was mounting intelligence that pointed to Saddam acquiring components of nuclear materials (Russian U-235 weapons-grade uranium) by way of Djibouti. President George Bush II was about to finish what his father had started. . . .

A Score to Settle

Two years after George W. Bush was inaugurated president of the United States, the antagonistic relations that had been smoldering between the United States and Iraq finally burst into incandescence. On March 20, 2003, at 2045 hours EST, President George W. Bush's Gulf War Two, or GW2 as it was informally dubbed, lit up the desert skies and the sprawling Iraqi capital of Baghdad, becoming full-fledged declared war.

Earlier that day, at 0545 hours local Iraq time, President Bush covertly sent five Special Forces ODAs (Operational Detachment Alpha) from the 10th SFG (Special Forces Group)—stationed at Fort Carson, Colorado—into northern Iraq. At the same time, he sent the 5th SFG (A), accompanied by the Florida National Guard, from Kuwait into the western desert of Iraq, and revved up the Air Force to maximum capacity. At last, the president of the United States would put an end to the Iraqi threat.

The U.S.-led coalition had forced Saddam Hussein out of Kuwait during the first Gulf War, but the coalition stopped short of going into Baghdad after a badly defeated Iraqi Army streamed home. The senior George Bush said that the United Nations, under whose mandate the American military was operating, had only called for removing Saddam from Kuwait, not for removing the dictator from his own country.

Ten years later, his son, George W. Bush, realized that Saddam was indeed plotting mass destruction of his enemies in Middle Eastern and world affairs. And Saddam was acquiring the weapons of mass destruction to do just that—almost daily, the White House received ominous warnings.

Through Djibouti, on the Horn of Africa, cargo planes were landing for refueling and maintenance. Spies from Somalia, with leanings toward the United States, warned that there was at least one transport aircraft landing in Djibouti each week, from Russia. These planes were landing with large refrigeration systems, which had to be attached to ground electrical systems to keep them working. One crew member was watching at all times, to make sure the refrigeration units were operative.

This could only mean that radioactive and nuclear substances were being transported. These shipments were being paid for with large amounts of U.S. dollars originating from Saddam's oil-smuggling operations based in Basra, Iraq's Arabian Gulf port. The administration could no longer risk standing by until Saddam was able to launch a nuclear weapon toward any part of the world.

Special Forces Groups left the United States over a week before, scheduled to fly into Iraq. They were planning to take off from the large airbase the United States had rebuilt in Kosovo, the former Yugoslavian military headquarters brought down by NATO. The 10th Special Forces Group ended up leaving for Iraq from Constanta, Romania, that very day.

Special Forces Companies, or B-Teams (ODBs), are comprised of a group of A-Teams under them, much like the Army has platoons. One Company Commander—generally a major—has up to six A-Teams or ODAs in his command. SGM (Sergeant Major) Tim Strong was the noncommissioned officer in charge of the B-Team, comprising the five A-Teams of this first expeditionary force of Green Berets to openly invade northern Iraq. The five ODAs were not all from the same company. SGM Tim Strong and his B-Team were only the skeleton of the company that would soon be augmented by thousands of native Kurdish tribesmen. Known as Peshmerga, the Kurd warriors

were indigenous to the mountainous area in the north of Iraq, and almost immune to the raids of ordinary Iraqi soldiers. They collectively
hated the lowlanders whose leader, Saddam Hussein, and his cousin,
"Chemical Ali," had launched the gas attack that had killed thousands
of Kurds in the late 1980s.

Before the five A-Teams could go into action against the Iraqis,
they had to reach their destination as quietly as possible, and meet up
with the awaiting Peshmerga and their commander of the Irbil sector,
General Mustafa.

In England, at Biggin Hill, an airbase about forty miles north of Lon-
don, LTC (Lieutenant Colonel) Mark Alsid was one of the pilots who
fly the particularly dangerous and most difficult missions the U.S. Air
Force has to offer, as part of the 352nd Special Operations Group
(SOG). This was to be no exception. Alsid took off from Constanta,
Romania, with four other American pilots, each piloting a huge
MC-130 transport filled with crew and supplies to be used by the
A-Teams.

At the same time, units from the Florida National Guard were waiting to cross from Kuwait into southern Iraq, and start the march to
Baghdad. Also waiting in the wings for their cue into Iraq were the
British Royal Marines, Parabats (Parachute Battalions) and Tank
Regiment—their job being to control the southern port of Basra and
secure the route past it for the Florida National Guard, who would
head up to Baghdad. With everything prepared and ready, the forces
poised to invade Iraq had nothing to do but wait—a common malaise
at the beginning of wartime action.

While the Special Forces were waiting for the "green light," or go-
ahead, the intelligence contingents were scratching their heads, wondering if they could perhaps knock out Saddam Hussein and prove
he'd been killed—thus ending the war before it started.

As the 10th Group ODAs waited with their pilots, ready to fly, a
top-secret group made up of Special Forces and Delta Force was on
patrol inside of Baghdad, hoping to determine Saddam Hussein's ex-

act location. As they interrogated their assets regarding the dictator's present whereabouts, they finally got a break—a clue as to where Saddam was at that very moment. They learned he was most likely deep down in the subbasement structure of the house of a Ba'ath Party general, a veritable underground fortress and bomb shelter, with fifty-foot-deep roots. Relaying the information to call in Close Air Support (CAS) attachments, the Special Forces intelligence group moved as far away from the target area as possible. No one wanted to be taken out by friendly fire or stray bombs dropped by their own planes before the war even began.

Task Force 20 (the super-secret Special Operations Task Force with one purpose: hunting down Saddam and his henchmen) gave the go-ahead, and a two-thousand-pound smart bomb was dropped from an F-117/A Nighthawk, directly onto the house where Saddam was suspected to be hiding. The entire city shook as the JDAM (Joint Direct Attack Munitions) bomb hit and exploded after penetrating close to one hundred feet into the ground.

If the dictator was in or near the building that was destroyed, he would never be seen again.

And this was the problem. It appeared that Saddam might well have been killed and his body destroyed beyond all recognition—in fact, it seemed probable that this was the case. But where, then, was the all-important proof? Within a day, possible Saddam look-alikes began to appear. There was simply no telling whether he was alive or not, and thus Saddam's army was itself doubtful whether to resist the anticipated invasion, or to give up and surrender, saving their lives.

For days following the bombing, Iraqi officials were effectively doing their job, broadcasting that Hussein was alive and well. This type of propaganda continued throughout the war. Later, Baghdad Bob, a self-appointed spokesman and ultimately a spot of comic relief, joined the fray, reporting to Iraqi citizens and the rest of the world that not only was Saddam Hussein alive and well, but that there were absolutely no Americans or any foreign troops in Baghdad. Directly behind him and all around him, American and British tanks and troops proved otherwise.

Task Force VIKING

Concede Nothing

On March 20, 2003, at 1930 hours local Iraq time, five MC-130 "Combat Talon" transport planes from the U.S. Air Force's 352nd Special Operations Group lifted off from a runway in Constanta, Romania. The first three specially modified transport planes held members of the 10th SFG (A), the last two were loaded with members of the 3rd Battalion, SFG (A).

All were now part of the same task force, the "Combined Joint Special Operations Task Force-North," or CJSOTF-N. For security, the planes split into two groups, and flew different routes. The first three Talons flew a tedious, low-level, three-and-a-half-hour route, nicknamed "The Ugly Baby," north along the Syrian-Iraq border before banking east and into the northern tip of Iraq.

The three planes were cross-loaded with half of the members of five ODAs (Operational Detachment Alpha, or A-Teams) on each plane, and half of a B-Team, or ODB, on each plane, along with the B-Team's communication augmentation and equipment. Altogether, there were about sixty A-Team operators and fourteen to sixteen B-Team members. If one of the birds went down, only a part of each A-Team and a part of the B-Team would be lost.

Correspondingly, the commander of the newly formed CJSOTF-N,

Task Force VIKING

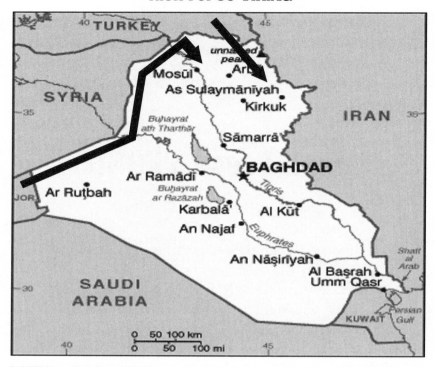

CJSOTF-N, or Task Force VIKING, was comprised of members of the 3rd and 10th Special Forces Groups (Airborne). They infiltrated into northern Iraq through two routes: The "Ugly Baby," through Turkey into the As-Sulaymaniyah region, and through "SAM Alley," along the Syria-Iraq border, into the Duhok Airfield, northeast of Mosul. *Courtesy:* CIA World Factbook 2003

COL (Colonel) Charles Cleveland, flew in the first MC-130, and the Company SGM Tim Strong followed behind in the second. Keeping the commander and the sergeant major on separate planes was part of the SOP (Standard Operating Procedure) for Special Forces.

CJSOTF-N was code-named Task Force VIKING. Their motto was "Concede Nothing." They would live up to that name in the weeks to come. True to their fearless credo, one of TF VIKING's fire bases—a temporary front-lines camp where Special Forces soldiers live while in their AO (Area of Operations)—Fire Base Zeb, had a cardboard sign fashioned by a Green Beret from ODA 065 that read:

"WE'RE 065 AND THIS IS AS FAR AS THOSE
BASTARDS ARE GOING!"

SAM Alley

The 352nd Special Operations Group's adept pilots flew the "Ugly Baby" route from Constanta, Romania, totally blacked out, with no lights at all, first along Jordan's border, then along the Syria-Iraq border, before banking straight east into northern Iraq into what SF operators deemed "SAM Alley." SAMs, or Surface-to-Air missiles, were one of the main concerns during the white-knuckled infiltration into Iraq.

AAA (Anti-aircraft artillery) soon became the bigger concern, as battery after battery of enemy AAA guns fired salvos of shells at the MC-130s as they flew along SAM Alley. The Air Force pilots' quick-thinking solution was to dive the plane low to the ground, bringing the Talons' flight paths under the Iraqi AAA guns' arc of fire. Once raised into position, one SF operator explained, the enemy artillery pieces could not be quickly lowered, so their arcs of fire went right over the top of the MC-130s.

"How we survived that triple-A fire, we'll never know, to this day," SGM Tim Strong later recalled.

The first MC-130 to cross the Iraqi radar screens along "SAM Alley" set off the warning systems on Iraqi radar. The AAA began to fire, and the second plane flew under the arc of the guns. The third plane was not so lucky, as the anti-aircraft gunners finally zeroed in.

The third Combat Talon was hit by flak from one of seven batteries of Iraqi AAA flak as it flew through Iraqi airspace north of Mosul. The pilot rerouted to Turkey for an emergency landing, with more than forty holes in the aircraft's skin, the largest over a foot and a half in diameter. Luckily, all forty-eight of the crippled MC-130's passengers safely landed in Turkey.

The first and second MC-130s made it all the way past Mosul and into Bashir airfield unscathed. The 10th Special Forces Group's commander, now the commander of CJSOTF-N, recalled that at the time, he had no way of knowing the status of the other two MC-130s of the group, which were assigned to 3rd Battalion, 10th SFG (A) and infiltrated into Iraq along a new flight path to different coordinates. The rumor had been that they also made it into Iraq in one piece; thankfully this proved to be true. Their planes were destined for As-Sulaymaniyah to the east, where they landed without incident.

Three ODAs, including ODA 043 and ODA 045, were already inside Iraq and had linked up with Kurdish Irbil sector commander General Mustafa, when the last two birds touched down, bringing the strength of 10th SFG (A) in northwestern Iraq up to 108 men, a total of nine A-Teams, of a dozen Green Berets each. ODA 043 and ODA 045 later became a QRF (Quick Reaction Force) that could be called in to back up another A-Team if they were overwhelmed. They also had the secondary function as a Combat Reconnaissance Force (CRF). As a CRF, they would be called upon for their firepower more than a few times in the following days of battle. As a CRF, ODA 043 and ODA 045 would do reconnaissance missions of enemy positions in their armed Land Rovers and call in CAS.

The ODAs were also supplemented by Air Force Combat Controllers. An Air Force Combat Controller is a single Air Force man attached to an A-Team for the purpose of bringing the bombs in precisely on target. This brought the total strength of Task Force VIKING to twenty ODAs in northern Iraq.

General Mustafa

After touching down on their Landing Zone (LZ) at Bashir airfield at approximately 0130 hours on March 23, the five newly arrived A-Teams and their Operational Detachment B-Team (ODB) loaded into the waiting vehicles and began a long, grueling drive along winding mountain roads to General Mustafa's compound, northeast of Irbil.

There, in the dawn's early light, they discussed their first moves with Mustafa and his commanders. Most of the men had yet to see the country they had just invaded. Within hours of this first meeting, the A-Teams moved out to the battlefield to join the Peshmerga guerrilla warriors in their defensive positions, known as TAIs, or Targeted Areas of Interdiction.

In Kurdish culture, the name Peshmerga means "ready to die," or "those who face death." The Peshmerga are a faction of Kurdish people indigenous to northern Iraq and Kurdistan. Historical records make note of the Kurds as far back as 3000 B.C. Even in those early times, they had a reputation as fierce warriors, though largely in the context of defending their own territory. The Peshmerga (or "Pesh," as the Green Berets took to calling them) belong to one of two key political groups in northern Iraq: the KDP, or Kurdistan Democratic Party (largely in the western Kurdish Autonomous Zone, where the 2nd BN 10th SFG were located), and the PUK, or Patriotic Union of Kurdistan (largely in the eastern Kurdish Autonomous Zone, where the 3rd BN 10th SFG were located). The KDP and the PUK, on and off again at war with each other, are now united in opposition to Saddam's regime.

The Peshmerga under General Mustafa's command were only too glad to join the Special Forces in the efforts to oust the dictator who had wreaked such harm upon them. As one 10th Group operator recalled: "General Mustafa ran the whole sector, so we co-located with [him]. That way we could basically do a combined campaign with the Kurds. [Mustafa] set us up, and had no problem giving us whatever support we needed."

General Mustafa was a quiet, soft-spoken man, and when the Green Berets first linked up with him, some were unsure if he was the right guy. But they soon learned that behind Mustafa's soft-spoken demeanor stood thousands of battle-hardened fighters who would fight and die for him and for the Green Berets of TF VIKING.

General Mustafa had been an Iraqi POW for six years and had no fond feelings toward Saddam and his regime. According to the SF operators who dealt with him, Mustafa was a very scrupulous and honorable man. And the Special Operators on the ground made it clear that the Kurds were a great and invaluable asset. When the Green

Berets asked for their support, the Kurds would show up, almost always without hesitation and with little in the way of negotiations—ready and willing.

By dinnertime (1800) on March 23, the ODAs were already in place with their new Pesh allies on the hilltops of northern Iraq. One such A-Team, ODA 056, linked up with the Peshmerga on a hilltop OP (Observation Post) named "Hill 725." ODA 056's team leader (a captain), its assistant detachment commander (a warrant officer), and team sergeant (a master sergeant) conducted a leader's recon to determine their plan of attack. Because of the extremely muddy terrain on the hill, the rest of the ODA turned their SUVs around and headed back to Duhok.

During the night, a nearby Peshmerga checkpoint was hit with two incoming Iraqi artillery rounds, but it was already clear that the Coalition was attacking in full force: Mosul, the northern Iraqi stronghold, was lit up by American bombing runs that were clearly visible in the distance to the west, to the A-Teams in Duhok.

At 0500, the next morning, March 24, the Special Operators of Task Force VIKING began calling in CAS (close air support) on Iraqi positions near the Peshmerga's defensive lines, from the top of Hill 725. It took a great deal of convincing to get General Mustafa to understand the magnitude of the technology and firepower that the Special Forces could wield in the form of CAS and man-portable Javelin Weapons Systems.

At first, General Mustafa and his staff thought that with just a few handfuls of Green Berets the Iraqi armor units would just roll right over them if they tried to mount an offensive. But soon, General Mustafa had his first taste of U.S. firepower in action. In the Irbil sector, the 2nd BN 10th SFG called in two American F/A-18 Hornets. Their mission was to clear the ridgeline overlooking the Northwest Irbil Airfield to allow the unimpeded flow of military and humanitarian aid. The F/A-18s dropped two five-hundred-pound bombs on the enemy positions, killing eight Iraqis and wounding sixteen.

Later in the day, in the eastern sector, ODA 056 spotted enemy troop movements and positions to the north of the town of Ayn Sifni from their hilltop OP. But by that time, winds were gusting fiercely between 15 and 30 knots, and the weather grew cold and overcast. The next three days were even cloudier, and CAS was ruled out completely until March 29.

April Fool's Day

Good weather for the Green Berets and their CAS missions was vital. Clouds, rain, and fog lead to poor visibility; heavy winds could affect accuracy. As demonstrated in the following excerpt from an ODA's daily BDA (Bomb Damage Assessment) journal, the correlation between weather and success is a strong one. It is particularly evident on April 1, when the Special Forces had the chance to target hundreds of Iraqi soldiers at once, had only the weather permitted.

25 March 2003
—*Maintained observation of TAI 2 and OP site. No air due to weather—overcast.*

26 March 2003
—*Maintained two OP sites—Hill 725 overlooking TAI 2 intersection and vic LF531707 overlooking north of Ayn Sifni. Targets have been plotted but still no air.*

27 March 2003
—*0500Z, CW2* **[censored]**, *SFC* **[censored]**, *and SSG* **[censored]** *move off OP site, move back to 12th Supay Barracks for refit, still no air.*

28 March 2003
—*0600Z, went to Duhok to speak to the CDR about air and then back up to Hill 725.*

29 March 2003

—*1400Z, Still operating OP on Hill 725 and established a new OP site vic. Peshmerga checkpoint below Hill 725. Received CAS with 2 × F-18s at 2030Z (dropped 2 × 500lb JDAMS & 6 × 500lb LGBU) on bunker complex N of Ayn Sifni. Then worked a B-52 w/ 12 × 2000lb JDAMS (dropped 6 bombs on EN positions at 2230Z, 24 EN KIA, 50 EN WIA and 6 bombs on a suspected logistics site).*

30 March 2003

—*1400Z, moved 3 man OP vic. 512673 still continue to observe TAI 2 from main OP on 725.*

31 March 2003

—*0400Z, CAS with 2 sorties; 2 × F-14s and 2 × F/A-18s 6 × 500lb bombs dropped vic. Hill 613 (5 KIA & 10 WIA).*
—*1100Z, IZ moved two 57mm ADA pieces to the west of Ayn Sifni, OP on 725 worked 2 × F-14s dropping 8 × 500lb bombs— destroying 1 × 57mm. (AC[-130] had hard time identifying second 57mm and hit the destroyed 57mm 4 additional times).*
—*1600Z, CAS with 2 × F/A-18s 2 × 2000lb JDAMS dropped on Hill 613, slightly off target.*

01 April 2003

—*0900Z, begin observation of what appears to be a withdrawal by the Iraqis from positions 5 kms south of OP 725, sent SALUTE to higher, requested CAS, "NO CAS" and then watched 500 Iraqi soldiers load 6 buses and safely depart area heading south towards Mosul.*
—*1100Z, conducted recon along east ridgeline of Hill 725, for possible Raid.*

Kirkuk

Route 4 runs from Chamchamal to As-Sulaymaniyah, going through a mountain pass with steep, near-impassable angles that are a fatal "choke point" to any attacking force. The Kurds had always held their ground here; the Iraqis had never made it up this far. If an armored force such as Saddam's army ever made it as far as the pass on Route 4, it would be routed at once. The last great wide-open area was a ridgeline far to the south, which lay in front of Kirkuk. This was where the Iraqi Army had been massed for the last ten years.

Oil-rich Kirkuk had been home to the Iraqi 8th Infantry Division and the Iraqi 5th Mechanized (Motorized) Infantry Divisions. Through the years of fighting against the Peshmerga, they had moved little by little up Route 4, all the way to the pass into As-Sulaymaniyah, where they could go no farther. What was now left was more a unit of stragglers than a combat-effective force. The Green Berets of 3rd SFG (A) made short work of the remaining Iraqi forces, with CAS in the first few days after they had arrived, though the Iraqis tried to hold their ground on Route 4. This showed the PUK that the operators were worth their weight in gold, and they took them up to where the real fight would be—Chamchamal.

Chamchamal sat on the main road, some twenty-five miles east of Kirkuk City. The ultimate objective of seizing Kirkuk went hand in hand with 10th SFG (A)'s objective of liberating Mosul—the two northern cities would be used to resupply and reinforce army units in Baghdad once the ground war began to make its way northward from Kuwait and Saudi Arabia.

Chamchamal was a far cry from As-Sulaymaniyah, which sat in the protected northeast corner of the Kurdish autonomous zone. In As-Sulaymaniyah, the city was clean. There were Internet cafés on practically every corner, satellite television was popular, and children attended schools in uniforms that reminded the Green Berets of American parochial schools. Chamchamal was the polar opposite. It was not in the safe haven of well within the no-fly zone. It was on the very fringes of Saddam's Iraq, and here the Peshmerga people felt his brutality the keenest.

The green line (the area that unofficially separated "Kurdish territory") ran directly through the town of Chamchamal. A ridge to the immediate west of Chamchamal was home to a dug-in, completely fortified Iraqi Army battalion. That was their deliberate defense, and unknowingly their closest line of troops to the newly arrived Green Berets. These Iraqi positions had been manned for over a decade: well-reinforced bunkers, many trench lines, huge minefields, and one thousand five hundred meters of "no-man's-land" directly in front of it.

The Green Berets found a perfect home—a castle right in Chamchamal. The Special Operators watched the Iraqis across the flat, land mine–infested no-man's-land from the parapets, and calculated their first moves. More soldiers watched from rooftops.

No-man's-land was ruined ground; sheep and cattle could not graze on it, and it was hated and feared as much by the people of Chamchamal as it was by the Iraqi soldiers who occupied the mountainside to the west. Not only did the minefields of the no-man's-land frighten the people, but Iraqi troops had for years fired random shots from their trenches into the town on nothing more than a whim.

Chamchamal was described by one of the Green Berets from ODA 083 as "comparable to 'Barter Town,'" which was featured in the 1985 Mel Gibson film *Mad Max Beyond Thunderdome*. When the Special Operators arrived in the spring of 2003 it was nearly deserted, yet it had once been home to over fifty thousand inhabitants.

By April of 2003, after a decade of constant threat, the number of inhabitants had dwindled to only a few hundred solemn-faced Peshmerga fighters, who walked the streets with AK-47s and other rifles slung on their backs. No one stood around idly, and the only event that happened like clockwork, sadly enough, was that the Iraqis shelled the town daily between 1700 and 1800 hours.

The Peshmerga had set up a vehicle checkpoint right on the edge of town, fashioned out of an old Conex-style metal shipping container. In the words of one of the operators, "That [Conex] had been hit with so many mortars [rounds] . . . I don't know what kind of crazy guys could use that [Conex] as a vehicle checkpoint, because basically it was used for target practice by the Iraqis." It resembled Swiss cheese, totally mangled beyond recognition.

The road from Chamchamal wound west to Kirkuk through a small mountain pass. On the other side of the pass, less than a thousand meters away, sat the Iraqi checkpoint on the Kirkuk side. The Iraqis could have rolled over Chamchamal at any point, but had chosen instead to keep the citizens of the Peshmerga town under constant threat.

The condition of the Iraqi soldiers on the ridgelines, however, was worse than the condition of the Peshmerga. The bunkers the Iraqis were forced to live in as they held guard over the town and gateway to Kirkuk were "horrible . . . terrible," according to a Green Beret who witnessed the spartan squalor of the Iraqi bunkers firsthand.

Upon arrival, the Kurds of Chamchamal were wary of the Green Berets. "You never really could trust who was who in that town," explained a Special Operator. The town's population was made up of all male soldiers, so there was always the chance that one of the denizens was an Iraqi agent. If the word got out that there were American soldiers present in the town, it could spark an offensive by the Iraqi Army. Tensions ran extremely high.

The members of ODA 083 dressed like Peshmerga, and were led at night to a rooftop where they could spot the Iraqi battalion on the ridgeline across the no-man's-land. The next day, every Iraqi position was targeted. It was a free observation post, and the Iraqi emplacements were close enough to be visible to the naked eye.

Coupled with NRO (National Reconnaissance Office) satellite imagery that the team had brought with them, the targeting process became very easy. Targeting enemy positions with just a map alone was far more difficult, and the chance of misreading the map or the terrain (especially in an area with similar landmarks) not only increased the chance of a miss, but could potentially increase the chance of friendly fire. Friendly fire had devastated the men of ODA 574 in Afghanistan, and accidentally killing Kurds would be just as horrific. A rapport had not yet been developed, and as the 10th SFG were learning in their sector, a mistake of this kind could potentially be quite costly.

What wasn't clearly mapped out from NRO imagery was clearly explained by the Peshmerga HUMINT (Human Intelligence). They had been facing these Iraqis for more than a decade. The Pesh knew exactly what every building contained, and if one bunker looked like a company command post, but was virtually indistinguishable from the one next to it, the answer was given to the Green Berets. Whether it was water-pumping stations or anything else, the PUK militia knew the layout. Previously, the Kurds had been unable to act on their intelligence; now it was put to good use. The permanently fixed Iraqi targets wouldn't know what had hit them when the Special Forces were through.

Not only did the Pesh know every nook and cranny of the Iraqi complex, they knew every path that would take the Special Operators to whichever destination in the immediate area that they wanted, and safely. Trust and the initial rapport were forged with the Kurds, which was difficult. Though a little leery at first, the Pesh proved to be very helpful.

The Kurds in the 3rd SFG (A)'s Area of Operations were right in the middle of Saddam's "Arabization" Project. Most, if not all of them, were displaced refugees. They were very motivated to get back their land, and most importantly, their oil-rich city of Kirkuk. A tie to certain areas unfathomable to most people drove the Kurds to want their land back more than anything.

At secret meetings with PUK representatives, the Special Forces were surprised by how Saddam's legacy of brutality hit home for the Peshmerga in the region. Almost every single one of the Kurds sitting around the table had a story of how Saddam and his regime had killed a loved one. This war was personal.

One Green Beret said it best: "I did not meet a single Kurdish male between the ages of fifteen and sixty that had not either been in prison and tortured, at one point in time or another, or that had a brother or father killed [by Saddam]."

The same operator's interpreter had been in prison four years, and tortured the entire time. According to Amnesty International reports, favored methods used by the SSS included beatings on the feet, extinguishing cigarettes on the soles of the feet and all over the body, beatings on the back with cables, hoses, canes, and other objects, pulling out fingernails and toenails, and applying electric current to the victim's genitalia.

The interpreter had scars all over his body from various torture methods, and both his father and brother had been murdered. Saddam's SSS had found out that he was part of the resistance. That was the price he paid for wanting freedom and autonomy for his people. There was a brief amnesty period, where the Iraqi government was to treat the Kurds like "ordinary citizens," but brief it was. Rumors abounded that it had been a ploy to gather intelligence on, and identify, Kurdish leaders who were then swept up and tortured.

The goal of the "Arabization" Project was to concentrate the Kurds into several large population centers. Saddam's regime had destroyed over a thousand villages in the Chamchamal sector alone. The usual method was for the Iraqi government to move all of the people out of their homes before bulldozing them to the ground. Nothing was left of the villages. Once a sector was razed and "cleared," anyone caught back in the area of his or her village was immediately killed. With the Kurds concentrated in certain spots, they could be "killed wholesale."

The stories of torture and murder reminded the Green Berets of the genocide of the Jews in Nazi Germany. This included the infamous poison gas/chemical warfare attacks on entire populations, which were an experiment in the killing effectiveness versus the effort which Saddam's forces wanted or needed to expend. The Kurds were so spooked by their experiences with gas attacks that any white smoke or dust caused them to panic. Lining up the Kurds in front of trenches and shooting them, or telling the Kurds to get into the trenches first, before shooting them, was also a common story. Later, when Kirkuk itself was liberated, one Green Beret described the city as being filled with mass graves.

"Everywhere you went, you were tripping over a mass grave," he said. The Kurds told the Special Forces that the toll stood at over

250,000 of their people killed by Saddam. At first, the operators thought that number might be inflated, but after seeing the mass graves firsthand, it was easy to agree.

In 1991, after Saddam had beaten down the Kurdish people through "Arabization," no-man's-land zones were put up between the Kurdish autonomous zones and the borders of the Iraqi regime.

The chance that the Kurds might seek vengeance was a real cause for concern with the Green Berets, so they explained that the United States, and its laws of warfare, did not permit or tolerate such atrocities. The Kurds agreed. On the whole, they did not want to sink to Saddam's level, no matter how terribly they themselves had been treated.

The more the newly arrived Green Berets learned of the Kurdish mind-set and their chief political party in that sector, the PUK, the more they understood. They wanted to take part in anything that was different from the Iraqi regime, and tolerated many different Islamic groups, Socialist groups, labor groups, and myriad others. With all of these parties, it wasn't a true democracy—everybody had a gun, and many ruled by force, but it was as close as they could get. One operator reasoned that perhaps this haphazard governance was why extreme groups like the Ansar al-Islam flourished.

But the PUK had an enemy in Ansar as well, because of the Ansar's desire to get control over the area away from Jalal Talabani, so that they could operate without restrictions as a terrorist base in the region. The PUK had frowned on it, but had done nothing to stop them. Soon, there were car bombs exploding around As-Sulaymaniyah, and Katucha rocket attacks by the Ansar on likely PUK locations. The Ansar would be dealt with severely in less than a week—it would be called Operation VIKING HAMMER and the story is told in this book.

The Kurds of Chamchamal respected the Green Berets immensely once the initial rapport was established. The older Peshmerga chastised the younger fighters by telling them that the Americans came from halfway around the world to fight their fight for them, so they had better be very brave in their presence. Also, they knew the high premium on American lives, and that the Special Forces needed the Kurds to watch their backs. In turn, fathers would instruct their sons to never leave the sides of the Special Operators when in battle.

Many of the Special Operators had already spent a good deal of time with the Kurds during Operation PROVIDE COMFORT during the 1990s, and they knew both the Kurdish people and the stark landscape of northern Iraq very well. The Kurds came to feel that the Green Berets were brothers instead of outsiders.

"Kak Salah," short for Saladin, was the Kurdish leader in Chamchamal. He was named after a great Kurdish fighter. "Kak" meant "Mister," but he was a lieutenant colonel as well as a worldly man who spoke Arabic like a true Arab. This was a great skill to have in Iraq as a Kurd so close to the green line.

The first day, one of the PUK commanders told the Green Berets of a particularly brutal incident that had happened at the Iraqi checkpoint not long before the Green Berets arrived. An elderly Kurdish woman (reportedly eighty to ninety years old) approached the Iraqi checkpoint with a can of gasoline she was carrying back to Chamchamal from Kirkuk. Kirkuk is rich in petroleum products, but to the Kurds on the other side of the green line, gasoline was a luxury. The Iraqi soldiers snatched her gasoline can away, and poured the contents over her, igniting it and burning her alive.

When the Green Berets heard of this, they dropped a JDAM (Joint Direct Attack Munitions) on the guard shack, putting the five-hundred-pound bomb right through the roof of the little building during the first air strike the next day. The Iraqis responded with a rocket and artillery attack on the town. A thirteen-year-old boy died in the attack, and a Kurdish woman lost her legs.

The Green Berets responded with "Game on," and unleashed the full force of the USAF and U.S. Navy aviators on them the day after. Even though the bombing of the guard shack resulted in several Kurdish deaths by retaliatory Iraqi shelling, it showed the Kurds of Chamchamal exactly what the Americans could do. It was not simply a lucky shot. These bombs could land with pinpoint accuracy—

nothing the Kurds or the Iraqis could really fathom before seeing it firsthand.

The first day on the rooftop in Chamchamal was spent targeting; the second day was spent calling in aircraft and dropping precision-guided bombs. The rooftop was less than twelve hundred meters from where the bombs were being dropped. The Green Berets could see Iraqi vehicles moving about in ignorant bliss, unaware that many of them would soon be vaporized. Due to the sloping topography, the ridgeline could only be seen from this distance, or from kilometers away, where the land sloped up.

With the satellite imagery and the help of the Kurdish HUMINT, the targets of highest priority were taken out first. High above the earth, the faint vapor trails of a B-52 Stratofortress made such fine white lines in the atmosphere that one had to really squint to take notice. With an altitude of forty-five thousand feet, the nearly invisible heavy bomber let go a slew of twelve JDAM-equipped bombs; each one was locked onto its own target. The Iraqis would never know what hit them.

The Green Berets were calling in air strikes on the bunker systems by the end of their second day in Chamchamal. They operated in split-teams, as they had done in Afghanistan and elsewhere, with a third to a half of an ODA on each shift. That way, the CAS missions could be called in without a break in their devastating torrent, and the men of 3rd Group were never too fatigued to carry out the CAS missions with anything but the deadliest of accuracy.

The Iraqis who were left alive retreated back over the ridgeline and closer to Kirkuk. With the threat that had once been only twelve hundred meters away now on the other side of the mountain, Chamchamal became the new FOB (Forward Operating Base) for 3rd Group, moving down from As-Sulaymaniyah to the new front lines.

The entire Iraqi front collapsed around Kirkuk after four or five days of heavy bombing. Altogether, it was a total of about ten days of dedicated CAS missions, and the Iraqi units were overwhelmed with the intensity. There was no time for them to regroup or think of a strategy—the bombing never ceased, and they could not even fall back in an organized manner. It was "cut and run," every man for himself as they raced to make it to Kirkuk for a last stand with the Green Berets and the Kurds.

The 3rd SFG ODAs moved toward Kirkuk with thousands of Peshmerga soldiers. At a certain point, one operator commented, they had to finish off the Iraqis with a conventional attack. By this time, Saddam's forces were too few and too scattered to be bombed anymore. "It was like, we bombed them, we bombed them, and we bombed them. . . . The ones who were left were not giving up, so we knew it was time for a ground assault."

The Green Berets had planned to perform ground assaults on the Iraqi Army all along—it was standard practice. Once a target is destroyed, the SOP is to clear the objective before continuing onward. But before the Special Operators and their Pesh fighters could get there, the Iraqis who had not been killed in the bombing had already retreated. Only when the last of the die-hards remained, and there was nowhere to retreat, did the Green Berets launch a ground attack.

It wasn't easy for some ODAs, however, and there was some steady resistance among the Iraqis. It was never anything the Green Berets couldn't handle, but rather it was a little surprising, considering that the intelligence they had received had indicated that the Iraqis were ready to give up.

The ground attacks were organized by the Green Berets in what they deemed "textbook Ranger School assaults." This included two assault lines and at least one support-by-fire position to cover the assaulters while they moved across their objective. The discipline of the Ranger-style strikes eliminated the chance of fratricide among the normally wild Peshmerga, and maximized the chances of success with minimum casualties.

The PUK were broken down into 150 to 200–man assault teams, and mortar teams were organized for support-by-fire positions. The Green Berets supplemented this with vehicle-mounted MK-19 automatic grenade launchers. The Iraqis had never been on the business end of an automatic grenade launcher before, and it "really spooked them," said one operator. They either ran or stayed in their bunkers until the bunkers were destroyed by CAS. The CAS was provided by "fast movers" as well as a B-1, a B-2, and a B-52 bomber. The B-1 and B-2 flew even higher than the B-52, with nearly invisible contrails. The only way the Green Berets could tell the bomber had dropped its payload was to count the seconds on their watches after the "Bombs Away!" command had been heard over the radios. Almost to the second, the calculations of the Air Force crews matched up with the resultant explosions.

The Iraqis that were captured and became POWs were deathly afraid of the Americans. "They thought we were going to execute them," one Green Beret recalled.

Kirkuk fell quickly. The city, essentially a military depot because of its strategic importance, was so well equipped that every Kurd was literally driving around in a new army vehicle after the city fell. Everything had been abandoned—hundreds of T-55 and T-72 Russian tanks, ammo depots full of every imaginable weapon and corresponding ammunition, even uniforms. Thousands of Iraqi uniforms lay in heaps in locations all over the city, as the soldiers stripped and melted into the population. This virtual osmosis would play a big part in the insurgency later in the war, pro-Saddam and otherwise.

Operation VIKING HAMMER

Perhaps the largest Special Operations assault in history occurred a stone's throw from the Iranian border, east of As-Sulaymaniyah, the 3rd Special Forces Group's FOB. The massive uphill battle, through rocky, rough terrain and sometimes ankle-deep mud, was done under some of the most intense enemy fire imaginable.

The battle lasted for two days and ended with the destruction of the largest terrorist camp in the world. The incident has remained in the shadows of the war, however, and has received virtually no press coverage at all. Until now, the "Quiet Professionals" of Special Forces have been silent about what may have been the biggest victory in the

Global War on Terror since vanquishing the Taliban and Al Qaeda in Afghanistan.

On March 28, 2003, at 0600 hours fifty of the Green Berets from 3rd BN, 3rd SFG (A) and between eight to ten thousand Peshmerga fighters moved east along two "prongs," toward their objective: the secret mountain base of the terrorist organization known as Ansar al-Islam. Intelligence indicated that the area off the roads had been heavily mined—and the Green Berets weren't about to test the accuracy of those reports. Even if the intel turned out to be off, as it often turned out to be, there was no need to venture there unnecessarily.

The fear of treading through minefields kept the Special Operators and their massive Peshmerga force strictly to the roads and mountain trails, where they moved as "ducks in a row" instead of in the wedge-shaped assault formations typically used when engagement with enemy forces is likely or imminent.

The twin prongs of the assault force were broken up into fast-moving advance elements, which could move at a high rate of speed as they engaged the enemy terrorists with assault rifles and light machine guns. The Pesh guerrillas in the lead elements were lightly armed with AK-47s and PKs (Pulemyot Kalashnikova—Russian general-purpose machine guns with between 100 and 200 rounds of ammunition per man). The Green Berets had their M-4 carbines and M-240B SAW (Squad Automatic Weapon) light machine guns, but they were never ones to go easy on the ammo, regardless of how fast they needed to move.

Three hundred meters behind the lead force of each group was the support force: Green Berets in trucks with .50 caliber machine guns and MK-19 belt-fed grenade launchers, and Peshmerga heavy weapons men with ZSU 23mm Soviet anti-aircraft machine guns and mortar tubes on wheeled trailers. On this mission, there was no dedicated CAS, so if there wasn't an aircraft in the area, the Green Berets and their new allies were going to be on their own.

The northern prong included ODA 093, while the southern one, which ran two kilometers south, and parallel to the northern prong, contained the men of ODAs 094 and 095. The fight began just after 0600 hours, as they drew closer to the edge of the mountains. Here, the enemy would always have the high ground, and in the early morning light, the first sporadic bursts of light machine gun fire started to rain down on the advancing Peshmerga—a drizzle at first.

The drizzle quickly turned into a downpour as they drew closer. The fire came from members of Ansar al-Islam, and they were heavily defended. The popping of light machine gun fire turned into the *clang, clang, clang* of 23mm ZSU fire and the *whoosh* of Katucha rockets. The Peshmerga and their Special Forces comrades had no choice but to charge forward up the hill, straight at the terrorists, as the fire rained down around them. Here and there a Kurdish soldier fell on the battlefield.

The support elements began launching their own Katuchas and ZSU fire. Then to that they added the force of the American .50 cals (fifty caliber) and the devastating fire of the MK-19 automatic grenade launchers. The MK-19 is particularly effective because it covers what is known in the military as "dead space": those areas unseen, such as behind berms or ridges and in low-lying depressions an enemy force may use for potential cover and concealment.

When an MK-19 is fired, the 40mm High Explosive (HE) projectiles look a great deal like baseballs, moving at about the same velocity as a pop fly to center field. The Green Berets of 3rd Group arced those 40mm rounds right into the nests of the terrorists, and within thirty minutes, the first ridgeline was seized and the PUK militiamen stormed the hilltop in victory.

It was too soon to celebrate, however. This was only the beginning, and the first ridgeline was only the initial outlying enemy position. Now came the dangerous part: they would first have to move down the road toward the tiny village of Dekon, where part of the Ansar al-Islam was headquartered. After that first lookout post was destroyed, there was no doubt that the enemy camp was gearing up for a desperate last stand.

Once Dekon was seized, they had to take a road north to the second objective, a village called Gulp. To get to Gulp, the attackers would have to continue climbing into the mountains, and navigate a switchback in the road that looked on the maps like a textbook "ambush alley." If they made it that far, there would still be the final approach to the third village, named Varogat.

Varogat itself would be even more hazardous, as it sat in a bowl-shaped depression surrounded on three sides by steep, high ground that would obviously be used for defensible positions by the Ansar. As it happened, it would turn into the enemy's "Alamo," as one Special Operator described it.

The assault on Gulp itself, along narrow footpaths, became harrowing as the combined force swept into the village and across the objective. The enemies had retreated onto the high ground again, where their weapons were trained down upon the advancing force. If the rain of fire had been a downpour before, it was now an absolute deluge.

The Green Berets and the PUK guerrillas were pinned: they could do nothing but lie there and hope that the support teams behind them could suppress the torrent of enemy fire that blasted all around them. It was 0715 hours.

Luckily, an Air Force Combat Controller attached to one of the ODAs was able to locate a Navy F/A-18 Hornet streaking by in the distance. On command, the pilot loosed two five-hundred-pound bombs on the hilltops, and the fire let up a bit from the enemy emplacements. Not good enough for the Green Berets—the now sporadic fire had to be entirely stopped. Not one of the Americans had been hit yet, but the erratic fire was deadly serious, nonetheless.

The adept Navy pilot ignored the SOP of maintaining a thirty-five-thousand-foot ceiling, and dropped in fast and low for a Vietnam-style gun run on the last remaining enemy pockets on the high ground northeast of Gulp. His 25mm auto cannons ripped through the terrorists with a pinpoint precision that amazed the Peshmerga assault force. The battle was effectively over, forty-five minutes after it had begun.

The Pesh took the high ground, and the village of Gulp was swept through and cleared. The remaining stragglers from the Ansar dropped their weapons and feigned surrender—but the Green Berets knew their schemes from their Afghan experience only a year earlier. From a safe and armed distance, they instructed those who remained to drop to their knees and begin disrobing.

The few outwitted terrorists who were left detonated their hidden suicide vests, evaporating in a puff of smoke and a rooster tail of wet dirt, leaving behind nothing but a small pothole in the mud of the village. These fanatics would not be taken alive: they were a different breed of men than the virtual cowards of Saddam's army, and it sent a chill through the Kurdish line.

The Ansar defenders who had not been captured or killed in the gun run disappeared over the crest of the hill, toward the Iranian border, and toward the third and final objective, Varogat. Varogat was more or less saddled across the border between the two nations. This was no doubt the ideal spot for a terrorist camp.

The dangerous trek along the road and up through the switchback began about a mile from the edge of Gulp. Just as the Green Berets had anticipated, they were attacked right in the center of the switchback, with a volley of fire even more ferocious than before. They had no choice but to dig into the mud of the trail, and hope for the best.

The enemy began lobbing mortar rounds down on the attackers—an effective meteor shower of shells, which blasted clumps of mud high into the air all around the pinned-down lead force of about fifty Pesh and seven Green Berets.

One Special Operator recalls laying facedown in the mud, looking over at his medic, Bobby, who was crouched in a small bit of cover nearby. The fire continued—more than ten minutes of absolutely the most intense fire they had ever seen. A mortar round hit the earth right in front of the Special Operator, and a clod of wet mud hit his face squarely like a pie in a slapstick comedy routine.

The medic and the mud-covered Special Operator looked at each other and began laughing out loud—there was nothing else they could do until the support forces could get around the switchback or the Ansar ran out of ammunition altogether.

The Green Berets finally began to suppress the enemy with their M-240B SAW light machine guns and a few MK-19s that had been carried into the switchback under direct enemy fire. The enemy were suppressed just enough for the Peshmerga to make a run for the side of the switchback and begin a flanking maneuver.

It worked. The Ansar al-Islam fighters withdrew around the switchback, and into their Alamo, where they would rearm and await their fate. The Special Operators and their battle-weary guerrilla fighters reloaded their magazines and readied for another battle charge. This time it was around the hairpin and into the bowl-shaped village of Varogat, where they no doubt would make easy targets.

Miraculously, there were hardly any casualties for the eight-to-ten-thousand-man force. Somehow, luck was on their side this morning. What had taken the Special Operators and their Pesh only two and a half hours had been estimated to take from six to twelve in their pre-battle calculations. Things were looking good.

Around the switchback, the Green Berets and the Pesh began taking sporadic fire as they were within eyesight of Varogat. By this point, the combined forces were so desensitized to the heavy fire they had been taking all morning that they moved on unflinchingly. To the terrorists on the high ground surrounding their Alamo, it must have been horrifying. The Americans and the Peshmerga just kept advancing and advancing, and now they were simply ignoring the bullets that cracked by their heads.

"We literally didn't think much of it at all," one Green Beret recalled. "Being shot at was normal to us at that point. We thought, 'Hey, maybe this will just be a little burst of fire, and be over in ten minutes.'" Ten minutes of heavy enemy fire was no big deal at that point.

Coolness under fire was nothing new to the battle-hardened Green Berets, who came around the switchback ten feet tall and bulletproof, doing three- to five-second rushes (also known as IADs, or Immediate Action Drills) as they gained the ground a few feet at a time.

The first truck had come around the switchback at this point. While under heavy, direct enemy fire, the Special Operators unloaded the fifty-caliber M2HB, walked over to a suitable location, and began setting it up.

Soon, the machine gun was "rocking and rolling," piling up brass casings as its barrel began to smoke, and the enemy fire died down. It grew eerily quiet, with only small bursts of fire here and there in the distance. It reminded one of the operators of training back in Fort Carson, where the still air of the Rocky Mountains would echo with the distant fire from shooting ranges and exercises that dotted the landscape of the Army post.

The Pesh took advantage of the lull in return fire that the .50 cal created, and swarmed up the hill like angry hornets. It was almost noon, and they wanted to get this over with. But it was clear that it couldn't be over: they could see small mud huts dotting the hillside and cresting the mountain, right over the top and over the downslope, where the Iranian border intersected the side of the mountain.

The Green Berets and the PUK fighters took shelter under a cliff face, and ate lunch. The SF medics dressed wounds, water was chugged, and faces were stuffed. All this fighting burned calories! The whole day seemed surreal—hands down, this was certainly the most horrific, intense firefight that anyone had ever been in. Spirits were high and the men felt invincible as they laughed, rested, and finally got ready to finish the fight, before the terrorists could escape across the border.

They would have continued sooner, but the intensity of the enemy fire had been so ferocious that the Green Berets felt the Ansar al-Islam would rather die than to retreat past the end of their encampments, and it gave the Green Berets time to regroup. Perhaps there was something here that they knew they would have to die for, and it was becoming obvious to the Special Operators that this was the largest terrorist camp they had ever heard of. According to Special Forces, it was the largest known in the world.

The mass of soldiers and Pesh guerrillas began the climb up the final slope on the Iraqi side of the border. This was the heaviest territory they had seen thus far; the Green Berets were now so far ahead that the heavy weapons force behind them hadn't yet been set up. But they wanted to get this over with, and pushed on.

Once again they faced the heavy enemy fire, but now for the final time. The Green Berets of 3rd SFG (A) took cover behind mud huts as their .50 cals and MK-19s began to suppress the last of the terrorists. The Pesh unloaded their heavy-barreled DHSK ("Dishka") Russian machine guns, and they lobbed mortar rounds up the mountainside, ignoring the terrorists' last stand as if they were invisible, or just annoying mosquitoes.

The enemy fire ceased, this time for good. It was now after sundown, and the mopping up began. The entire objective was swept over, and intelligence gathered. Only a handful of Ansar al-Islam had been captured alive—the rest had either fought to the death or blown themselves up.

As the Special Forces swept through the village, the size and scale of this multinational terrorist stronghold became evident, and it sent a chill up the spine. One of the few terrorists left alive was a Palestinian, another reportedly a Syrian. Identification found on the scores of bodies pointed to almost every country in the Middle East: IDs, passports, and plane tickets from Yemen, Qatar, the United Arab Emirates, and several undisclosed European nations were found on the bodies or left inside of the crude huts.

Links to HAMAS, Abu-Sayaaf in the Philippines, and potentially Al Qaeda were found, along with stacks of documents that linked the camp to a web of terrorism that stretched all over the globe. The Green Berets, then the Peshmerga commanders, interrogated the few prisoners. Then the POWs were zip-tied, sandbags pulled over their heads, and they were escorted back down the mountain in trucks to the FOB at As-Sulaymaniyah. They were imprisoned in what one Green Beret described as a "Mini Guantanamo Bay" they had hastily constructed in the FOB for just this purpose.

Start to finish, the entire operation lasted just over forty-eight hours. It was the fiercest, most intense battle anyone present had ever witnessed—yet amazingly, not a single Special Operator had been even slightly wounded, and the casualties among the thousands of Kurd militia were minimal. Final figures: seventy-five to eighty Pesh wounded in action, twenty-four KIA. Perhaps the single biggest success in Special Operations history, this story can finally be told.

The Domino Effect

Despite their similarities, the Peshmerga's division into two political groups was along basic lines. Massoud Barzani is head of the Kurdistan Democratic Party (KDP), founded in 1946. The KDP is secular, with a goal of Kurdish autonomy and independence. They had forty-five thousand infantrymen and militia at the start of the war, and obtained most of their funding from taxes, duties, and customs fees with Turkey. The KDP were mainly north of As-Sulaymaniyah, where they share a border with Turkey.

The second group, the Patriotic Union of Kurdistan (PUK), split from the Kurdish Democratic Party (KDP) in 1975, under the leadership of Jalal Talabani. As of December 2003, the PUK was still led by Jalal Talabani. Talabani's group has the same overall goals as the KDP, but differs in that it is socialist. The PUK maintains ties with Iran, its border nation, and is largely concerned with stopping the actions of Islamic fundamentalists, including Ansar al-Islam. Talabani had over 25,000 light fighters before the start of the war, and his area of control extended from the north of As-Sulaymaniyah south to just east of Baghdad. After the war, Talabani also had a seat on Iraq's Governing Council.

The flag of the Kurds, called "Iraqi Kurdistan," is a blazing yellow sun over the center of the Iraqi flag of red, white, and green. Since the first Gulf War, the Kurds in the "autonomous zone," the mountainous areas of northern Iraq, northeastern Syria, western Iran, and eastern Turkey, have developed viable political, military, and social structures. The one structure that the Kurds lack is a solid economic base, and it is exactly this that the four Kurd-occupied nations fear the most.

If the Kurds gained their independence, it would, according to official sources, have a "Domino Effect" of destabilization on all of the four nations, Turkey being the most affected. With border control, thriving trade routes, and a fairly large standing army, Iraqi Kurdistan has fought tooth and nail for everything they have gained over the last

Iraq

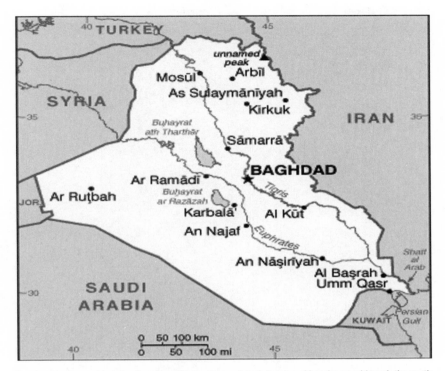

Iraq is an area roughly twice the size of Idaho. It is mainly flat plains of hot desert, although the north of the country is part of the "fertile crescent" and home to the Kurdish people—victims of Saddam's "Arabization" and genocide. The south, lands east of An Nasiriyah, was home to another indigenous group, the Marsh Arabs. These people were also brutalized by Saddam Hussein, who drained their marshes to drive them from their lands and kill their livelihood. *Courtesy:* CIA World Factbook 2003

decade, and is very reluctant to give up what land they have gained since 1991.

Kurds became persona non grata in their own homelands after World War I, with the division of the Ottoman Empire. These indigenous peoples were left out in the cold—literally and figuratively, when they weren't factored into the postwar division of the lands, in part prompted by the discovery of oil in Mosul.

Given the large number of Kurds displaced from their homes and businesses during Saddam's "Arabization," many problems lie ahead in the resettling of cities like Mosul and Kirkuk.

Iraqi Minority Areas

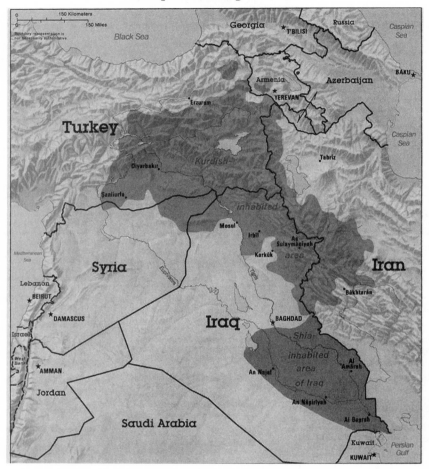

Iraq's two ethnic minorities, the Kurds and the Shi'ia, or "Marsh Arabs," were the subject of Saddam's genocide and torture experiments. The Northern and Southern No-Fly Zones were established to protect these oppressed minority groups. *Courtesy:* CIA (a Map Folio, 1992) and the University of Texas

Camp Loki

It took a couple more days' worth of coaxing and negotiations to get Mustafa and his men to assist the Green Berets in retaking the Northwest Irbil Airfield, especially given that the CAS had been halted by the inclement weather. The men of 10th Group explained to General

Mustafa that without the airfield, they could not ship in the necessary weapons, ammunition, and supplies to adequately equip their joint forces.

The Green Berets told the Pesh that their first vitally important operation to date would be to clear out the AAA positions surrounding the airfield. It would also be their first challenge. The AAA batteries surrounding the Northwest Irbil Airfield made it impossible to land a C-130 supply plane, or even fly by close enough to airdrop supplies to the troops. Without supplies, the situation could only get worse.

On March 26, the Kurds and the U.S. troops prepared themselves, and the combined forces assaulted the airfield in a wave of strength and righteousness. With Javelin man-pack antitank missiles, the Special Operators fired on the Iraqi tanks, Armored Personnel Carriers (APCs), and AAA guns that were dug in around the airstrip. The Peshmerga rebels assaulted the enemy positions with their AK-47s and other small arms. A small contingent of Kurds also manned several mortars and heavy machine guns.

That same day, 10th SFG (A) and a contingent of Pesh fighters secured a DZ (Drop Zone) for the 173rd Airborne Brigade's insertion into northern Iraq in the same vicinity. The 173rd would be the first regular infantry unit to infiltrate into Irbil, followed by 2nd BN (Battalion) 14th INF (Infantry), and the 10th Mountain Division, who were to set up security and guard the airfield. The first helicopter stationed in northern Iraq, a 352nd Special Operations Group MH-53, landed at Irbil on March 26, as well. The 26th of March was a victorious and productive day for TF VIKING and their new airfield. The old SUVs were replaced with armored Land Rovers (nicknamed "pinkies" by the Brits), which afforded more protection, maneuverability, and hard points to mount crew-served weapons such as .50 caliber machine guns, Javelin missiles, and Mark-19 grenade launchers.

The armored "pinkies" positively bristled with radio antennae and portable satellite uplinks. Rucksacks, gear, and ammo were strapped along their front and sides, giving the Rovers an otherworldly appearance.

The Northwest Irbil Airfield was renamed "Camp Loki," after the mischievous Norse god, and an apt name it was, as its members were true to the Nordic spirit of Task Force VIKING.

The "bare bones" of Camp Loki quickly took shape with hard work from VIKING's TF SPT (Task Force Support) and the soldiers of Bravo Company, 528th SOSB (Special Operations Support Battalion). The headquarters for CJSOTF-N was moved to Irbil from Salah ad Din on March 29, the same day that the first MC-130 landed on the airstrip. Within weeks, Northwest Irbil Airfield would support over one thousand five hundred soldiers, sailors, and airmen, and the large contingent of Kurd warriors.

The Special Forces contingent tasked with defending the Irbil sector (AOB 040) was a company-sized element of nine ODAs, commanded by MAJ (Major) Eric Howard and SGM Tim Strong, and code-named ALPHA 210. It was an area of over one hundred kilometers of "frontline trace" to cover, stretching from the northwest up to Aski Kalak, down to Shaqlawah, Mahkmur, and Dibs, with a total area of between 10,000 and 15,000 kilometers of ground to cover, with little more than one hundred Green Berets to do the job.

Consequently, intelligence was minimal, and based on terrain analysis and past skirmishes. Because of the way the Iraqis had attacked Irbil in 1996, MAJ Howard decided it would be best to defend the key avenues of approach, and allocated teams to those "high-speed avenues" that would most likely be used in an attack by Iraqi armored and mechanized forces.

MAJ Howard's A-Teams set up Observation Posts on the best terrain available before asking the KDP guerrillas to join them. This cautious approach to setting up a defense would keep the signatures low and minimize the risk of being attacked by Saddam's forces before the Green Berets of TF VIKING were ready.

Objective STONE

Every day, the numbers of the Kurdish forces grew in VIKING's sector. The ranks of Mustafa's indigenous fighters swelled significantly after they witnessed the devastation that the Special Forces unleashed on the Iraqis' defenses, and the precision with which the air strikes were directed. The Green Berets' air assets flew in from every direction in support; from Navy carriers, and from airfields practically everywhere: Jordan, Afghanistan, Qatar, and Saudi Arabia, to name a few. The Peshmerga realized they would finally have a fighting chance against their oppressors.

By April 3, TF VIKING's commander and General Mustafa agreed that they had enough forces in their sector to start launching multiple hit-and-run guerrilla attacks on the front lines of Iraqi armor, which were dug in to protect a bridge at Aski Kalak.

10th Group's ODAs began sending recon elements to find weak points in the Iraqi lines near the bridge. Probing the Iraqi defenses was not without its dangers; there were a large number of Iraqi troops in the area, and the A-Teams and their Kurdish allies came under heavy volumes of fire, from both enemy small arms and tank rounds. The Green Berets were lucky; they came out unscathed. The Pesh suffered casualties, but very few. The bridge at Aski Kalak and the Iraqi armored company that stood their ground there was code-named Objective STONE, and was the focus of a combined Special Forces/Pesh offensive operation.

It was ODA 065's mission to seize Objective STONE. ODA 065 was commanded by MSG (Master Sergeant) Pat Quinn and CPT (Captain) Carver. The battle over the bridge lasted a bloody seven days, with vicious fighting back and forth. On three occasions that week, a QRF (Quick Reaction Force) consisting of two ODAs (043 and 045) and a force of Kurds had to roll into the area surrounding the bridge, because ODA 065 was on the verge of being overrun by the Iraqis.

On April 5, the last day of the fighting on the bridge, MAJ Howard observed from a hilltop as the Green Berets and the KDP guerrillas advanced six times, were beaten back six times, and finally took the bridge at Aski Kalak on their seventh try. The Green Berets and their Kurdish allies took heavy fire from machine guns, mortars, and artillery. Iraqi tank rounds ricocheted down the streets at the troops, tearing the bumpers off cars parked along the street to the bridge and wreaking great havoc.

The Iraqi armored task force that was dug in around the Aski Kalak Bridge attempted numerous counterattacks, but the Green Berets were unstoppable. Every piece of enemy armor was destroyed with CAS and the Green Berets' Javelin man-pack missile systems. "Not a single [Coalition] tank was available, nor needed," said one Special Operator, to support Task Force VIKING in their attacks on the entrenched Iraqis.

Before the end of the first week, the combined U.S./Kurdish forces and their QRF had fought their way through the Iraqi armor, and were on to planning an offensive operation on an enemy stronghold near the town of Debecka, the gateway to the city of Mosul.

Objective ROCK

The next fierce assault on Iraqi armor units took place along the ridgeline of the Debecka Gap, code-named Objective ROCK. The first time the Special Forces laid eyes on the massive expanse of embedded Iraqi armor, it was, in the words of one of the operators, "phenomenal, and pretty scary." There were literally entire battalions, perhaps even a division, dug in and protected, as far as the eye could see.

Debecka was an extremely hard TIA (Target Interdiction Area). Hard-core Ba'ath Party commandos dug into a remarkable system of three- to four-feet-deep trenches along the ridgelines. Bomb after bomb was dropped on the enemy ridgelines by U.S. Air Force B-52 bombers that circled the area in lazy figure eights, barely visible at their extremely high altitude. Still, the Iraqis hung on and defended their positions with tenacity.

By April 6, there was a clear path that ran approximately eighteen kilometers through the gap, straight to the bridge. The "run" down through the Debecka Gap, staying low and avoiding enemy fire, became known as "Sandoval's Run," named after SGT (Sergeant) Tom Sandoval.

Sandoval's team went straight through the gap in the ridge, and all the way down to the crossroads of Highway 2. The ODA and their Pesh fighters now had several avenues of approach. The problem, however, was that the Debecka crossroads were also protected by Iraqi armored battalions.

Elements from the 3rd Special Forces Group accompanied the 10th Group strike teams. They carried Javelin Weapons Systems, which they launched at the Iraqi armor on their way down Sandoval's Run.

10th Special Forces Group (A) ODAs from FOB 102 and their Peshmerga counterparts assaulted the ridgeline and destroyed a company-sized element of Iraqi tanks and APCs, again with the use of Javelins. Special Forces were really starting to appreciate the surface-to-surface antitank missile at this point. They would later be dubbed "Javelin aces" in the *New York Times*.

The Javelins were an impressive piece of weaponry. Once launched, the Javelin missiles would arc high in the sky before coming straight down on the tops of their targets and detonating, catching the Iraqi units completely off guard. Without horizontal flight paths to trace back to the missiles' origins, the Iraqis had no idea where the Javelins were fired from, or where to shoot back.

One 10th Group officer remarked: "Those things [Javelins] just fly, and they go up and come down [seemingly out of the bare sky], so when it hits two or three tanks, the tanks don't detect it. And so the people, the tank, the other tanks were like 'where are these coming from?' "

Unfortunately, the Special Operators didn't have that element of surprise when it came to their other weapons. The *thump-thump* of Mark-19s and the tracer-fire of their M2HB machine guns made it easier for the enemy to pinpoint the location of the attack.

Objective STONE and Objective ROCK were TF VIKING's first two primary obstacles to a huge push in forward momentum for the American/Pesh combined forces, and it wasn't long before both of the hostile objectives were cleared.

These objectives may have been the most important ones, but they were not the only offensive operations in the first few weeks of the war. One Special Forces source on the scene said that there were a total of thirteen A-Teams on the ground in this sector of Iraq between

April 2 and April 10, and all thirteen were engaged in offensive operations, either against Iraqi "task force armored battalions" or Iraqi infantry "regiments."

There were ODAs on the ground, as well as the CA (Civil Affairs)
and PSYOPS (Psychological Operations) units attached to them. Accounts of the numbers of Pesh with the ODAs vary depending on the
source, with one estimate conservatively placing their numbers at
over six thousand of General Mustafa's KDP soldiers now under Special Forces command, while others have claimed the number to be
around twenty thousand.

General Mustafa's KDP "division" was trained by the Special
Forces and fought alongside them, but they were not armed by them.
The Peshmerga had their own weapons and equipment, in varying
states of usability. The Green Berets helped them service, clean, and
maintain what they already had, and trained them on effective
weaponry. Preventative Maintenance Checks and Services, or PMCS,
a concept previously unheard of by the Pesh, could make all the difference in the world when bullets started to fly. Weapon or equipment
failure was a matter of life and death, and the Green Berets needed to
minimize that variable to the best of their ability.

The Raid on Ayn Sifni

On April 6, at precisely 0600 hours, the raid on the town of Ayn Sifni
was launched by 10th SFG (A) A-Teams and a total of one thousand
five hundred Peshmerga.

The attack was four-pronged, and used the Observation Posts on
Hill 613 to the north/northeast to provide CAS and fire support with a
Peshmerga 82mm mortar platoon on Hill 613.

Assaulting elements came from Hill 725, with ODA 056 and three
hundred Pesh fighters coming from the west. At the same time, ODA
055, accompanied by a Pesh heavy weapons element, came straight
down the road from the north to block a northern Iraqi escape route.

It took thirty minutes for a combined element of ODA 051 and a

Raid on Ayn Sifni: Operational Map

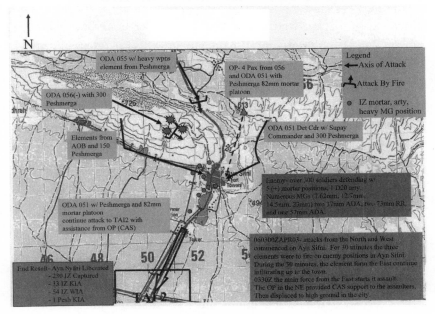

This is the Operational Map with the results of the raid and the plan of attack used by the combined Green Beret/Kurdish force. *Courtesy:* US Special Forces, 10th Group

Supay commander (unit commander) with three hundred Pesh to infiltrate in from the east. They reached the objective around 0630.

Ayn Sifni was an Iraqi stronghold. It sat at the crossroads, and was well defended, with a fort and towers, and a body of water on the southern end. A road ran from north to south through Ayn Sifni, and from the town's center, another road shot straight west.

Ayn Sifni was defended by more than three hundred Iraqi soldiers, with five mortar positions, numerous heavy machine guns (7.62mm, 12.7mm, 14.5mm, and 23mm ZSUs), two 37mm ADA (Air Defense Artillery) pieces, two 73mm RRs (Recoilless Rifles), and one 57mm ADA gun.

The OP on Hill 613 called in bomb after bomb, dropped on the enemy's heavy weapons emplacements. Four F-14 Tomcats and four F/A-18 Hornets loosed fifteen 1,000- to 2,000-pound JDAMs and strafed the Iraqi positions with two 20mm gun runs. The Iraqis were overwhelmed. After the main battle, the remaining Iraqis retreated down the road to the south.

There, the fleeing Iraqis were met by an element from ODA 051 and another Pesh 82mm mortar detachment at TAI 2, where the attack continued until every enemy soldier had either been KIA or had laid down their weapons and surrendered.

The raid on Ayn Sifni bolstered the confidence of the Pesh, and got them one step closer to Mosul, a city that had once been their own. The body count from the raid stood at 33 Iraqi KIA, 40–54 WIA, and 230–240 enemy POWs captured (estimates vary slightly, depending on the source).

The Green Berets were again unscathed, but sadly the Pesh suffered the loss of a commander during their charge into the town, and a total of twenty WIA.

The KDP mourned the loss of their commander, but celebrated their liberation of the first major town in northern Iraq. Several Green Berets attended the fallen commander's funeral, which helped to patch any resentment or anger over the KDP's loss of one of their best men.

Gaining Momentum

As the A-Teams and their Pesh fighters gained momentum toward Mosul, they began to witness General Mustafa's sense of honor and morality firsthand. Initially, the Pesh were a well-mannered, disciplined bunch; but as they charged south and began sweeping through Iraqi towns and cities with intoxicating victory and liberation, there was the occasional report of KDP fighters looting or rioting.

When this occurred, it would usually happen in the very front ranks of the advancing Kurds, and when Mustafa arrived in town with his entourage, he would immediately take control of the situation and put a halt to any acts of revenge or pillage. For the Kurds who took part in the looting and rioting, it was revenge and a fair turn for what they had endured at the hands of Saddam and his regime. To Mustafa, it was no way to set an example or to treat others, even if they were the enemy Iraqi.

Mustafa dealt with the infractions severely. He would immediately have the offenders seized, arrested, and jailed. Through his long ordeal as a POW, Mustafa knew that he would not let his people sink down to the levels of the Iraqis who had oppressed them for so many years. He would lead his men by example.

According to the operators on the ground, the KDP treated their Iraqi prisoners very well, even as "brothers in arms," to quote one Green Beret. The Kurds were observed being civil and even friendly to the captured Iraqi soldiers. Any Iraqi who came under arrest was treated with the same respect the Kurds felt they deserved, had the situation been reversed. The Kurds realized that many of Saddam's soldiers were there only because they had no choice—they did not necessarily want to be there, and many wanted to be liberated from Saddam just as badly as the KDP wanted to be liberated. Camaraderie quickly developed, and it was a "good scene" to witness, according to some of the Green Berets who watched it unfold.

After taking the Debecka Gap, the Aski Kalak Bridge, and Ayn Sifni, 10th SFG and General Mustafa headed due south and liberated Mahkmur. According to SGM Tim Strong, the Iraqi Army was caught so off guard that pots of tea were still hot and steeping on their stoves when the Special Forces rolled into Mahkmur.

On April 8, the Green Berets moved again, this time to Altun Kupri and Dibs on the east, across the Great Zab river. The Green Berets pushed west, east, and south, taking one objective after another.

According to one Special Forces commander, seven to nine cities were liberated with General Mustafa over the course of one single day, April 9.

The usual tactic was the Green Berets' fire support for the Pesh in the form of CAS and Javelin missiles. The Pesh would follow this up with an on-line infantry assault across the objective. The three 3rd SFG "Mobility ODAs" assigned to work with Task Force VIKING were outfitted with mounted, belt-fed MK-19 automatic 40mm grenade launchers, M-60 7.62mm GPMGs (General Purpose Machine Guns), and .50 caliber M2HB machine guns. These fast, armored weapons platforms quickly swept across the objectives and aided the combined Green Beret/Pesh forces with valuable fire support. These efforts, in no small way, contributed to a swift and purposeful war.

Apocalypse Now

Mosul, a city of over one million people, was liberated by a single Special Forces battalion. Their first nighttime drive into the chaos was later described by one SF leader who was there: "It was worse than *Apocalypse Now,* driving up the Mekong, with all the burning buildings and people. The city was on fire, there was looting . . . it was out of control."

And chaos it was. There were firefights between property owners and looters on every street. An AC-130 Spectre gunship loomed overhead, able to provide precise and devastating fire support to the ODAs in downtown Mosul in literally an instant. The SF teams patrolled the city in what is known as "Force Projection," showing the Iraqis that they were now in control.

While the scene may have appeared to be like *Apocalypse Now* to the U.S. troops, chaos was not at all new to Mosul. This third largest city in Iraq has been a center for twentieth-century revolt: major upheavals happened in 1920, 1963, and again in 1968. Crude oil was discovered after the fall of the Ottoman Empire and its post–World War I division, and there has been much strife and controversy there ever since. Mosul is strategic economically, with significant oil storage and refinery facilities. It is also the major economic hub for northern Iraq.

Saddam Hussein's "Arabization" Project had displaced large numbers of ethnic Kurds and Turkomen from their homes in Mosul, paying Arabs to move into the Kurds' homes and take over their businesses while the rightful residents were herded and chased into refugee camps in the mountains. Although Mosul is not generally regarded by the Kurds as within their claimed areas, it is within close proximity to the green line, and rests just south of the 1970 Kurdish maximal demands.

This close proximity, according to military sources, has led to the Turkish rhetoric of "playing up" the Kurdish intent to occupy Mosul, an attempt by Turkey to keep Iraqi pressure on the Kurds. Turkey has long been fearful of an independent Kurd nation; Turkey is the nation with the most land to lose should the Kurds gain their independence.

10th SFG drove through Mosul, arriving at the city's airfield at approximately 0100 hours. The next day the city was broken down into sectors by 10th Group's battalion commander. Each ODA had its own sector, and they proceeded to tear down roadblocks, establish some peace, law, and order, and let the citizens of Mosul know that the Americans were there and the people of Mosul were now free.

On April 12, ODA 065 discovered a huge ASP (Ammo Storage Point), and determined that an eight-kilometer-square section of the city needed to be secured by them immediately, until follow-on units could arrive to replace them. They held security on the area until the next morning.

Two days later, 065 found an area in the Mosul Polymer/Carbon Production plant that may have been a BIO/CHEM/missile production facility. The plant was stocked with chemical suits and protective gear; one building reeked of ammonia, with various chemicals spilled on the floor.

The next day, a room with several dead pigeons on the floor was discovered in Mosul's prison complex. Every situation had to be treated as contaminated; Coalition forces could not be too careful. This time, there was no evidence to substantiate the cause for concern. The pigeons probably didn't die from exposure to or testing of a poisonous agent, but dead birds will always spark some anxiety. After all, canaries have been used by miners to detect carbon monoxide, and other natural gases, and are much more sensitive to the toxic effects of chemicals and gases.

Within four days, the 101st Airborne Division arrived in Mosul. The city was turned over to the Screaming Eagles on April 19, 2003, without the loss of a single Special Operator. "We were so lucky we didn't lose anybody, and that's what's so amazing. We didn't lose one single American. I mean, it's not the jungles of Vietnam that you [Robin Moore] wrote about, but . . . war is war, and it doesn't matter where you're at," recalled SGM Tim Strong.

"We were in our Range Rovers, we always had our ballistic armor on, and we basically took no shit. People got in our way; we got 'em off the road. Anything that was considered a threat, we neutralized. We didn't fuck around."

The Screaming Eagles

Hearts and Minds: An Author's Note

On an early October morning, I climbed into a waiting Black Hawk helicopter for the two-and-a-half-hour flight from Baghdad to Mosul. I was with my long-time Green Beret friend and Iraq traveling companion, Russell Cummings, on our way to the headquarters of COL Joe Anderson and his "Screaming Eagles," the 101st Airborne.

The Baghdad outskirts flashed below me, miles and miles of crops and date palms growing in the Euphrates and Tigris fertile valley, helped along by a huge irrigation program. An hour out of Baghdad, we passed over Tikrit. Below us, we could see the palaces in the city of Saddam Hussein's youth.

Huge rocks and endless sand covered the ground below—a veritable no-man's-land of desolation. I thought of the Green Berets of the 10th Special Forces Group (Airborne) who, a few months earlier, had landed in Bashir. They must have been discouraged at best, with their shot-up airplanes flying over such desolate territory.

I was certainly happy to be in a functional Black Hawk as we approached our landing at the helipad, owned presently by the 101st Airborne Division. You had to be a tiger in the air to survive this area, surrounded as it was by such inhospitable wasteland. Yet, as we settled into the helipad, I could see the grand palaces that defied the hardscrabble city surrounding them.

We landed in Mosul and were met by a delegation from the Strike Brigade and "Strike Six," COL Joe Anderson. We were quickly whisked away with our impedimenta, and taken to the HQ of the 101st Airborne Division, a palace complex that had been looted by the Iraqis, and then made functional again by the 101st. Our first stop was the palace that had been acquired by the officers in charge of the Air Force contingent.

The usual group of Public Affairs Officers (PAOs) greeted us. They had managed to set up their offices in the finest areas of the most luxurious palace available. We were introduced to the various commanders of the Mosul units, after which we were taken by MG (Major General) David Petraeus to a briefing on the Screaming Eagles and their activities as they tried to create order from a greatly disordered city. I'm afraid that I, having Parkinson's and the dry irritable eyes that accompany this affliction, had to close my eyes for a few minutes of the briefing. I assure the reader (and the general) that I not only absorbed every word of the briefing, but made sure to include them in the following pages.

After his presentation, we took our leave of the general, and walked to the HQ palace where COL Joe Anderson was waiting for us. I immediately felt a kinship with the colonel. We discussed some of his group's exploits over the past three months since the Screaming Eagles had invaded Iraq from Kuwait via the outskirts of Basra.

The most recent newsworthy event of the war at that time was claimed by Anderson's brigade, when only months before, they had located and dispatched the two sons and a grandson of Saddam Hussein in Mosul.

Before the briefing, CSM (Captain Sergeant Major) Jerry Lee Wilson introduced himself to me. He was obviously close friends with the colonel; much more so than the ordinary bond of an NCO and his commander.

In the course of getting to know each other, COL Anderson showed me some photographs of himself and his activities since his arrival in Mosul. There were videotapes taken from the inside of the cars and humvees that they drove around in.

"Weren't you afraid of getting shot at by the pro-Saddam Iraqis and their Al Qaeda friends?" I asked.

"No," the command sergeant major answered. "We kept our eyes open and were prepared to shoot our way out if we had to."

It didn't surprise me that the troops weren't particularly worried about the terrorists in the area. I noticed that almost every soldier I met in Iraq wore a black bulletproof vest in addition to their camouflage flak jackets, and they usually carried an M16A2 assault rifle, frequently with a 40mm M203 barrel mounted underneath for firing grenades. I, too, had taken to wearing the black bulletproof vest as a matter of course, although civilians were not allowed to carry machine guns. My particular vest had been loaned to me by my friend COL Bob Morris; it was the same one he wore when traveling in foreign countries where the population was suspect.

I spent the rest of the afternoon and evening talking to "Smokin' Joe" Anderson, as he was known by his friends. Listening to his war experiences, fighting his way up from Basra to Mosul for four weeks, I was completely fascinated with the baldheaded colonel. We both decided that if a movie were made of the war, the perfect actor to play the part of him would be Yul Brynner. Unfortunately, Brynner had died in 1985 from cancer, caused by smoking.

I had hoped that perhaps "Smokin' Joe" would invite Russell and me to go out with him on his nightly foray looking for the bad guys. He said he had just received some information about two terrorists and their Iraqi friend who were in the area and were going to be causing trouble that night.

However, COL Anderson did not ask me to go with him on this trip for the obvious reason that I was carrying a cane, and my Parkinson's could have thrown me off balance, thereby endangering the whole operation. Looking at it from Joe's point of view, I could see why he would not want a seventy-eight-year-old parkinsonian to be sitting in a humvee with him if he got into a firefight with a few pro-Saddam insurgents or the Al Qaeda. We were later informed that at about

0400 hours, Anderson and his soldiers had indeed found, engaged, and shot the Al Qaeda and Hussein loyalists.

After I had returned to the United States, it was with great sadness that I picked up a newspaper and learned that CSM Jerry Lee Wilson had been assassinated by a group of terrorists who cornered his jeep and sprayed him with AK-47 fire. The newspapers said that the bodies had been dragged from their vehicle and desecrated by anti-American Iraqis.

When I asked Joe about this by e-mail, he assured me that was not the true story. The attack had taken place unexpectedly and the terrorists who had fired the shots had killed him but then had immediately disappeared. To this day, I do not know the whole truth of the matter. It has brought to light the great effort of the military to suggest to the American public, through the press, that the soldiers in Iraq were winning the hearts and minds of the people there. More importantly, they tried to show that the local residents did not appreciate the work of a few terrorists. This entire "hearts and minds" subject, which I had dealt with in Vietnam on two visits, was something everybody talked about, but had not really seen too often—just as the terrorists had emerged from nowhere to kill Jerry Lee, the Viet Cong had struck and disappeared back into the indigenous population in Vietnam. Many of us in Vietnam and in other terrorist areas agree that "if you get them by the balls, their hearts and minds will surely follow."

The Associated Press (AP), FOX News, Reuters, and other news agencies had reporters embedded with troops at many of the sites, and even with the Special Forces. War is won with information as well as fighting, and the war could not be won if the Iraqi people and the rest of the world, particularly the Arab world, could not see the "ground truth" firsthand.

In October 2003, at the Sheraton in Baghdad, I met Dana Lewis, who had been in Iraq previously, reporting for NBC TV, and later, for FOX News. Dana had been an embedded reporter with the 101st Airborne, from before the time they crossed the Kuwaiti border until they had entered Baghdad. Dana was great friends with COL Anderson, and told me much about the Strike Brigade and his journey with them into Iraq. We exchanged contact information, and kept in touch after I returned to the States. Dana has kept me abreast of the continuing situation in Iraq, and is still there as of the date of this book's publication.

Back Stateside, I asked for Dana's view of the story—the war as seen through his eyes. Part of what follows in the next section is Dana Lewis's "War Diary," which documented his experience and tells the stories of the Screaming Eagles in Iraq better than anyone else could hope to. Dana rolled all the way into Baghdad with the 101st, witnessing the events from the military side, but through civilian eyes. Here is his story, re-created from the pages of his daily journal and written interviews.

The Beginning

[Dana Lewis]

We had just finished a week of chemical/biological training, and another week of battlefield survival skills. The instructors had gone so far as to suggest Iraq may be too dangerous, but somehow it really didn't register with me. I had covered wars in Afghanistan, Kosovo, and the Middle East. It didn't register until my producer delivered my Army-style dog tags.

"Dana Lewis; NBC; blood type and allergy to penicillin."

The thing was—there were two of those tags to wear around my neck.

"Why two?" I had asked.

"Well, one stays with your body, and the other is for Army records if you die," she said.

I never went to Iraq to die.

I had promised my wife and family that I was a survivor, and would come home. But everyone knew the risks were real; the chances of getting wounded were extremely high. What I know is that every dangerous assignment always seems worse when you're thinking about going. I kept telling myself, "Once you're on the

The Screaming Eagles

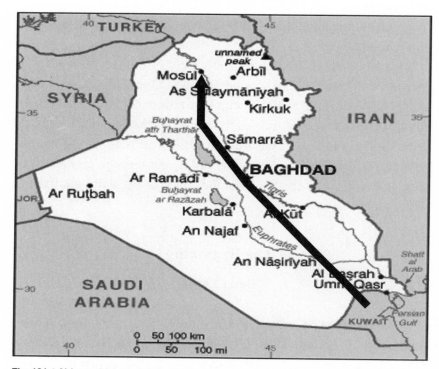

The 101st Airborne Division (Air Assault) was commanded by MG David Petraeus. Known as the "Screaming Eagles," they performed two of the longest air assault missions in history as they fought their way up the gut of Iraq during Operation DESERT EAGLE II, making their way through Baghdad, and ending up in the city of Mosul, where they took over the northern city from Task Force VIKING's Green Berets. *Courtesy:* CIA World Factbook 2003

ground, Dana, you feel your way, you feel your feet on the ground and it's not so scary or difficult."

I thought this time I was kidding myself. It was scarier and more difficult than anything I had ever done.

Kuwait

COL Joe Anderson is the commander of Strike Brigade, the second of three brigades of the Screaming Eagles, 101st Airborne, based out of Fort Campbell, Kentucky. He's known to those around him as "Smokin' Joe." When asked, Joe explained to me, "That [moniker] started as a boxer at West Point and continued as a LT and CPT because of my fitness, aggressiveness, and personality. As a Ranger Company Commander, I led the Joint Special Operations Task Force main effort in [Operation] JUST CAUSE (B Co, 2-75 Ranger Regiment). [Operation JUST CAUSE was the invasion of Panama, which deposed Manuel Noriega in December 1989.]

"We combat airborne assaulted onto Rio Hato to fight the Macho de Monte Company (Panamanian Rangers) and a motorized company. Both of these companies were loyal to Noriega and responded to the coup in the fall of '89—that is why they were the main objective for the invasion. We then moved downtown to secure the U.S. Embassy and then took control of the town and area of Alcalde Diaz. I was one of six Bronze Star recipients for the 2nd Ranger Battalion—those medals weren't given out like they were for DESERT STORM or OEF/OIF."

Joe is a friend. I first met him in Kosovo when U.S. forces rolled tanks into previously Serb-held areas. I liked him because he didn't just welcome reporters, he understood that we are the first draft of history, and COL Anderson felt if the U.S. Army is making history, someone ought to be there to report it.

We lectured together at the Naval War College one year before. He had invited me, believing young officers needed to know about the media, and how it could even change the shape of a war.

His gift to me was the book *We Were Soldiers Once . . . And Young.* It was written by a U.S. colonel and a reporter who together went to Vietnam and wrote it all down. That colonel wanted the bravery and honor of his soldiers told to the world, as did "Strike Six," Joe Anderson.

Despite the debate about the freedom of embedded reporters, I had agreed to go with the 101st because my friend the colonel promised me "open skies. Don't give our positions away, but you could broadcast what you want when you want it," and that's pretty much the way it turned out.

The 101st was deployed to the war late in the game, just weeks before the conflict began. That meant I arrived in Kuwait before the Screaming Eagles ever got there, so I was waiting at the port when their first of half a dozen ships arrived. The pace was frantic. If the 101st wanted to make the war, they would have to move fast, off-loading a massive amount of equipment to arm some fifteen thousand soldiers, about five thousand of them in the 2nd Brigade. The equipment included two hundred and seventy helicopters: Black Hawks, Apaches, and Kiowas—which make the 101st an Air Assault (AASLT) division.

The ships were late leaving the United States, and the 101st was under intense pressure. As it turned out, all of the needed gear, including humvees and artillery and ammunition, didn't reach the port of Kuwait until just a couple of days before "G-Day," the beginning of the ground war. And as we moved out, the Strike Brigade was still receiving its battle gear up to the very last minute, and in the nick of time.

The Desert

The 2nd Brigade was assigned to a temporary staging area in the Kuwaiti desert, appropriately named Camp New York. COL Anderson, a native New Yorker, had me phone the governor's office in New York and ask for a city flag to be mailed out to our Kuwaiti bureau ASAP.

NBC delivered the flag to Camp New York. COL Anderson carried the flag into battle in honor of those who died in the World Trade Center on September 11, 2001.

The camp was a sprawling series of tents sheltering up to sixteen soldiers. I moved into one tent, with my team of three: producer, cameraman, and engineer Sam Sambeterro.

Sam's "baby," as we called it, was a six-foot portable satellite dish that would allow us to feed our video material and go live whenever NBC wanted us to. It also had six New York telephone lines.

Word quickly spread across Camp New York that we would allow free use of the phones, and soldiers who had not seen or talked to their families since leaving the United States lined up to phone home.

Right next to the phones, I had a picnic table that I used to write my stories for NBC. I will never forget those nights under a star-lit sky, listening to young men talk to wives and children and mothers and fathers. There was no way not to listen. It left me with a lump in my throat hearing one young man whose wife was just days away from giving birth to their first child, trying to calm her fears, and another whose father was sick in the hospital.

It still strikes me how wide-eyed and baby-faced the soldiers from the Screaming Eagles appeared while they phoned home.

All of them came to thank me after those calls. Many would tell me they didn't look forward to war, just the hope it would be a short conflict and they would soon be heading back to the United States.

Missiles

Dressing for war was a complicated balance between not taking enough and getting worn out from carrying too much. One little waist bag I tried never to leave behind was my gas mask. Inside it were self-injecting needles with antidotes to nerve agent (atropine) and antidotes to biological weapons.

The Velcro cover of that bag was worn out within a matter of several frightening days in Kuwait.

The first siren at Camp New York sounded at 1245 hours in the afternoon. We had already practiced the drill of getting into above-ground concrete bunkers, but nothing prepares you for the real thing. You have just nine seconds to get a gas mask out of your bag and put it on, while on the run for that bunker.

As an Iraqi missile screamed over the desert, our hearts raced, wondering if we'd be hit with deadly chemicals, or as one soldier put it—"human insecticide."

There was silence in the bunker as soldiers waited and wondered and feared. I don't know what they thought as I tried frantically to call NBC News, and started reporting live as we were under attack.

Over the course of the same day, there were four more Iraqi missile attacks. In one hour, three sirens.

I quickly decided that I would try to stay out of the bunker and re-port live, which I did, for NBC. It was a personal choice, my reason-ing being that if the missile hit our bunker, which had no doors and was open to the outside, we wouldn't survive anyway. My producer hid in the bunker, and only with a bit of coaxing did I manage to get cameraman Bill Angelucci to come out.

Over the next few days, the rush of adrenaline was followed by fatigue and frustration when the "all clear" signal came. It wore on everyone.

I went from fear to anger; from not wanting to mask-up at all to re-minding myself there could be chemical weapons in one of those warheads, which, while falling harmlessly in the desert, could be blown into our camp with lethal consequences.

My producer who had decided to stay in the bunker told me she saw one young soldier, tears visible through the gas mask eye pieces. The 3rd Mechanized had passed into Iraq. We were sitting ducks un-til the word would come for us to move out and into Iraq.

Camp Pennsylvania

Getting psyched up to go into combat is a lifelong pursuit for com-manders training young soldiers: how to turn fear into something that motivates. The attack on Camp Pennsylvania, just down the road from our base, bruised the morale of many in the 101st. It was an at-tack from one of their own, and one of the most confusing sequences of events I had witnessed in the Kuwaiti desert.

An American soldier was alleged to have thrown grenades into three of his commander's tents. He also opened fire as a soldier tried to come out and investigate the source of the blasts. One soldier lay dead, while nineteen were injured, including the commander.

At Camp New York, there was pandemonium as first word spread of the attack and then another explosion erupted into the night sky. I looked up and saw a huge orange fireball slowly falling to earth not far from our camp. Then the alarm sounded for us to put on gas masks. Soldiers, believing there was a coordinated terror attack on the Camps, took up defensive positions, crawling on the ground around our tent and aiming their weapons at the perimeter fences.

As the hunt was underway for the wanted American soldier at Camp Pennsylvania, in an unrelated incident, one of the camp's Patriot missile batteries mistakenly identified a British fighter jet as an incoming missile, and launched. We heard the launch, and the fireball I saw turned out not to be a downed missile as we first reported, but the aftermath of two British pilots being blown out of the sky.

Unrelated events, but in the end connected. As soldiers rushed into bunkers, the wanted American soldier who had carried out the attack was seen in a bunker with blood on his clothes, tackled, and arrested.

Despite the obvious news value of the attack, some questioned our reporting, because it actually delayed the departure of the 3rd Brigade. COL Joe Anderson, who attended the memorial ceremony the next day at Camp Pennsylvania, left us behind at Camp New York. His view was, "The story is a day old; we have a war to fight. I can't imagine why you're still reporting that."

The colonel never tried to stop us from reporting, but the incident demonstrated one way of controlling reports coming from embeds. The Army won't censor your material, but they can control what you have access to. We relied on their transportation, their goodwill to take us where we wanted to go, and sometimes they weren't interested in allowing us to see what we thought was news.

Mission Planning

It deserves to be written now that overall, during the war, I was provided remarkable access by the 101st. Not all commanders were as open as COL Anderson. He trusted me as a professional, enough so that I was privy to witnessing the actual mission planning as it happened. I was allowed to walk in and out of what is known as the TOC, or Tactical Operations Center. Inside there were computer screens with real-time information on troop movements. In battle planning, we heard when troops would move before they did. I also saw American intelligence estimates showing the estimated strength and locations of Iraqi forces. All of this helped me cover the war for the American public in a most efficient manner as an embedded reporter.

Because of his confidence in me not to report mission plans, which would surely cost American lives, I can say that the embed process allowed me a deep understanding of the war from beginning to end. I did not consider it a compromise to not report something the moment I knew it. And it was because of COL Anderson's trust that I came to know that complicated mission plans were often turned upside down.

Almost daily, the 101st received changes in battle plans, and planners became deeply frustrated. 101st MAJ Mike Hamlet, who led mission planning, told me, "I have never seen anything like *this* in war planning."

As an example, one day, the 2nd Brigade was tasked to take Saddam International Airport. Another day it was a target code-named BEARS—the road leading out of Baghdad to Saddam's hometown of Tikrit. In the end, the Strike Brigade was never tasked to take those targets. The 3rd Infantry Division moved faster than anyone imagined and mission plans went up in smoke.

Final Dinner

"Easy Company," the famous company of soldiers from World War II profiled in movies and TV programs like *Band of Brothers,* was part of the 101st.

Soldiers from Easy Company told me that when waiting for paratrooper missions in England, they never knew when they would be sent to fight—except for one signal: the night before combat, they were given a special meal. That meant they would go to war the very next day. There were so many canceled missions after these meals that they seemed a mixed blessing.

In a dining tent set up for hundreds, at Camp New York, we lined up for our special meal. Steak and lobster were served to soldiers who now knew they were being deployed to Iraq.

Soldiers from other bases got wind of the menu, and decided they deserved a good dinner, too, so as a result, the lines were so long I never actually tasted the steak. But the lobster tail was the last good meal I would eat for weeks. In the dining hall, soldiers were wearing their chemical (MOPP) suits; the call to move out early the next day had come. There are many stories of the tricky intricate planning in wartime; now I know it goes right down to the last lobster tail served up with melted butter in a tent in the middle of the Kuwaiti desert!

Road to Iraq

The 101st has a saying about how quickly it can deploy: faster, deeper, further. Light infantry, rapid-deployment airborne units can move much faster than heavy, mechanized divisions that need monstrous amounts of supplies to keep them going. We didn't cross the border first, but when the Strike Brigade moved, it was fast. Traveling only in humvees, we crossed the border into Iraq. Being in the back of a cramped humvee with a cameraman was about as comfortable as being squeezed into a tin can.

Excluding a few fuel stops and eating Army food on the hoods of our vehicles, we drove north toward Baghdad for a straight thirty hours. It was exhausting and nerve wracking. The danger and fear were that Iraqi forces would launch a preemptive assault on our convoy of several hundred vehicles. Humvees are not bulletproof. They are "soft" vehicles and offer little protection, so much of the time we drove at night. No lights. All the while, the drivers were wearing night vision goggles and trying not to fall asleep or run into the vehicle in front.

It is difficult to describe the massive amount of U.S. military supplies moving north. For example, we were told the 3rd ID was literally running out of gas. Huge tankers, convoys of thirty and more, raced up the highway to refuel tanks waiting to assault Baghdad.

One tanker overturned in front of us, when a convoy was told there was intelligence that an Iraqi attack might occur on their roadside base, and they moved out too quickly.

On the road, we saw dizzying amounts of burned-out Iraqi vehicles. And, while it received little media attention at the time, we also saw burned-out U.S. M1A1 Abrams tanks. Soldiers were shocked because no U.S. tanks had been destroyed by Iraqi forces in the last Gulf War, yet outside Baghdad alone we saw three of them damaged beyond use.

The First Mission

The Strike Brigade's first mission involved relieving mechanized units from the Iraqi town of Kifil, a little town with a very large battle.

Kifil, south of Baghdad and near An-Najaf, is a gateway across the Euphrates River, and where the Iraqis put up a major fight. As we entered the town, the first bridge had been half exploded. We drove across what was left only to find out a few days later there were explosives under the bridge that luckily didn't detonate as we crossed.

When the 3rd ID quickly pressed forward to Baghdad before us, they often skirted towns and cities, leaving them still occupied by Iraqi Army units and paramilitaries.

Our first meeting with the mechanized units took place on the north side of town, and it ended in mayhem. Iraqi forces, knowing our location, fired mortars on our position.

My cameraman, Bill Angelucci, jumped into a crater left over by the Coalition air campaign, and took cover. I was stuck outside. I first ran for cover beside a building, but then thought the wall might come down on top of me. I ran out into the open, praying the shells now landing 150 feet away wouldn't kill us.

Within seconds, the Army wisely signaled that we were moving out.

But it wasn't over. As we drove down the road, enemy sniper fire was directed at soldiers guarding the road. This time I took cover next to a ditch while the soldiers frantically searched for the source of the sniper fire.

All the fears of urban warfare were suddenly realized: The sound of fire echoes off buildings and there's no way to tell where it's coming from. You take cover and scan the buildings but often the gunman fires and moves before troops can return fire.

Members of the 101st shook their heads at the damage done by tank fire to the town of Kifil. There was barely a storefront or home along the main street that wasn't bullet ridden. The bodies of Iraqi paramilitaries shot to death in their vehicles remained. It was a gruesome scene, as starving dogs fed on the bodies.

I will never love dogs quite the way I used to.

Kifil Soda

Kifil, a town most Americans have never heard of, soon became famous among the Coalition troops. The 101st Airborne (AASLT) took over a soda factory as its temporary base. Huge stockpiles of apple-flavored soda, orange soda, and cola soon started appearing on military units moving toward Baghdad. Some soldiers would probably drink that soda before long, in Baghdad!

The Army told us they planned to write a check to the owner of the factory—if he ever turned up.

The Kifil soda factory also bottled water. After days of 100-degree heat, wearing chemical gear that felt like a sauna, we had our first showers. One of the soldiers used a plastic laundry tub and placed it on a second-floor platform inside the soda factory. With a hose as a shower head, and gravity working to draw the water down to the first floor, I was able to get sixty seconds of water.

Ten seconds to get wet and soap up.

Fifty seconds to wash off.

The water was freezing cold.

Still, that soda factory proved to be one of the most comfortable nights we had in Iraq.

Sleeping

When we slept, most of our time was spent on the ground, under the stars, in humvees, or on portable cots—if we could get them.

There were times that we left our gear behind, believing we'd be back to a temporary base—only to be stuck in an area of conflict with nothing. I will never forget the searing daytime heat of Iraq followed by the freezing nighttime temperatures.

In the city of An-Najaf, I slept for two nights on the ground behind a school. With only my clothes and a bulletproof vest to keep me warm, I spent the night miserable and shivering, dreaming the "heater," or Iraqi sunrise, would come soon. My bulletproof vest often doubled as my pillow. Not very soft, but enough to keep my head off the ground, where I worried about scorpions.

In the end, I only saw one scorpion next to my bedroll, which didn't bother me. It was a spider that decided I was good enough to eat. For two weeks after the war, I suffered stomach swelling and eventually underwent surgery for the poisonous bite.

An-Najaf—Mines!

An-Najaf is a holy city to the Iraqi Shi'ia, housing the Tomb of Ali, the son-in-law of Mohammed, who the Shi'ia believe was the Prophet's true successor. An-Najaf was one of the places the Shi'ia rose up against Saddam Hussein after the first Gulf War, only to be slaughtered by Iraqi forces. Soldiers from the Strike Brigade took the city from the north while other members of the 101st fought their way into the southern half.

I stood and watched LTC Bill Bennett from the 101st call in his artillery strikes. The first artillery shells were smoke, to shelter the hundreds of U.S. soldiers moving into residential areas, then came the actual artillery fire directed at the rooftops that were used by the pro-Saddam loyalists to resist the Coalition attack.

Suddenly, out of the smoke we saw a Shi'ia man emerge and approach commanders. He was speaking Arabic while signaling that there was something on the ground we were walking on: land mines!

We had walked onto a minefield, and now we had to get back out. Mines are buried and designed to hide just below the topsoil, until someone steps on them with devastating results. Two of our tanks had already crossed the field safely, so we quickly moved onto those tracks, cautiously walking our way through the danger.

When we got to the other side, our cocky COL Anderson remarked: "Ha! I think that there were no mines—that guy just told us that so we wouldn't spoil his field."

Not ten minutes later, there was an explosion as a humvee crossed the field and ran over a mine. Luckily, the passenger seat was empty. The vehicle was destroyed by the blast, but the two soldiers inside the vehicle were unharmed.

LTC Bennett and the others noted how incredible it was the Iraqi risked his life to warn us. It was a sign that the "welcome mat" was out for U.S. forces. But it was also a sign there would be resistance—a lot of it. It was not until months after President Bush declared an end to major hostilities in Iraq that anyone would know how fearsome and costly that resistance would be.

In the streets of An-Najaf the soldiers were guarded. They worried that the residents might try to attack. But as we crossed the road to talk to Shi'ia residents, I was welcomed and surrounded by smiling locals. I was asked for food and water, which the Army couldn't provide. It was hard to tell people we barely had enough water for ourselves. The Army promised that once the fighting stopped, they would help repair An-Najaf's water system to win the hearts of the people.

I asked the colonel on camera: "When will you get these people electricity and water?"

"Not our job right now," he said. "Our goal is regime change; then we'll see."

Off camera, the colonel said, "What the fuck was that all about. Why were you bothering me with that?"

But later, U.S. commanders would come to realize that making life return to some normal level in Iraq was critical to winning the long-term battle for Iraqi hearts and minds, and the U.S. government would have to make an investment of tens of billions of dollars in order to do so.

Highway to Hell

An Army commander told me it was going to be a demonstration mission, just a show of force not even worth watching. U.S. soldiers from the 101st, led by tanks from the 2-70 Armor unit, were to drive north from Kifil to distract Iraqi soldiers, while the 3rd Mechanized Division, east of us, would push toward Baghdad.

The plan was called a "fade," or diversion, so that the Iraqi forces would concentrate on the 101st, while the 3rd ID hit them to the east. No one expected much resistance. They were wrong.

As the tanks pushed north of Kifil, just south of the town of Al-Hillah, Iraqi troops waited in ambush. As one tank commander described it, a "rain of rocket-propelled grenades and machine gun fire" hit the column.

U.S. forces returned the fire and soon artillery exchanges came into play; the big guns from both sides fired 105mm shells, leaving huge craters in the road where they fell. One soldier from the 101st died when he was struck by a bullet while on top of a tank.

A commander told me he hoped he would get a Silver Star from the heroics that day. There were plenty of heroics: the enemy fought hard, and several quick moves limited the U.S. death toll to one. But the next day I was able to talk to soldiers from the 2-70 Armor element. I was surprised at their description of the fight.

One major just shook his head, saying: "It was terrible, a blood-bath, no one wanted to be in that kind of fight." Tanks were forced, he said, to "open up" on men running at them armed only with AK-47 assault rifles. "We had to shoot dozens and dozens, it was a bloody shooting gallery," he said as he described the battle.

The 101st Airborne put the death toll on the Iraqi side at two to three hundred. The 2-70 Armor said it was more like one hundred. I wanted to see it for myself.

To get to the scene, I left the 101st and asked the 2-70 Armor to take me north. When we arrived, the carnage on that highway was unforgettable. Burned trees stood as eerie symbols of the death that enveloped everything on the road. There were dead animals that had been caught in the crossfire. The dead bodies of Iraqi soldiers hung out of trucks and jeeps, and were being eaten by insects.

What I will never forget is the smell of death. Many of the Iraqis were killed by tank fire as they fired from buildings. Their bodies remained in those buildings in the hot sun, and the smell hit me like a steamroller.

We witnessed the aftermath of a battle that was seen very differently by the soldiers who fought it. For some it was victory over an enemy. A battle fought and won with honor. But other soldiers told me, "This is not what we trained for."

Tank commanders who spent their military careers preparing to fight enemy tanks had been forced to cut down an enemy who was driving cars, and in one case, a dump truck.

Make no mistake about it, those cars and trucks and the Iraqis inside them were a threat. They had weapons that threatened tanks, and they killed one American soldier. But it's just that the fight was one-sided, American forces were so easily outgunning the enemy. Some of the soldiers from the battle will never boast about the fight.

A commander from 2-70 Armor, who didn't hope for a Silver Star, later got one for that battle.

The Danger

The danger was ever present as we moved through Iraq. In Karbala, as we got ready to join a U.S. infantry patrol to clear pockets of resistance in the city, RPGs (rocket-propelled grenades) were fired at Bradley Fighting Vehicles just a few feet away from my position. The Bradleys returned fire with their 23mm cannons, and I watched as part of the front of a building crumbled before my eyes.

On patrol we often heard sniper fire along with the explosions. That particular day in Karbala, the temperature climbed to over 100°F. We marched with the patrol for six hours. It was almost unbearable. I wanted to drop my bulletproof vest and take off my helmet, but we all knew that just one stray bullet and we would wish we'd had it on. So, I drank as much water as I could and pressed onward.

In Karbala, we had just rounded a bend on the way to a command post, when tanks and soldiers opened fire on a house. The Army was pumping grenades into the front of the house, which was being used as a shelter for Iraqi paramilitaries. The intensity of American firepower was awesome. Soon, the house was burning, and Kiowa helicopters were called in to track the enemy on the rooftops.

Kiowas

The Kiowa is basically a Bell Jet Ranger helicopter, packed with weapons like rockets and machine guns, and electronics that can spot and track enemy positions. They are scouts, though, and are not normally supposed to be the stars of the helicopter war. That's left to the Apache gunships.

Throughout the Operation IRAQI FREEDOM, though, we constantly saw the fast-moving, low-flying Kiowas flying over and taking the fight to the enemy. The Apaches were, in fact, grounded from night flying by the commander of the 101st. The Apaches often flew on the edges of cities, but because they proved so susceptible to small arms fire in the early stages of the war, rarely did they venture over the urban warfare environment.

We heard several commanders voice their disappointment that the Apaches wouldn't engage the enemy in urban fighting, all because a general had decided he didn't want to lose any more to ground fire.

The Kiowas flew directly over the enemy. Kiowa pilot LTC Stephen Schiller of 2-17 Cavalry, and his copilot CW4 Douglas Ford, told me that their helicopter had taken several bullets, including one that lodged directly under Schiller's seat. He still carries the bullet as a good luck charm.

We couldn't fly with the 101st's combat helicopters, but we did have them take one of our cameras along. We aired the video and spoke to enough pilots to realize that the Apaches didn't have a starring role in the war. The Kiowas won the part, and LTC Schiller received the Distinguished Flying Cross.

Baghdad

Twenty miles outside Baghdad, the 101st was told to stop. COL Anderson expressed frustration with the mission planners back in their bunkers in Qatar, who couldn't keep up with the battle. Baghdad was being looted and burned, and we could have entered a day earlier than we did, but we had to spend the night at a former Iraqi missile base, waiting almost twenty-four hours before getting the green light to move forward.

Was there a pause in the war? Officially, the Pentagon said "No." But in the prewar planning, sitting in Kuwait inside the 101st's Tactical Operations Center (TOC), we had heard about the "pause" over and over again. As U.S. forces approached Karbala Pass, the so-called "trigger point" where Saddam might use chemical or biological weapons, war plans had called for a twenty-four-hour pause, where Hussein would be given a final chance to step down and leave Iraq.

In the end, as we lingered on the edge of Baghdad, there *was* a pause. But because the war had happened so quickly, and Saddam might already be dead, that "last chance for Saddam" was never issued. But the pause was forced. One 101st Airborne officer confirmed that they "*had* to pause."

The Coalition, and the 3rd ID (Mechanized) in particular, had pushed too fast too far, and were out of fuel and ammo. "We, the

101st, had to give them some of our artillery and other stocks so they could push forward. The pause was about resupply, and in the middle of it, sandstorms had swept across Iraq making any further progress impossible," explained the Screaming Eagle officer.

But, in any event, there *was* a pause, and battle planners will have to admit one day that the supply lines got strung out, disorganized, and vulnerable to attack. That doesn't stop the campaign from being anything but a fast victory in anyone's mind, but it wasn't quite the ballet Washington had made it out to be.

When we got inside Baghdad, we saw huge crowds of looters on the road, pulling, pushing, dragging, and carrying everything they could from nearby factories and businesses. The 101st did nothing to discourage the looters. The initial decision was made to ignore civil disorder and concentrate on finding the enemy.

We went to one of Saddam's palaces near the International Airport. We videotaped looters taking toilets, chandeliers, window frames—anything they could pry loose and fit into a car or truck, or carry on their backs. Again, the 101st decided that civil disorder was outside of their mission. It would be several days until the order came to start clamping down on looters.

In Baghdad, the 101st's lead element claimed a water treatment facility as its new temporary headquarters. Every few days we had taken over schools or factories or slept out in sand dunes; now it was a water plant. It had the first real toilet that we had seen in weeks—no small luxury!

At night in the outskirts of Baghdad, the shooting never seemed to stop. You went to sleep hearing it. I sometimes awakened to explosions coming very close. These sounds remained in my dreams for weeks after I left war-torn Iraq.

Several days into our stay, our compound was fired upon. I was getting ready to go on air—live, with a group of soldiers who had been ambushed the day before, when suddenly automatic machine gun fire sounded over the wall.

Our interview was off. The soldiers began returning fire over the wall at Iraqi gunmen, who shot at the American forces. Incredibly, the fight wasn't about control of the city; the Iraqi gunmen were involved in a rent dispute. The lawlessness of Baghdad had landed on our doorstep.

The embed process was not perfect. It was, at times, a select but limited window on the war. But it's important to stress again that we were never censored or stopped from reporting. And all of those small windows from embeds add up to a very big picture, a picture called the Iraq War. It is a picture that without the existence of embeds would never have been provided to the American public.

101st LTC Darcy Horner told me that before the war, when he heard reporters were coming to sleep and eat and live with the military, he responded, "Well, why don't we just invite enemy soldiers into our bases, too?"

In the end, he saw the media wasn't the enemy after all.

A young captain from the Strike Brigade turned to me after a day of patrols and fighting in Karbala, and said, "Dana, it's been an honor to have you with us." I was surprised. In the first days of the embeds, the soldiers told me they didn't like the media. Now, after weeks of living together and weeks of facing the same dangers, they had come to see us as friends.

When I told the Strike Brigade I intended to leave them and Iraq, no less than a dozen soldiers told me they couldn't believe I was leaving. We had become their link to the outside world, and the outside world's link to the soldiers' well-being. Their families could know where they were and that they were okay, by watching the news.

The embeds were, and are, the Army's greatest engagement. Units and soldiers showed how great they could be. Reporters were allowed to slip away from the PAOs (Public Affairs Officers) and get one-on-one with American soldiers, who were well trained and well intentioned.

After seven weeks of being embedded with the one-oh-one, I had to admit I felt honored to have had a ringside seat, as gallant and courageous young American soldiers went to war.

I left Iraq and the 101st at the end of April 2003. Soldiers were talking of "mopping-up operations." The worst was over, or so they thought. The 101st was moved north, to the city of Mosul. In comparison to the fighting, Mosul seemed at first like it would be a cakewalk.

Broke-down Palace

[Robin Moore]

"This is another type of warfare.
New in its intensity; ancient in its origin.
War by guerrillas, subversives, insurgents, assassins.
War by ambush, instead of by combat.
By infiltration, instead of aggression.
Seeking victory by eroding and exhausting the enemy,
instead of engaging him."

—John F. Kennedy

The 101st Airborne Division (AASLT) entered Mosul on April 22, 2003. The 10th Special Forces Group (A), about a battalion strong, left when the Screaming Eagles arrived, and they pulled out of the area quickly. There was tremendous looting after the collapse of the security forces in Mosul, and one of the early challenges that the 101st had was to reestablish the shattered security.

"It was a fairly chaotic situation when we got here," said MG David Petraeus, the 101st's commanding officer.

There had been a riot in Mosul a few days before the 101st arrived. Close to a dozen Iraqi civilians were killed in the riot, after the riot apparently threatened part of the battalion-sized USMC unit that was also here. The riot moved toward the airfield the Marines were guarding, and they felt the airfield was being threatened. Once their duties of securing the airfield were over, the Marines were redeployed back to their ship in the Mediterranean Ocean, and the 101st Airborne took over the AO.

The 101st Airborne is headquartered on the northwest side of Mosul; the airport is on the southeast side of the city, diagonal to it. Initially, the HQ was at Mosul Airfield, but the commander of the Screaming Eagles wanted his men out of "tentage" and into a "hard stand," because he felt they would be there for a while.

The only place large enough was the palace area of Mosul. Initially, the 101st occupied a small area of the palace complex, which still had residents, or "squatters," as MG Petraeus referred to them. Internally displaced people, living in bungalows, were given money for relocating before the area was cleaned out.

When the 101st arrived at Saddam's palace, it had been completely looted. The only things that remained were piles of trash, which were at least ankle deep most everywhere. Everything else was gone. Every light in the place was gone; anything that could be taken had been taken, or had been smashed and destroyed, right down to the toilets and heating systems. Even the copper wire had been pulled through the walls. There was not a single pane of glass left in the entire palace when MG Petraeus and his men arrived. Determined, the 101st rolled up their shirtsleeves and after six months of hard work, the palace was once again organized and functional.

Law and Order

The first month in Mosul was focused on regaining order in the city. The first day, April 22, the 101st met with city leaders and worked out a plan of action. They helped to get businesses open again, put some police forces together and back out onto streets, and persuaded a retired police chief to take over. "He lasted about a month," MG Petraeus recalled.

The second police chief lasted only a month, too. As of late October, the third police chief was still there.

The schools and universities were then reopened, and the streets were cleaned. There were private armies and gangs, which needed to be disbanded. It seemed as if every local leader had pickup trucks full of thugs with weapons and heavy machine guns following them around. Before the war had started, all of the power in Iraq was concentrated in the central government. Little, if any, power had been given to the governors of the provinces. They were now scrambling to get whatever they could in the shadow of Saddam's toppled image.

There were a lot of self-proclaimed "governors," and with the enormous vacuum in power and the huge number of people vying for control, the 101st came up with a solution. They ran an election, which started in late April and finished on May 5. The election was an intense, ten-day process, and convened 271 delegates for positions on a "Province Council." Then, the council elected a governor from within their delegates. Sometimes called the mayor, he is "double-hatted" as the province governor and the mayor of Mosul.

The results of early democracy have been great, MG Petraeus said. "It's quite a representative organization of the people." The governor was a general who had been forcibly retired in 1993, when his brother and cousin were killed by Saddam. The vice-governor is a Kurd, who was born in Mosul. He did leave the country in the 1990s and returned to Mosul after it was liberated. There are two assistant governors; one is a Syrian Christian, the other is a Turkoman. Two other Kurds are on the Province Council; one is from the Kurdistan Democratic Party (KDP) and one is from the Patriotic Union of Kurdistan (PUK), and there are a number of Syrian Christians on the council, as well. There are sheiks on the council, businessmen, a bishop—really a good cross section of the province.

There are many Arabs both inside and outside of Mosul. The ones inside the city seem to be more technocratic, with the chancellor of the university sitting on the Province Council, along with many doctors, lawyers, dentists, and retired generals. There are actually over eleven hundred retired generals in this province; they made up an important interest group, and had to be represented in the city council.

An important question had to be asked: since these were all Saddam's generals at one time or another, at what point did they fall out of favor with Saddam? This was key, with regard to their loyalty.

As soon as they saw an Iraqi face as head of their council, the people of Mosul began to take charge of their own destinies, control of their lives, and the rebuilding of their city. "They have a lot of initiative," MG Petraeus explained. "The governor has already traveled to the UAE [United Arab Emirates]. He'd been to Syria twice, and he helped broker a resumption of trade with Syria that was critically important to northern Iraq's recovery and reconstruction."

Major General Petraeus

[Robin Moore—Interview with MG David Petraeus]

"Well, fire away!" MG Petraeus, the commander of the 101st Airborne Division exclaimed as the author sat down and pushed the "record" button on his microcassette recorder.

"It's a fascinating place . . . I'm not the one to tell how Mosul fell, or the north fell, 10th (Special Forces) Group can tell that far better than I could. The Peshmerga are indigenous to the area above the 'green line,' to the east, and northeast of [Mosul]. The Pesh did come down here initially, all around Mosul and all around the Syrian border . . . cities like Sinjar, and they did in fact secure the huge hydroelectric dam that is to the northwest of Mosul, on the lake.

"There were thousands and thousands of Peshmerga in Ninevah Province when we got here. One of the tasks was to get them back into the Iraqi Kurdish area. In many cases they were, at the very least, an intimidating force to the non-Kurdish population in the areas they were occupying. The Kurdish leaders smoothly coordinated that with the 101st; it took us probably about a month to coordinate the withdrawal of the Peshmerga when we got here.

"The Screaming Eagles had a horrible week in July. Ironically, it was also the time of one of their greatest successes," MG Petraeus said.

The same week in July that Uday and Qusay Hussein were killed, the 101st lost six soldiers in ambushes planned and financed by former regime leaders. A week or so before the interview, three MPs bearing the Screaming Eagle patch, but detached from the unit and working in the Karbala region, were also killed—supposedly by Shi'ia militia.

The money for ambushes on Coalition troops was abundant in Iraq. An estimated $1.3 million in Iraqi dinars, U.S. dollars, and valuables was found with the bodies of Uday and Qusay. Two nights later, soldiers picked up a Fedayeen Saddam colonel with $350,000 on his person. A massive amount of money was stolen from the Iraqi people, according to MG Petraeus; it is this money that keeps the RPG attacks, bombings, shootings, and improvised explosives used against Coalition troops so prevalent, even now. The one-hundred-dollar reward to shoot an RPG round at some U.S. troops was a month's pay to most Iraqis, so the offers are tempting, especially for the criminals. Saddam had emptied all of his jails before the war started; the criminals were freed and the prisons were looted. Rebuilding and repairing the prisons of Iraq was another task the Coalition had to master. Moreover, all of the police stations had been burned or completely looted, so the Coalition had to repair or rebuild the stations themselves, in addition to issuing new uniforms, vehicles, weapons, radios, and all of the other equipment a modern police force needs.

In September 2003, a well-armed gang of looters tried to break into a grain warehouse, guarded by Iraqi Security Protection Forces and supplemented by a squad of 101st paratroopers. One of the Americans was killed.

Regardless, MG Petraeus was confident that the Coalition's mission in Iraq would succeed. "The most important factor is money," MG Petraeus said.

As of November 2003, there were over twelve thousand Iraqis on the payroll, and the momentum had to be kept up on the reconstruction projects as well. There had been more than thirty-eight hundred different reconstruction projects in the 101st's sector of Iraq, with costs totaling $29 million through fall of 2003. "Those [projects] are enormously important in the winning of the hearts and minds [of Iraqis]," MG Petraeus said.

Coalition forces anticipate that the various Iraqi Ministries will soon take over part of the financing and payroll, which will alleviate some of the strain on Coalition budgets and help to build Iraqi independence.

An emerging Iraqi independence is evident in the decrease of Coalition presence in some areas—a sign of trust in the new Iraq, and a feeling that Iraqis are able to rebuild and protect their cities and society without a Coalition military presence to back them up. By way of example, for every two ammo dumps still guarded by Coalition troops, there are three that are now guarded solely by the Iraqis. The ratio will only improve over time. "They [Iraqi guards] have been shot at a couple of times, and they shoot back; they do a good job," MG Petraeus said.

The Coalition presence in police stations has also lessened, from fourteen joint police stations, to just three in November 2003. The rest are Iraqi run. Gradually the infrastructure is being built up for larger military base camps, so that many of the base camps around Mosul can be broken down and combined into a few larger ones. This will reduce the "footprint" of the Coalition presence on Iraqi soil, and may help ease the frustrations of the Iraqis. The consolidation of base camps also makes it easier for a relief force to take over.

For the Iraqis, training the Iraqis will only become more refined as time goes on. There are two police academies: an interim academy that lasts three weeks and an advanced academy that runs eight to nine weeks. A Primary Leadership Development Course for Iraqi military and police NCOs (Noncommissioned Officers) will be starting up as well.

In MG Petraeus's opinion, most of the future work to be done will be "repairs," i.e., the replacement of Iraqi officers, soldiers, guards, or policemen with qualified and properly trained personnel, when they are killed, fired, or injured.

The Iraqi police force was long feared and reviled by the citizens of Iraq for its use of torture, its corruption, and manipulation by Saddam's regime to do his bidding. The notions of honor, integrity, and selfless service, along with the American police motto, "To protect and serve," are being indoctrinated in the new Iraqi police. The policemen are now paid a "decent" $120 per month salary when they complete the interim course.

"Is there anything you'd like to ensure is in this book?" the author asked of MG Petraeus as the interview came to a close. "It's a historical account, and we'd like to have everything in there . . ."

"Well, just the fact that Screaming Eagle soldiers came in here with a rifle in one hand and a shovel in the other, if you will," the general replied.

"And I think they've maintained, achieved a good balance between killing or capturing bad guys and reconstruction. There's been a tremendous sensitivity to the need to win hearts and minds. Every operation we do, for example, we test it by asking whether it will create more bad guys than it takes off the street by the way we conduct it. After we conduct an operation, we go back to the neighborhood the following morning, and explain what we did and why we did it, what the results were, ask them what their needs are, hand out Beanie Babies, which are given to our chaplain by the thousands by some supporters on the Internet. Or soccer balls with the Screaming Eagle patch on them, or water, or whatever. . . .

"Our lawyers have done a phenomenal job, we have a fantastic legal team in everything we've ever done . . . helping to open an international border, or whatever . . . it's always done in accordance with UN Security Council resolutions, and all the relevant legal documents out there at any given time. I think again, our commanders and our soldiers work very, very hard to be seen as an army of liberation rather than as an army of occupation. The latest thing that we're doing right now is we're conducting about forty-five of what we call 'goat grabs.'

"A goat grab is basically a local tradition of having a big long table where they put out platters of rice, vegetables, and literally hunks of sheep that have been on a spit, roasting and so forth. You just dig in, you grab sheep or lamb, or fish, or what have you. But we're doing them, every battalion commander is doing at least one of them, some are doing more. Those are great events for maintaining the engagement with the locals.

"This part of the world is all about personal relationships, and you have to invest in those. We've been fortunate to be in the same place for about six months to be able to build those relationships. So, when we have a crisis, we're more going to meet the Imam for the first time, or the Muktar, the neighborhood clerk.

"We actually brief all of the neighborhood clerks for Mosul, for example, there are a huge number. We do the left bank, and then the right bank, over the course of a two-day period every month. We have biweekly meetings with the Imams, and a biweekly meeting with the Christian bishops. We have a biweekly interfaith council; we have engagement at every level. There's somebody responsible for everything. You name every function, and there's somebody responsible for it. There's medical: the Division Surgeon, and the combat support hospital. If it's the Telecommunications Ministry, it's the Signal Battalion . . . a university has one of our aviation brigades. The school system had . . . elementary and high schools, separate from the university, had the Corps' Support Group commander. The Assistant Division Commander of Support does airfields, trains, and taxis and buses. Everybody is overlaid on something . . .

"We have Civil Affairs battalions, too, and they overlay on these areas in the peace . . . [Take] a captain, or maybe a major, of a CA battalion, who is doing education—he might be a teacher back home, and now he's interfacing with a fifty-five- or maybe sixty-five-year-old chancellor of a university of eighteen thousand. And now we take the old colonel, aviation brigade commander, and add him to that mix, and again now, he brings helicopters that can fly this guy to and from Baghdad, he can get him into the office with the CPA [Coalition Provisional Authority] adviser to that ministry. There's a lot more he can do, plus he has the assets of these command emergency reconstruction programs because he's an O-6 commander. All of that makes a big, big difference.

"The Division Support Commander does youth activities in most of Ninevah Province. Basically, every ministry activity, we have someone laid on top of, and . . . ideally, with expertise in it, but if you don't, then you just put a good guy in and tell him to get after it.

"Because the number one winner, in our slide of winners and losers in Operation IRAQI FREEDOM, are flexible, adaptable leaders and troopers. I don't know how we get that, but I think it's partly the

American culture. I think it's partly our military institutions and school systems, and it's partly just the experience that a lot of our soldiers have had. I mean, a lot of us have done this stuff before. I just came from Bosnia last summer; we were taking command of a division where I spent a year doing this kind of stuff, and also doing counterterrorism, which is ideally suited for what we're dealing with when we're going after the bad guys. That's really the way we're doing this. This is not. These are all targeted, intelligence-driven, provided by interagency . . . fusion. Targeted raids—they're not dragnet operations, they're not street sweeps or search-and-destroy or anything like that. They are targeted, focused, and as precise as possible, operations.

"And, by the way, we take the Iraqi police and the Muktars with us whenever we can. We don't [search] mosques, the police will [search] a mosque for us . . . that was said in the slide briefing yesterday. We don't [search] women; we have women soldiers who do that, or again, the police . . . it's just an extraordinary team of people to have in the 101st, and all the additional assets given to us. And then, the great Iraqi partners, who have really stepped up to the plate, and so forth. And really, again, I just can't say enough about the team that has been provided to us here, and how fortunate we are to have such talented people, at all levels.

"But you've got to go after the bad guys at the same time, because they are trying to come in and take down what is, you know, arguably a success story for Iraq. Certainly the Iraqis here feel that they are leading the way for the rest of Iraq. They are 'setting the standard,' to use a military term."

HVT#2 and HVT#3

The second and third most-wanted Iraqis, HVT (High-Value Target) #2 and HVT#3, were none other than Uday and Qusay, the two sons of Saddam Hussein. For months before the raid that killed the sons, U.S. forces, and in particular a super-secret Special Operations Task

Force (SOTF), had been hunting high and low for the fugitives, chasing down false leads and keeping intelligence efforts at full force.

Uday Saddam Hussein was, at one time, the infamous chief of the Fedayeen Saddam, the Iraqi Olympic chairman, and an Iraqi National Assembly member. His torture of Olympic athletes, documented in *Sports Illustrated* magazine, was especially cruel, and gave the world a glimpse into his realm of power and horror. Reports have described Uday as punishing athletes who lost a game, with severe jail sentences during which they were beaten and tortured. One particularly gruesome method of torture was to have athletes dragged across pavement or a rocky surface, then dipped in blood and sewage to ensure infection.

During Operation IRAQI FREEDOM, Uday was known as the "Ace of Hearts," and his picture was in the hands of every Coalition soldier with a deck of playing cards issued by United States Central Command.

Uday founded the Fedayeen Saddam, "men of sacrifice," in 1994 or 1995 (reports vary) to support his father against domestic opponents and crush potential dissenters. The Fedayeen also performed antismuggling operations and patrols, and their ranks were filled with young, promising, idealistic soldiers from pro-Saddam regions of Iraq.

According to intelligence reports, Uday was relieved of command in September 1996 when his father discovered that he had been transferring high-tech weapons from elite Republican Guard units to his Fedayeen militia. Control was passed to his brother Qusay. Not only were the Fedayeen Saddam royal guards, but the thirty thousand to forty thousand martyrs reported directly to the Presidential Palace instead of the army command, and were well trusted and politically reliable.

Qusay Saddam Hussein was designated the "Ace of Clubs." In 1996, he took the reins of the Fedayeen from his brother, which added to his power and control of Iraqi intelligence. Qusay was also the supervisor of Al Amn al-Khas, or Special Security Service (SSS), and the deputy chairman of the Ba'ath Party's Military Bureau.

The SSS (also called SSO—Special Security Organization, or the

Presidential Affairs Department) was described as "the least known but most feared Ba'athist organ of repression." Its official function was to protect the Ba'ath leadership, most importantly Saddam. Unofficially, according to reliable sources, including *Jane's Intelligence Review,* the SSS secretly set up a network of front companies to acquire special equipment and materials used in the production of chemical, nuclear, and biological weapons during the 1980s.

The SSS also conducted surveillance on members of the Iraqi military and intelligence officers with sensitive positions. They were the most trusted of Saddam's elite, and held a special position with special rewards—especially the SSS members who survived and protected the leader during an assassination attempt. The only people that Saddam trusted enough to supervise these highly secret organizations were his own sons. That alone granted them status as Numbers Two and Three on the Coalition's target list.

On June 29, 2003, Uday and Qusay Hussein arrived at the door of a huge stone and concrete home in the Falah district of Mosul. The two sons arrived with five others; they were all wearing traditional off-white Arab dress, called *dishdashas*. Uday had shaved his head and sported a curly "Quaker-style" beard without a moustache. Qusay sported longer hair and the early growth of a new beard. Also with them was a man named Summet, believed to be a bodyguard, and Qusay's fourteen-year-old son, Mustafa.

The party arrived in two separate vehicles: an extended-cab, four-door white Toyota pickup, and a black Mercedes-Benz. The next day, the Toyota's Baghdad license plate was changed to a Tikrit one. According to the tipster who ratted on the infamous brothers, the license plates were swapped frequently.

When the tipster came to the 101st, he provided quite a lot of information. Initially, the 101st didn't believe all of it: it was just too good to be true. The informant told of Uday's and Qusay's requests for him to steal another car and get more weapons, and explained how the brothers were plotting to send a car packed with explosives into the Ninevah Hotel in Mosul. They also wanted the tipster to score them some phony Syrian passports.

COL Joe Anderson, 2nd Brigade's commander, immediately contacted Task Force 20, the secret operations group tasked with hunting down Saddam and his two sons. The brothers had already been holed up in the house for about three weeks longer than they originally told the source they had expected to be. Letters were brought back and forth between the sons and people on the outside, and the source claimed that he had heard conversations he believed were with Saddam Hussein himself.

The sons of Saddam and their henchmen brought bags and pieces of luggage with them. One bag alone, about two-by-two feet in size, was stuffed full of American dollars and Iraqi dinars, totaling $500,000. Another bag full of jewelry was found under the bed that Qusay had been sleeping in. Additional bags contained five assault rifles and one RPK light machine gun.

For three weeks, Uday and Qusay remained holed up in the house, and according to the tipster, sometimes stayed up all night long plotting attacks against U.S. forces. On July 19, Qusay's son, Mustafa, left the house, walking from the hideout with another of the henchmen, a man named Munam. Munam was Summet the bodyguard's brother, and the former manager of Saddam's palace in Baghdad. Mustafa and Munam returned the next day with a white four-door Toyota, and two bags of clothing.

The Raid

The operation began on July 22, 2003, at precisely 1000 hours. The cordon was in place; the 101st's 2nd BDE (Brigade) had a support-by-fire position on the south side of the building and a support-by-fire position on the northeast side of the building. There were additional troops situated on the road parallel to the target house.

The assault force from Task Force 20 was standing by, three build-ings over, ready to move around and storm into the target house when the time came.

An interpreter with a bullhorn was used to contact the targets from a position right next to the garage, the entranceway to which was sit-uated near the front door. Vacant lots were on either side of the house, and the Bashar Kalunder mosque was located diagonally to the house, across the street.

This was a wealthy neighborhood. From the air over Mosul, green lawns could be seen behind the high, gated stone and stucco walls that surrounded most of the houses. All of the houses had two stories, with patios on the flat, low-walled roofs. Also worth noting was the width of the streets, with large sidewalks and multiple lanes. This was a neighborhood of privilege.

The only people in the target house at the time of the assault were Uday and Qusay, the bodyguard, and Mustafa's son. The owner of the property, Nawaf al-Zaidan, owned a total of five houses. He pur-portedly was a self-proclaimed cousin of Saddam Hussein; a lie that led to his being jailed years ago. But he did have business associa-tions with the family, under the auspices of the UN Oil-for-Food program, which eventually led to Uday and Qusay seeking refuge in his house.

At 1010 hours, Task Force 20's assault force came around the northern, rear side of the house, into the carport. They had just begun working their way into the building when they came under fire from either assault rifles or light machine guns.

Four soldiers were hit; three were Task Force 20 operators on the way up the stairs, and one was a 2nd BDE trooper in the street, felled by a round from the Hussein bodyguard, who fired from an upstairs bedroom window.

A Black Hawk medevac chopper dusted off from a nearby field to evacuate the four men wounded in the firefight. The first entry was botched.

At 1030 hours, the 101st opened up on the hideout with their vehicle-mounted, .50 caliber machine guns to soften the fugitives, so that Task Force 20 could attempt another entry. Again, the return fire from inside the house held them at bay.

At 1045, COL Anderson cranked up the heat. AT-4 rockets were eagerly pulled from rucksacks, and the air rang with the *clacks* of charging handles from the vehicle-mounted Mark-19 automatic grenade launchers that surrounded the residence. The Screaming Eagles started to "prep" the hideout a little more before TF 20 moved in for another go at it. Even light antitank rockets and 40mm HE grenades weren't enough, however; return fire from the house continued.

By 1100, COL Anderson had called up a team of two Kiowa Warrior helicopters on the radio. The Kiowas flew from an airfield about an hour's drive south of Mosul, zeroed in on the target house, and armed their weapons systems. The lightning-fast gunships came from southeast to northwest, screaming toward the house as they let four 2.75-inch rockets and their belt-fed .50s loose. One rocket struck pay dirt, while three arced wide and to the left, missing their mark.

"It was unusual for this many rockets to miss," Anderson said. "But this is July, and they hadn't fired any since April."

Also, the Kiowa is very unstable when firing, because of its slight stature. Kiowa pilots prefer not to fire their weapons systems at all while hovering.

The Kiowas made one more gun run before the QRF (Quick Reaction Force) platoon was called in. A platoon from the "Widow Makers," 3/502nd (3rd Battalion, 2nd Brigade) of the 101st, was in position downhill by the river, and moved up at 1150 hours. A tactical Psychological Operations (PSYOPS) team and the Military Police's QRF team were also on the move. Blocking positions were set up along the south of the house to hold back the crowds gathering to watch Targets Number Two and Number Three make their last stand. Later in the day, one of the people in the crowd fired at the American soldiers.

At noontime, shots rang out from a two-story pink building across the street, which had a store below and some apartments on top. Five minutes later, Task Force 20 made another move. They moved in the same way as before, and again took fire when they topped the stairs inside the house. This time, Task Force 20 retreated to the north, to a home across a parking lot.

Next, COL Anderson ordered "Prepping, Phase Two" on the holed-up Hussein sons—.50 calibers and Mark-19s were again on the menu. Fifteen minutes later, TOW (Tube launched, Optically tracked, Wire guided) missiles—among the heaviest weapons they had—were launched. Volley fires were aimed at the house, and eighteen TOWs flew in from every which way, impacting the mansion and punching holes through the structure's two-foot-thick concrete walls.

The goal of the eighteen-missile volley was, according to COL Anderson, "A combination of shocking them if they were still alive, and damaging the building structurally so that it was unfeasible to fight in."

Task Force 20 had reported that there had been a stronghold-type safe room near the bedroom, probably specially reinforced and designed with a "last stand" in mind. On their first entrance attempt, there was movement from a sitting room and a room by the corner. When Task Force 20 soldiers once again entered the house, there was no movement at all.

All four inside were dead. Blasted furniture was everywhere, and the walls were pockmarked and gouged with bullet holes, or completely blown out altogether by grenades, rockets, and missiles.

The house was bulldozed the next day, because the building was not structurally sound after all the explosions. Columns that had framed the front of the house were now skeletons of rebar and wire. Also, the razing of the structure would keep souvenir hunters out of the area, where they could potentially get hurt.

In a later interview with COL Anderson, he talked about the raid that resulted in the deaths of Uday and Qusay: "We had a tip they were in the house. But we had many tips like that before. I just knew we had some bad guys when our soldiers approached the house and they opened up from the balcony. They fired on some of our soldiers, wounding several."

However, did the Coalition want to kill Uday and Qusay, or capture them alive? To this question, a senior officer in the 101st ABN

(AASLT) replied, "We just kept ramping it up in response to them. They obviously were not going to give up. I had wounded men. They fired; we fired back. I brought in more and more soldiers. They fired more. I ramped it up more. Eventually, we put antitank missiles through the window. That was that."

The officer also stated that violent raids such as the showdown with Uday and Qusay might have been a mistake by those above (i.e., Administrator L. Paul Bremer III) to attempt to very quickly alienate the former Ba'ath Party members. Many of them had felt disenfranchised by the new Provisional Authority. With no promise of a new future, Ba'athists eagerly helped in the insurgency. "The important question is, what are your intentions *now*," Bremer had said. "Based on certain professions, there was a big pool of Ba'ath (like schoolteachers); you just can't say the guy was Ba'ath. It's what does that mean *now?*" Bremer explained. "Were you a dues-paying member, or an active supporter of the [Saddam] regime?"

By the end of the year, Bremer had softened his stand on Ba'ath Party members, allowing them to join the new Iraq Army and the police force in what the United States dubbed the "de-Ba'athification" of Iraq.

A Touch of Home

The morale of the troops in any war zone is absolutely vital. It is said that an army marches on its stomach, but an army in good spirits can go hungry in a pinch, and can succeed where others would fail, often against overwhelming odds.

The war in Iraq had generated mixed reaction among the Democrats and Republicans, the liberals and the conservatives. But when the commander in chief makes the decision to put our soldiers' lives on the line on a new front in the Global War on Terror, the public should be behind these brave servicemen and -women 100 percent. By their very nature, our troops are without opinion; they must follow orders, and do their best in the situation they have been given. Thus, troop morale is of the utmost importance.

The confidence of the troops can be raised in many ways—mail from back home, and care packages full of candy and treats do much to warm the spirits. But when mail call is held one day a month, if the troops are lucky, there is often the fearful anticipation of a "Dear John" letter, or none at all. Some soldiers would rather not hear from their loved ones at all, until they are home safe in the arms of those they cherish. It is often too much to bear, and too distracting when on the front lines of combat.

But one thing that the soldiers would never complain about is a good old-fashioned USO-style concert. Any celebrity who could entertain the troops while they are at war would boost their spirits and be burned in their fondest memories until their final day. And one of the toughest parts of being a soldier is the uncertainty of not knowing just when that final day will be.

People in the public eye may have ulterior motives for wanting to visit Iraq, and the American public is not blind—the crossed fingers of young soldiers while shaking the hand of Hillary Clinton can attest to that. Some people may have criticized President George W. Bush for landing on the deck of the aircraft carrier USS *Abraham Lincoln* to announce the ending of open warfare against Saddam's regime, but it will forever bring a smile to the faces of those who were there serving their country, and that is most important.

As this is being written, President Bush's father has planned to parachute out of an airplane to celebrate his eightieth birthday. This won't be the first time—the former president was shot down south of Japan in World War II and parachuted to safety, by necessity. But in 1997, thanks to publicist and media whiz Linda Credeur, Bush Sr. was inspired to do it once again, finally bringing closure to the bad memories. The former president's eightieth birthday, on June 12, 2004, will hopefully mark the third jump he has made since his bailout during World War II.

Aside from publicity stunts and derring-do, what delights the average American serviceman and servicewoman is the opportunity to

meet a blockbuster Hollywood star, there with the soldiers not for publicity or to promote a new film. He or she is there because they want to
do their part and express their gratitude for our nation's young, who
have pledged to give the ultimate sacrifice when duty calls.

In Vietnam, the Special Forces had actress and comedienne "Colonel Maggie," known to stateside Americans as Martha Raye. She
spent many a night in the A-camps and fire bases on the front lines,
clad in tight-fitting tiger stripe fatigues and a well-worn green beret,
cocktail in hand, and a joke at the ready. Her California mansion had
open doors and was a welcome refuge for many SF troopers who
needed a pit stop before going home, or had no home to go to at all.
She truly cared and will never be forgotten.

A new breed of supporters has taken up the reins from Colonel
Maggie, and have shown their support in any way they can. Actress
Bo Derek has visited the wounded soldiers of Special Forces on many
occasions, and has recently brought with her another enthusiast, eager
to put a smile on the faces of the casualties of war, Jennifer Love-
Hewitt.

Hewitt is a young, beautiful film and television actress and vocal-
ist. Her photograph, taken while visiting Special Forces soldiers with
Bo Derek, had made its way into *The Drop,* the official magazine of
the Special Forces Association. Chris Thompson, my writing assistant and project coordinator, thought that she deserved credit on these
pages, just as we applauded Bo Derek in *The Hunt for Bin Laden,* after we witnessed her being awarded her honorary Green Beret at the
50th Anniversary of Special Forces in 2002.

Another celebrity who has gone above and beyond the call of duty
came to our attention while I interviewed COL Joe Anderson of the
Strike Brigade, 101st Airborne Division (Air Assault). We came
across a photograph of Bruce Willis, clad in desert BDUs (Battle
Dress Uniform) with the Screaming Eagle patch, emblazoned with
the Airborne and Ranger tabs above it, featured prominently on his
shoulder. Bruce was singing on stage in Tallifar, Iraq, on September
25, 2003, with his blues band, the Accelerators.

We received permission from COL Anderson to reproduce a

little-known photograph for the book, and to use quotes from the 101st's newsletter while in their AO, called "Iraqi Destiny." Bruce and his band's appearance in Iraq was the realization of a dream for the actor/musician, who first tried to join the military during Operation DESERT STORM. He was informed that he was too old to enlist.

Bruce had lobbied tirelessly for several weeks to arrange for a visit to the troops; finally he got the go-ahead from the Defense Department. After a lunch with CSM Marvin Hill, Bruce and the band flew into Tallifar on a CH-47 Chinook helicopter. Bruce, clad in a white shirt, with a shaved noggin reminiscent of COL Joe Anderson himself, peered out the side window of the Chinook, watching the Iraqi landscape through dark sunglasses.

Soon after the chopper touched down outside of Mosul, Strike Brigade Commander COL Michael Linnington stepped onstage, and introduced the much-appreciated Hollywood star, honoring him with the presentation of a 101st Airborne Division (Air Assault) flag.

COL Linnington then stripped off his uniform top, the name and rank were ripped off, and Bruce gladly donned it before heading onstage to the cheering crowd of several hundred 3rd BDE troopers. Bruce and The Accelerators played a one-hour set for the Strike Brigade. The songs were interspersed with commentary from Bruce, which sent the uniformed fans into a frenzy of applause.

Willis offered one million dollars in cash to any soldier who could place Saddam's head on his doorstep. The brawny star of *Tears of the Sun* and *Die Hard* also told the soldiers of the 101st, in quite inventive language, exactly what he would do if he had "four minutes with Saddam."

It was apparent to all present that Bruce Willis was genuinely glad to be with the troops. "I didn't see enough people coming out here and supporting the troops," Willis said. "Back home, the news is manipulated . . . by people who would like the American people to believe the war is unpopular. It's not unpopular, especially with the Iraqi indigenous people that are being helped. This is the War on Terrorism; it's worth fighting for."

Bruce Willis and The Accelerators ended their show with a simple message: "Stay safe, and God bless you all."

In his personal journal, entitled "Notes from Life," Willis described in his own words what the trip to Iraq meant to him. Bruce wrote the entry on October 2, 2003, a week after his return from Iraq. The following is an excerpt that seems to sum things up:

>   . . . We live in a great country, and I feel that now more than ever . . .
>
>   . . . It was a life-changing experience for me, and one I will never forget. But I do not look at myself as a hero. I wanted to help remind the men and women overseas that they are the Real heroes, and I got a chance to do that, for which I will be eternally grateful . . .
>
>   . . . Regardless of how these men and women feel about their situation, I never heard one complaint. Not one. And believe me, there were some things there that warranted complaints . . .

Thanks, Bruce.

Ali Baba and the Five Critical Basic Needs

LTC John E. Novalis Jr., the Brigade (BDE) XO (Executive Officer) for the 4th BDE of the 101st Airborne Division, discussed with me some of the major factors in rebuilding Iraq, and listed the vital needs of the Iraqi people in order of priority, something he called the "Critical Basic Needs."

According to Novalis, the first concern for the Iraqi people is electricity. You can't live in the twenty-first century without electricity, the type that goes on and stays on all the time. With electricity comes safety and security, which are vital in such a volatile environment.

Security is of high importance. Iraq is a country with perhaps the richest per capita oil supply in the world. One of the biggest refineries is Bashi, about twenty miles north of Baghdad. Crude oil from

Turkey travels to Iraqi refineries to be processed into fuel. Hundreds of tanker trucks are escorted by the 4th BDE all the way from Turkey to Baghdad every day.

"There are still a lot of 'Ali Babas' out there . . . who are out there just to steal things," Novalis explained. "They are corrupt; they don't have any other jobs, so that's all they can do."

Terrorists and hard-line Ba'ath Party Saddam loyalists don't only target the Coalition military; they also target the NGOs (Non-Government Organizations) that are working in Iraq. They want to slow down the process of rebuilding. Add people who are just plain criminals and bandits to the mix, and the rebuilding of Iraq becomes a virtual powder keg.

The black market was a huge economic force in prewar Iraq, and the power brokers in contraband were at the top of the criminal food chain. When Coalition forces first entered Baghdad, there were a lot of reports of illegal roadblocks and checkpoints set up by the bandits and black marketeers. They would stop all vehicle traffic, and steal everything they could find. Strict Darwinism blossomed in the vacuum of occupation. "Take their wares and send them on their way," Novalis described.

After electricity and security needs comes fresh water. Along with fresh water come the collateral issues of sanitation and sewage.

Medicine was fourth on LTC Novalis's list. Good, clean medical facilities and routine health care are necessary. Even now, flight surgeons from the 4th BDE go out to various Baghdad health clinics once a week. "Some of the things that they find in those clinics, the things that those guys work on . . . if they weren't there, those guys would have died," Novalis explained.

Simple ailments such as intestinal infections are often fatal, if left untreated for seven or more days. A Coalition doctor can deliver laxatives, antidiarrhea medications, and/or antibiotics all in one exam. The patient can be cured quite easily with the correct diagnosis and treatment in a dedicated full-time medical clinic. These clinics are new to much of Iraq, and are something "they just never had before," Novalis added.

The fifth Critical Basic Need is education. An education system must provide and staff schools in which children can learn to read and write. If this need is unmet, uneducated Iraqis will be at the mercy of their Arab neighbors. When a nation's GNP (Gross National Product) is primarily oil based, its people are at the mercy of those who can refine it. Oil refining is a complex chemical process. Higher education will also be vital for the Iraqis if they are to keep their newfound independence.

Novalis is hopeful for the future, however: "They have the potential, that's for sure."

On top of the "Critical Basic Needs" is the umbrella of power. "It's a power-hungry country; everybody wants power. Whether you get it through money, rank, knowledge of your position in life, all of the basic needs are under that power umbrella," Novalis explained. "Depending on what the guy who is in power wants to do, is how those five other areas get focused."

The 4th BDE flies daily, with lift aircraft (transports), attack helicopters, and scout aircraft. The scout aircraft mainly fly border patrol missions. There hadn't been a great deal of humanitarian missions, though there were some along the border early on in the war.

The mountain paths between Iran and Iraq are traversed by pilgrims, with little more than their sandals and a bottle of water. Droves of them began migrating from Iran into Iraq as cities were liberated. Sometimes humanitarian airdrops were necessary for the starving groups of travelers.

"The problem you have with that is that there are usually only three types of people who are coming into Iraq," Novalis said. "You have the pilgrims, who want to go to Karbala or some place like that, and express themselves religiously; you have former Iraqis who were forced by the former regime to Iran and now they want to get back to their homeland; the third group comprises those who want to join the movement against the Americans and the Coalition forces. The question is: how do you separate the three? The terrorists know that we [the United States] don't want to stop a pilgrimage, so they come to the border and tell us they are a pilgrim, but they could be a terrorist just as easily. So what we have done is, unless they have a valid passport, they can't enter Iraq."

Novalis explained that this helped to separate the three types, but it was not such a cut-and-dry solution. All of the 9/11 hijackers had valid passports, for example.

Pilgrims who made it over the mountains into Iraq were met with humanitarian-issued meals, or HDRs (Humanitarian Daily Rations), water, shelter, and security. The Coalition military handled this by themselves.

"You would have thought it would be a great spot for the NGOs, but you didn't see any of them out there," Novalis said. "We'd love to have NGOs out there, but right now, with the security risks, NGOs are just not lining up to come out."

The Postwar Dream

By the fall of 2003, pro-Saddam insurgents had gathered momentum. While regular military news conferences were designed to show success in Iraq, and stressed that the frequency of attacks on U.S. forces was falling in overall numbers, the numbers of Coalition military personnel were, in fact, slowly on the rise.

After spending seven weeks with the 101st Airborne at the outset of the war, Dana Lewis returned to Iraq late in 2003 as a correspondent for FOX News. He found a very different Iraq, one not unfolding quite the way America had hoped.

On October 21, 2003, Dana Lewis flew into Baghdad on a Royal Jordanian Airways twin-engine Dash 8 from Amman, Jordan. Onboard the flight, everyone was nervous about surface-to-air missiles. The aircraft first buzzed over Baghdad airport, then made a rapid descent to final approach. The worries of surface-to-air shoulder-launched weapons were legitimate.

Several weeks later, a DHL cargo plane was hit shortly after takeoff from the same airport, and had to make an emergency landing with its wing on fire and one engine out. Royal Jordanian airlines canceled all flights. So did DHL. On December 9, word spread that a military C-17 MAC (Military Airlift Command) flight was hit and had to shut down one of its engines.

The rhythm of attacks by insurgents, many of them former Saddam loyalists, some foreign fighters, reached a fever pitch in October and November of 2003. Dana Lewis was there to see the attacks and their aftermath firsthand. The following section is in his words, as he shares excerpts from his "bomb diary" and talks of the attacks and dangers in and around Baghdad.

Dana Lewis's "Bomb Diary,"
October and November 2003, Baghdad

Oct. 26—0610 hrs.: Al Rashid hotel hit by missiles launched from a trailer, the launcher hidden in a generator. I went live from near the hotel all day. Deputy Secretary of Defense Wolfowitz in hotel at time it got hit. Could have been killed. We are very worried about our hotel at Sheraton. Also a target. Numerous terror warnings out.

Oct. 27—0800 hrs.: Bomb blast heard all over Baghdad. My room shakes. 10 blocks away Red Cross building hit by ambulance bomb. Then 4 police stations hit by suicide bombers same day. I tape my windows in my room, scared of flying glass. Start sleeping with wedding ring and watch on. Asked my bed to be moved in between two concrete pillars . . . away from the windows!

Nov. 2—Chinook chopper shot down. Sixteen dead. We drive out thru Fallujah, a hot spot. Risky. Left the scene before nightfall.

Nov. 6—Drove two hours to Iraqi airbase. Memorial for soldiers killed. Slept over as it was too dangerous to drive back.

Nov. 8—Nighttime patrol with 1st Armored "Dirty Company" in Baghdad. In humvees. We went looking for roadside bombs. 5 minutes before we came down the road, another humvee got hit. Plastic explosive in paint can. We're exposed. It's very dangerous. Soldiers believe new Iraqi police may be involved in some attacks on American troops.

Nov. 21—Awoke to the sound of crashing and flying glass. Bolted out of bed. People running toward fire exits. Missile hit our hotel on 17th floor. Elevator crashed to ground floor. Glass atrium ceiling caved in on 5th floor and crashed 60 ft to lobby below. All of this around 0720. Missiles also hit the Palestine hotel next door. And the Oil Ministry. Donkey carts—with multiple rocket launchers. 4 fired here. 11 didn't go off. Thank God.

Insurgents were now targeting Iraqi police, U.S. contractors, aid agencies, and civilian targets. FOX News aired a segment about former Saddam loyalists who were running several dozen cells in Baghdad, paying people to plant bombs or launch RPGs on U.S. convoys.

"The price for killing a U.S. soldier?" I asked an American officer.

"Up to five thousand dollars," was the reply.

Mosul, where the 101st had gone and trumpeted unusual success in Iraq in winning the hearts and minds of locals, began to have big troubles, too.

A car bomb on a U.S. base outside of Mosul in the first week of December 2003 sent an estimated forty-one soldiers to the hospital. COL Anderson, who often traveled with little protection, was told by his general to start taking more gun truck escorts when he moved around, and he confided in me that a contract had been put out on a Coalition official in Mosul. When I asked the colonel who the intended target was, he said it was him.

The daily loss of soldiers' lives touched all of us. One loss in particular was personally devastating to the colonel and me.

November 23, the news broke that two soldiers traveling through Mosul had been ambushed and dragged out of their vehicle. Eyewitnesses said they were robbed, beaten, and left dead in the street for over an hour. The Army later denied reports that the two had their throats slit.

COL Anderson was the first to tell me one of the two dead soldiers was his sergeant major, Jerry Lee Wilson. I had ridden in the back of Jerry Lee's humvee for weeks at the outset of war. I'd viewed much of the early days of the war over his shoulder. CSM Wilson had stayed in the military to look after his colonel and longtime friend, Joe Anderson. He did that, but on that day he failed to look after himself while traveling with just his driver, in what was supposedly one of the safest areas of Iraq.

If the tide appeared to be turning on U.S. forces in Iraq, the Army continually tried to tell reporters that the support of Iraqi resistance was "not militarily significant."

COL Anderson had this to say about why the 101st was originally so successful in Mosul:

The situation in Mosul has not changed that much. The numbers of attacks are the same or actually less. What changed during November was the success that the enemy had. But if you remove the catastrophic helicopter crash, even the casualty rate is the same or less.

We won here primarily because of the type of force that we had—light infantry and helicopters. We were able to "flood the zone" and maintain constant presence with the populace. Our compounds are in and amongst the populace, not separate. We were able to cover a large area, yet remain concentrated where we needed to be. We rapidly engaged the population and continue to do so.

But as more attacks occurred in late November and early December, the colonel wrote this:

Ramadan was a factor, due to the increased martyrdom period. Another factor was our success. We were ahead of the rest of the country and the insurgents attempted to disrupt that progress.

Some would argue that we came on strong, but shifted to a heavy civil affairs focus, which allowed the FRLs [Former Regime Loyalists] to come out of hiding unscathed. We shifted back to the offensive on November 8 while still trying to win the hearts and minds of the people.

This is a double-edged sword: we cannot afford to alienate more people through offensive ops, but we cannot afford to get attacked while trying to restore stability to the region . . .

People here just don't understand freedom, democracy, and the principles of a free-market economy. There are huge cultural differences between our nations, and some of the traditions will never change. The education system wasn't/isn't great and people just don't know what they don't know. They are not "worldly."

In the short term, we can provide security and improve many functional areas (water, sewer, electricity, fuel, clinics, schools, etc.). These are restoration and improvement functions, not rebuilding. It will take a large investment of resources to rebuild this country over the long term. The infrastructure needs major repairs and the economy cannot bear this burden in the short term. It will take some painful years to get over the hump. Eliminating cronyism, corruption, and ineptitude will take some time as well.

Everyone wants something—not based on need, but on desires and equity. There are some ethnic hatreds and land/property resolution will take some time as well. Some points of reference span thousands of years.

According to some sources, the U.S. government was planning to speed up the formation of a transitional government for next spring, turn over power as quickly as possible, train the new civilian police force and Army, and get American forces out of the center of the cities by early spring 2004.

Another Vietnam?

Almost daily through the end of 2004, a soldier was being killed in a roadside bomb or attack on U.S. aircraft. Four helicopters were shot down. Two helicopters collided over Mosul, killing seventeen soldiers and crew. In Baghdad, rocket attacks hit the former palace of Saddam, now the main Coalition Authority Compound, on an almost nightly basis.

In reporting such events, journalists were constantly under fire from the U.S. military, who claimed that reports didn't show enough of the progress being made in Iraq.

1st Armored Division's BG (Brigadier General) Mark Hertling believed U.S. forces were winning in Iraq, and downplayed the sophistication and abilities of insurgents. In an e-mail to Dana Lewis, he provided a one-day list of activities in Iraq, to show the magnitude and scale of success U.S. forces were having in a Baghdad operation called IRON HAMMER. There had been a number of explosions that day, which Mark writes about, in addition to enclosing the censored list from the 1st Armored Division. The e-mail was as follows:

Dana:

Most of the large explosions were our work. There was, however, one 81mm rocket (a small one) that landed near Assassin's Gate (the north side of the green zone) at about 1953 hrs. No reports of injuries.

Most explosions were ours. We have the operation you are going on tomorrow, and another one (brigade sized, down south) tomorrow morning a little earlier than yours. Additionally, we have a large one going out tonight, but I won't tell you where, when, or what it is doing.

Have enclosed a partial listing of what we have accomplished.

Mark

(What follows is the enclosed list—one day of operations in Baghdad on November 15, 2003.)

15 NOV 03: Day 3 of Operation IRON HAMMER TF 1AD [Task Force 1st Armored Division] focused on capturing arms dealers and IED [Improvised Explosive Devices] makers. Using tips from local citizens, Military Police, and the Iraqi Police, captured two 107mm rockets, which were aimed at the Green Zone.

- *Based on a HUMINT [Human Intelligence], 1-36 IN conducted a cordon and search for individuals suspected in placing IEDs in 1-36 IN AOR. They captured one individual. Also confiscated were bomb-making components; a propane tank, ball bearings, wire, and explosives. The prisoner was transported to a holding cell interrogation.*
- *4-27 FA secured area and provided OPs [observation posts] for two Apache and one Kiowa helicopters to fire 200–250 rounds of 30mm at enemy mortar and rocket-launching sites in Zone* **[censored]**. *Anti-Coalition forces have used this area in the past to launch mortar attacks on U.S. forces. There were no U.S. injuries.*
- *60mm mortars impacted near the 1-13 FOB [Forward Operating Base]. 1-13 AR soldiers who were near the launch site, with the help of aerial assets, went to the site and searched a nearby residence. While searching the area, a white truck approached the patrol and fired two shots. The patrol returned fire, killing one local national and wounding another* **[censored]** *individuals were also captured.* **[censored]** . . . *prisoners were taken* **[censored]** *for interrogation. There were no injuries or damage.*
- *Using an aerial platform, TF 1AD fired 7 × 105mm rounds and 36 × 40mm rounds into a warehouse used by anti-Coalition forces to store ammunition. There were no U.S. injuries.*
- *2ACR conducted a raid on a suspected arms dealer. The target and one other individual were captured. In addition, (1)*

AK-47 and (1) AN/PRC-126 were confiscated. There were no U.S. casualties.

- *2ACR conducted another raid on another suspected arms dealer. The target was detained. In addition, (1) AK-47 was confiscated. There were no U.S. casualties.*
- *Iraqi Police Service Officers found three 107mm rockets in the Al Rashid district this morning at about 0930 hrs. Neighborhood residents told police that they saw several men setting up the rockets alongside a dirt mound. Police said the rockets were aimed at the Coalition Provisional Authority headquarters. The residents told police that they saw one of the rockets fired but it traveled a short distance and did not explode. The residents shot at the attackers with small arms but they were able to escape. Police seized the rockets and transported them to the Rushafa Police Headquarters where explosive ordnance disposal teams will examine them.*
- *Soldiers from the* **[censored]** *Brigade Combat Team and Iraqi Police Service Explosive Ordnance Disposal teams disarmed an improvised explosive device in the* **[censored]** *building at about 1345 hrs. A hand grenade was placed inside a soft drink can with the detonator protruding from the top.*
- *Task Force 1st Armored Division artillerymen conducted a counter-fire mission against a site confirmed as the point of origin within minutes after an earlier enemy mortar attack in northwestern Baghdad at 1915 hrs. Five 105mm artillery rounds were fired into the site, silencing the attack.*

The above excerpt provides an inside glimpse of the day-to-day efforts in Iraq. Winning the "official war" isn't enough. Coalition forces, while certainly making marked progress, are still fighting deep pockets of resistance and ever-present danger.

Dana Lewis traveled back to Mosul over Christmas. He followed Joe Anderson on many raids . . . and even to his weekly radio and TV message. He found some extremely tired men, drained perhaps more by the loss of close colleagues, including their CSM Jerry Lee Wilson, than by the long deployment to Iraq itself.

Jerry Lee's murder had left everyone in shock in the Strike Brigade. A fellow sergeant major said that he and Wilson had joked about not taking security as they drove across town.

"Jerry Lee didn't want to make a fuss, didn't want to ask for gun trucks and security just to drive to another base in the same city," he said. CSM Wilson paid for that decision with his life.

The killing of CSM Wilson and the downing of two Black Hawks in Mosul changed the direction of what until then had been the biggest success story in Iraq. The 101st went from velvet gloves to a new offensive in November.

In an intelligence briefing at the 101st, officers said they had arrested a handful of Al Qaeda in Mosul raids. "There is no doubt they are here," said one officer. Why the Army brass didn't announce this, and confirm the facts, left everyone wondering. Perhaps it was because they didn't want to tip off Al Qaeda. Perhaps it was political. Or it may be that the 101st's intelligence gleaned in raids wasn't convincing enough. However, the intel unit *was* convinced.

According to COL Anderson, "We couldn't *not* respond to attacks. We launched a new offensive. I personally began to approve every target based on intelligence. We wouldn't wait days to confirm and watch and wait when we got information. We moved on everything."

In one month, the 101st Airborne (AASLT) detained more insurgents than they previously had in four months!

In December 2003, in a background briefing in Baghdad, Dana Lewis recorded the comments of a senior military official: "We think Al Qaeda is here. But we also now know there are others who have joined the insurgency. Syrians, Iranians, Yemenis, and now for the first time we are tracking members of the Lebanese Hezbollah."

The Hezbollah, or "Party of God," which gained great experience fighting Israel in its occupation of a strip in southern Lebanon known as the Security Zone, is a group well experienced in guerrilla tactics, including explosives. Its emergence in Iraq has caused the U.S. Army great concern.

COL Anderson's new offensive had paid off. The attacks by insurgents seemed to decrease. The northern part of Iraq again seemed to be more peaceful. But postwar tactics in engaging the media were a roller coaster; Dana Lewis and his colleagues felt the pressure to keep reporting so-called "positive stories."

In Baghdad, BG Mark Hertling invited reporters to background briefings with his boss, CG (Commanding General) Dempsey. It was the "silver spoon" approach. Embedded reporters were offered more patrols and better access, in exchange for showing a different picture. Indeed the embeds tried to report the positive side, which showed a success in raids against insurgents, but the military seemed immensely frustrated by the fact that embeds continued to report the deaths of soldiers and the ongoing rocket and mortar attacks on not only U.S. bases, but even the former Palace of Saddam Hussein—now occupied by Paul Bremer and the new Governing Council.

Almost every night, according to Dana Lewis, BG Hertling would write him long e-mails, either criticizing or praising his work. Hertling was incredibly informative, but also seemed demanding in his attempts to have editorial input. According to Lewis, Hertling may have done this not only with him while he was working at FOX TV, but also with other news agencies in Baghdad.

One night, Dana reported on a demonstration outside a mosque following a raid by U.S. forces, in which they arrested the Imam, or spiritual leader, and were accused of tearing a Koran. In the same report, Lewis reported on the denials by U.S. commanders that they had done any damage to the mosque, and further, that they seized a large amount of weapons inside and called the mosque "a center for criminal and terrorist activity."

Despite what Dana Lewis thought was fair reporting, the curtain came down. BG Hertling sent a note to Dana's boss in New York, and threatened to cut FOX TV off because of their reporting.

In the previous week, Dana had asked for, and been promised, a profile on Hertling's CG Dempsey. The idea was that Dempsey would lead the reporter and cameraman through Baghdad, talking about the

Army's successes and plans for the future. Suddenly, BG Hertling
told Lewis that the granted interview was off until they (Dana's news
crew) proved themselves! Here is an excerpt of that correspondence,
provided by Lewis:

> Dana, not trying to leverage one story against another, and
> not trying to start a "process." Just trying to get you the things
> you need, within reason. And haven't threatened to "close
> down" anything, just telling you it will take more work for me to
> convince the CG that he should do a profile with Fox. Unfortu-
> nately, those are the consequences based on what he—and I—
> have seen lately. . . . [edit]
>
> Not trying to shut you out . . . really. You must admit we have
> been more open with you and given you more things than any
> other network. But it's still our call in what we give you [as]
> sanctions to cover within the division footprint. Just like it's
> your call to decide what you report.

It amazed Lewis that the Army would be so shortsighted. They
were giving BG Hertling and his boss CG Dempsey an opportunity.
According to Lewis, the Army shot themselves in the foot by using it
to leverage news coverage.

Lewis called his boss at FOX TV, John Moody, who supported his
decision to write back to Hertling and inform him that he was removing
his request for Dempsey. They needed to show the Army they could not
influence news coverage by "leveraging access," as Dana called it.

Lewis wrote CG Dempsey to discuss the matter but didn't get a reply.

It needs to be said that for the most part, BG Hertling believed pas-
sionately that the 1st Armored Division was winning the war against
the insurgency, even as he upped his estimates from seven to ten cells
operating in Baghdad (in November), to up to fourteen cells by December. He made an unprecedented attempt to engage Lewis to report
their side of the story, giving him a great amount of access, and ex-
changing many e-mails nightly to help FOX TV get the facts right.
But even the 1st Armored Division felt that the new Coalition Provi-

sional Authority (CPA) had badly organized press briefings. The Army's Central Command (CENTCOM) press desk was slow, and usually provided press releases on major news events twenty-four hours later, with little information.

If the Army had won the media war during the embed process and taking of Iraq, it lost a huge amount of ground in postwar hostilities by poorly engaging the media and getting its message out. According to Lewis, BG Hertling and CG Dempsey felt that the 1st Armored Division had to sidestep the CPA (Coalition Provisional Authority) and CPIC (Coalition Provisional Information Center) in order to reach out to the media, and the 1st Armored Division attempted to do so, with some success.

In the end, GEN (General) Dempsey did a FOX News interview. He invited Lewis to a briefing about the Army's success, and challenges ahead. BG Hertling later wrote Lewis a letter, in which he said that he had learned from his experiences. He started to write to Lewis again on an almost-nightly basis, telling him of raids carried out, and of captured bomb makers and financiers.

BG Hertling also praised Lewis for his coverage of the massive car bomb attack on the main Coalition compound in Baghdad on Sunday, January 18th, in which a suicide bomber detonated a thousand-pound bomb explosive outside the Assassin's Gate of the compound, killing more than two dozen, and wounding over one hundred people. As long as the reports included the Army's assertion that violence was on a decline, even in the midst of such a large attack, commanders felt "their side of the story" was being told.

Task Force DAGGER

LTC Christopher K. Haas

When I met with him in September 2003, LTC Christopher K. Haas was the deputy commander for 5th Special Forces Group (Airborne). During Operation IRAQI FREEDOM, Haas was the commander of 1st Battalion of the 5th SFG (A).

At the start of the war, according to Haas, his battalion was about fifty vehicles strong, packed to the gills with Green Beret and Aussie commandos, ready to breach through the berm in western Iraq on the first night of the war.

The Special Operators and their support had driven through the deserts of Jordan, down to Saudi Arabia, where there was an ideal location for them to infiltrate. Their support would be a unit from the Florida National Guard, who was there to do the actual breaching, while the SF troopers kept an eye out for signs of the enemy.

LTC Haas said his men had trained well for taking care of the breaches, with several months of drilling and focus on their executions before the war began. This made the Western Desert breaches incredibly smooth—the soldiers had it down to a fine art. Now it was time to apply that training.

The 5th SFG had just won their trial by combat in the deserts of

Task Force DAGGER

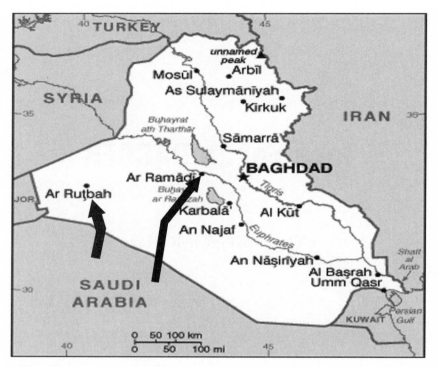

CJSOTF-W, or Task Force DAGGER, was comprised of the 5th Special Forces Group (Airborne). They infiltrated into western Iraq through two berms along the Saudi Arabian–Iraqi borders, and moved into western Iraq to two locations, Ar Rutbah and Ar Ramadi. Some locations have been changed at the request of Special Operations Security. *Courtesy:* CIA World Factbook 2003

Afghanistan. Their code name in Afghanistan, Task Force DAGGER, was resurrected once more, as they prepared to enter combat against a new and deadly foe.

The Breach

5th SFG (A)'s Bravo and Charlie Companies were poised in their vehicles, ready to hear the presidential orders that would give them the green light to simultaneously invade Iraq. A Florida National Guard Infantry Company was with them; the Guardsmen carried pickaxes and entrenching tools. By hand they would have to transform an impasse of dirt and stone marking the boundary into Iraq. They would do it, according to operators on the ground that night, in an inhumanly rapid time of two hours and fifteen minutes.

Picking the ideal spots for Task Force DAGGER to breach Saddam's barricades was not an easy task, however. Reconnaissance efforts were critical and Special Forces recon teams mapped out the best sites weeks in advance. The U.S. Air Force's Operation SOUTHERN WATCH flew sorties on Iraqi guard posts and ADA (Air Defense Artillery) nets or ground systems below the 38th parallel. Key enemy guard posts that could spot the breach and tip off Saddam were blown up ahead of time.

According to U.S. intelligence sources, Saddam's Iraqi border guards were "the weakest force they had in their inventory." Losing the element of surprise was more of a concern than the fight they might put up, so SOUTHERN WATCH took flight and punched a few holes in Saddam's security belt, guided in by the SF recon teams.

Bravo Company had a caravan of seventy-five vehicles for their detachment alone, which included their Australian SAS (Special Air Service) counterparts. The humvees and Pinkies (Land Rovers) were loaded down with rucksacks and gear, strapped to the bumpers and sides of the vehicle. Antennae and satellite uplinks bristled along the tops, and machine guns and belt-fed grenade launchers were mounted everywhere. It was a scene from out of a *Mad Max* movie, and viewing it through the green light of NVGs (Night Vision Goggles) added to the weirdness.

Here and there an SF sharpshooter stood atop the berm, facing the wind, and scanning the black horizon for signs of trouble. Through the green filter of the NVGs, the darkness of the desert took on an alienlike quality, looking like a scene from the surface of the moon. Bleak, flat, rocky soil spread out in all directions, making this giant berm the only geographic feature in what seemed like a hundred square miles.

The breach spot was twenty miles northwest of Judaiat al Hamir. Charlie Company would cross there, and enter a system of *sha'ibs* and wadis. Bravo Company would cross at a point north of there.

These dry riverbeds would hopefully conceal the Green Berets and their vehicles as they raced northeast.

A recall plan was put into place in the event that Saddam Hussein decided to "play ball" with President Bush at the last second and the invasion was to be called off.

Radio silence was the SOP, except for code words to the HQ when necessary; these were limited to their codes for "Commencing the breach," "First breach is complete," "Second breach commenced," "Second breach complete," and "First vehicle into Iraq." Also, there were code words for the companies when they hit their first phase lines or made contact with the enemy.

It was a clear and windy night; the moonlight was bright enough for some of the soldiers to keep their NVGs flipped up on top of their Kevlar helmets.

The operation was a "Go." Stone by stone, they pounded and tore away at the berm; one rock at a time it began to take the shape of a ramp instead of an obstacle.

The 160th SOAR (Special Operations Aviation Regiment) was on standby with Little Birds and Black Hawks, as well as a flight of USAF fighters. If the Iraqis got wind of these breaches, there would be gunships and fast-movers all over them. As the men dug the breach, the helicopters were in the air, choppers loosing rockets and chain guns at several guard towers south of Bravo Company.

As the choppers "lit up" the Iraqi towers, the SF commanders monitored the enemy radio transmissions; if they weren't wiped out, and called in for a QRF, the Coalition would know about it ahead of time.

Planning in this operation covered every variable the Green Berets could imagine. There was no room for errors, and they had warmed up for this with an unconventional war against the Taliban only a year earlier.

The vehicles topped the berm and crossed into Iraqi territory single file. In the military, this is called "ducks in a row."

An American flag was raised at the breach spot. The flag blew wildly in the windy night as the Green Berets and Australian SAS drove into enemy territory, racing across the flat sands toward their first objective: several areas in Iraq's Western Desert that were designated as being "primary launch sites" for missile attacks against Israel, Jordan, Saudi Arabia, or Kuwait.

SCUD Hunters

The Special Forces went as deep as they could into Iraq. They drove through the night and into the day, trying to get as far as possible.

Haas and his men were to "deny" the Iraqis the capability to launch a SCUD missile attack on anyone: that was their mission.

The Australians with the 5th SFG (A) infiltrated by vehicle at the breach sites, and were also airlifted by the 160th, but their mission was different: find and secure potential landing strips in the desert, so that more forces could be brought in.

COL Mulholland's intent was to be "omnipresent" in western Iraq within the first few hours, flood the west with as many Special Operations "bubbas" as he could, so that the Iraqis couldn't really figure out "Where are they *not?*" and could launch something.

By going in simultaneously close and deep, the Special Forces would have the Iraqis totally overwhelmed.

The seeming battlefield omnipresence of the Special Forces was achieved within eighteen hours. At dawn the following morning, the fight started against the Iraqi Army's counter-recon units, with a few minor contacts.

The morning of March 21 brought more counter-recon units to face the Green Berets. They came from the built-up areas in southwestern Iraq, and from the H-3 airfield in northwestern Iraq, just southeast of Ar Rutbah.

The area that the SF infiltrated was described as a "bowling alley," with terrain that certainly favored the Iraqi defenders in their counter-recon positions.

Over the next three days, Haas's men on the ground fought a

mounted battle against the Iraqi counter-recon units—the Green Berets came out of it clearly on top of the enemy, with better weapons systems, better technology, better vehicles, and better shots.

The Iraqis attacked in pickup trucks with Soviet DHSK "Dishka" mounted anti-aircraft machine guns and five to ten soldiers in the back. Groups of ten or so pickup trucks came out at first. This number dwindled down to four or five pickups after the first few engagements against the four-vehicle Special Forces teams.

According to LTC Haas, "Every team saw combat, and I had ten from my battalion, and three from 3rd Battalion; every team saw combat within the first four or five days."

When Haas saw the Iraqi tactic of trying to outnumber the SF team's vehicles with their own, he switched his tactics and combined the teams into two-team, eight-vehicle patrols instead. The next time the Iraqis came out with ten vehicles, now it was ten on eight instead of ten on four.

The ability of the SF teams to utterly destroy the Iraqi opposition and not have to retrograde or go into a defense gave LTC Haas a feeling of confidence. "It lessened my anxiety. We weren't running, we were destroying stuff," Haas recalled.

Within the first four days, SF teams under Haas's command destroyed over forty vehicles and killed more than one hundred Iraqi soldiers, just in the north, near Ar Rutbah. Charlie Company to the south had an equal damage assessment.

The Florida Army Reserve National Guard (FLARNG) Infantry Company attached to the 5th SFG (A) freed up SF to do what was most important: conduct the counter-recon fight. They had been working with 5th Group for over a month prior to the invasion and training full-time with the Special Forces.

Two of the FLARNG platoons were set up on strip alert as QRFs in case the Green Berets got in over their heads. They also guarded the H-1 Airfield inside Iraq and set up security on the resupply bundles when they came in.

Unfortunately, one of the Florida soldiers lost his life in a rollover crash at H-1 Airfield, but none fell on the battlefield.

A Company from the 10th Mountain Division eventually replaced the Guardsmen who supported 5th SFG (A). The Florida Guard unit was handed back over to Task Force SEMINOLE, responsible for taking care of detainees at H-1 that the SF teams picked up, as well as having a forward logistics site into the west to help out the British and Australians, who were deep inside Iraq.

Haas's battalion had the most ground to cover in the west of Iraq, so he set up his men along the major, high-speed avenues of approach.

TF DAGGER shared a center sector with the Australians, while the British SAS moved along the north. The way that the sectors were divided up was based on history—the launch sites that Iraqis had used during the first Gulf War, good terrain analysis, and new intelligence from NRO (National Reconnaissance Office) imaging satellites.

Underpasses on highways were favored hiding spots for Saddam's ballistic missiles, where they would hopefully be shielded from America's big eyes in the sky.

Unfortunately, this tactic was outdated, so the Special Forces knew that they might have something new up their sleeves. Saddam's most trusted intelligence lay within his Rocket Artillery Corps (the SCUD missile units), and they might try new techniques.

Previously, the SCUD units would lay in wait under a bridge or overpass and briefly emerge when a launch command was given. The missile would be raised and after the launch the vehicle would then retreat to its hide spot under the overpass. Civilian vehicles were used to transport missiles, parts, and supplies to the Iraqi soldiers manning the SCUDs, in an effort to keep a lower profile and keep satellite attention away.

This was Saddam's "Ace in the Hole," and he wanted to protect it as best he could.

Little did Saddam know that he would literally be an "ace in the hole" as well, when he was captured on December 13, 2003.

Based on the known ranges of SCUD missiles and the new locations of potential hide spots, the men of TF DAGGER knew they would have to go deep into Iraq to locate and destroy them. If they were to get to them in time, the Green Berets would have to go directly down Iraq's major highway systems. Forces were arrayed along the highways to prevent Saddam from ordering his missiles to be moved to a new location.

GEN Mosley of the JFACC (Joint Forces Air Component Command) located at PSAB (Prince Sultan Air Base) in Saudi Arabia was the "big boss" of the western Iraq SF mission.

Mosley put together an incredible "air package" available twenty-four hours a day, seven days a week, which provided "superb" air support for the western fight.

A-10 Warthogs, F-16 Eagles, E-3 AWACS (Airborne Warning and Control System) command and control planes, British Tornados— somewhere between sixteen to twenty aircraft were flying CAS missions for Mulholland's Green Berets and their SAS counterparts.

The ground to cover in the SCUD searches was broken up into "keypads," i.e., the sectors to cover were laid out in a grid like the numbers on a touch-tone telephone. The air and ground recon efforts were stacked up adjacent to each other, with real-time SATCOM (SATellite COMmunications) keeping the Green Berets and SAS on the ground constantly in touch with Mulholland and the CJSOTF-W. The aircraft covered different ground than the teams, avoiding duplication and wasted effort, but were near enough so they could be called on for support if the need arose.

The aircraft helped SF teams out of a jam on several occasions. ODA 525 was almost overrun by ten to fifteen Iraqi vehicles. Their call on the SCUDNET saved the team. An F-16 Eagle broke the ceiling, came down "on deck," and saw the enemy vehicles maneuvering on the detachment. The fast-mover "broke the enemy's back there," bringing in CAS right in close to the team and freeing up the ODA to counter-maneuver against the enemy.

The additions of Air Force combat controllers (TAC-Ps) to the SF teams allowed the Air Force's two-fold campaign of air interdiction and support for the SCUD fight, to be de-conflicted and run smoothly without losing assets for either fight because of improper organization or tasking.

Every day, the Israelis threatened to enter the conflict should even one SCUD missile be launched at their country. With this in mind, Mulholland, Haas, and the other Task Force DAGGER commanders were kept constantly on their toes.

According to SF commanders, one of the key lessons learned in the Western Desert SCUD fight was the importance of a Joint Fires Element to prevent green-on-green, or fratricide, and to maximize what both the ODAs and the aircraft could excel at on the battlefield.

All of this had been rehearsed prior to the war in Iraq at an exercise called EV, or EARLY VICTOR, at Nellis AFB in the United States.

Classes included calls for fire, concept of Joint Fires Element, and "live flies," with actual planes in the air and teams on the ground. How were teams to talk to the planes? How were the HQs going to talk to the AWACS? Code words and other intricacies of Saddam's "SCUDNET" were worked out for over two weeks in January 2003, before deployment. Continual rehearsals were performed on-site once the Green Berets arrived in the Middle East, as well.

The art of CAS, with an SF soldier on the ground, allowed for incredible precision and eliminated a great many potential friendly fire incidents and civilian casualties. In LTC Haas's Area of Operations (AO), in the city of Ar Rutbah, precision strikes on the Ba'ath Party headquarters were called in by Green Berets with their eyes on the target. There was much less of a chance of an errant bomb with an expert visually confirming the locations of enemy personnel. There was a Ba'ath Party defensive position in the city's old prison as well, and the Saddam loyalists were using the prison's fortifications—and the hapless inmates—to their advantage.

Signals Intelligence (SIGINT) is a major component of any army; operating without them is operating without communications and command and control (C&C). Major SIGINT stations in western Iraq were also a problem for Coalition bombers; without a man on the ground calling in the air strike, radio towers would be very hard to destroy. A skeletal steel frame and a tall, thin target could stay standing in place after scores of "dumb" bombing runs.

Again, it was the Special Forces eyes on the ground that saved an overexpenditure of ordnance as well as innocent lives. Those eyes on the ground also saved the Air Force time and money by driving up to radio towers and physically setting demo charges on the towers and blowing them up.

Another difficult target for the air assets was the Iraqis' German-built Roland missile systems. Here, Haas's men took out the crafty weapons systems with a combination of Javelin missiles, Mark-19 grenade launchers, and .50 cals.

The war in Iraq could not be won with air superiority alone, and if the Green Berets didn't call in the air strikes, they were neutralizing the enemy with what they had on hand. Both in the north and the west of Iraq, the three-fold arsenal of the Special Forces was always .50 cals, Mark-19s, and Javelins. They could hold their own against the Iraqis with only these three, but it was their mutually beneficial relationship with the joint air components that made the Coalition SCUD hunters unbeatable.

Urban Warfare

After the SCUD threat had been eliminated, CJSOTF-W's gaze was focused on removing the high-level Ba'ath Party officials from power. Throughout the southwestern cities of Iraq: Ar Rutbah, Nekayeb, Haburiayh, Mudaysis, the linkup of 5th Group's ODAs with the local Iraqi forces led to quick HUMINT and subsequent raids on the suspected hideouts.

CA assessments were drawn up at once, and the Civil Affairs teams basically came in "right on top of" the A-Teams. The Civil Affairs activities included the basic necessities—food, water, and supplies.

From Combat to Nation Building

"The people of southern and western Iraq are self-sufficient and independent," according to LTC Haas. "Hard core; they live pretty austere lives."

The Special Forces Civil Affairs teams established a city government in Ar Rutbah. MAJ Jim Gravillis, the B Company/5th SFG (A) commander in Ar Rutbah, "did some historical, fantastic stuff," according to Haas. Gravillis quickly put together a city election, organized a vote for mayor, and had a flag-raising ceremony celebrating Ar Rutbah's liberation from the Ba'ath Party. A police force was reestablished; humanitarian NGOs were brought in to repair the hospitals and get the electricity and water up and running.

Combat operations were immediately replaced with nation building.

At the same time, MAJ Gravillis's B Company ran two checkpoints: one in Tirbil, on the Jordanian-Iraqi border, and one up north on the Syrian-Jordanian border. 10th Mountain Division companies were brought in to augment the Special Forces teams. Hundreds, maybe thousands, of young Syrian males were turned away at the borders before they could enter Iraq to assist in the guerrilla fight against Coalition forces. They carried no weapons, but their MOs were easily discernible: lots of money (over $50,000 on some of the men) and directions on them as to who to link up with inside Iraq to fight the Americans.

The wannabe *jihadists* tried to come into Iraq on buses. There would be one bus with several families on it, then the next bus would be "loaded down" with fifty to sixty young males. They were interrogated and sent back across the border, while the "legitimate" families were allowed to proceed into Iraq to visit their relatives or reenter the country after fleeing before the start of the war. The 2nd BN/5th SFG (A) continued at Tirbil and Charlie Company from the 3rd BN/5th SFG (A) remained at the northern checkpoint.

According to Haas, MAJ Paul Ott "did fantastic work" in the Tehayab, Haburiyah, and Mudaysis airfield areas in the southwest.

SF's ability to blend in and care for the "host-nation" populace made the areas under their control very safe and friendly. They had gained experience in helping people in Afghanistan and this paid off when they built a rapport with the local Iraqis.

It became such a friendly, permissive environment for U.S. forces that LTC Haas was able to reposition Ott's company into the Akashat area to examine the phosphate mines there and to perform linkups with locals in that vicinity. Periodically, an A-Team or two would be sent back to their original southwest areas to ensure that everything was still under control. The close-knit tribal government there worked very efficiently and the locals were supplemented by airdrops of food and medical supplies, as well as work on their electricity and water sources.

This was dubbed by Haas as an "economy of force," which was moved northward to address problems along the Syria-Iraq border, where the ODAs were needed the most.

Private Contractors

Sheraton: An Author's Note

When I landed in Iraq in October 2003, the first place I went was the front door of the Baghdad International Airport, dragging my suitcase behind me, my travel companion Russell Cummings following. We were both eager to get out of the airport and into the city of Baghdad. At the entrance, a very tall American-looking guy waiting there introduced himself as John Jones of KBR (Kellogg, Brown & Root).

KBR is a major contracting and recruiting company for military men who still want to work in a related field after their retirement. It has rapidly become a club for former Special Forces men who are accustomed to an exciting and sometimes violent existence and who are grateful to find employment of the sort they feel most comfortable with. At an average salary of $100,000 per year, retired Special Forces men between the ages of thirty-five and fifty are delighted to go back to work for a few years, particularly in the field of security and in areas of difficult circumstance and unrest.

Jones was looking for his assistant, another American, who oversees airport security for KBR. It seems we weren't leaving the airport as quickly or easily as we thought. We waited for about half an hour before the security man arrived with the news that we were all set to go into the city of Baghdad, to the Sheraton Hotel.

From reading the newspapers, I had no idea of the level of danger awaiting anyone who landed at Baghdad International Airport. If you were not picked up by a military convoy, you were severely placing your life at risk. Even the convoys at times were attacked on the way back to Baghdad.

The drive from the airport to Baghdad took about an hour. We had to proceed quite slowly, with alternating bursts of speed as we negotiated "ambush alley," which went on for about seven miles. You never knew when someone with an RPG (rocket-propelled grenade) would shoot across your bow.

We navigated "ambush alley" successfully and arrived safely at the Sheraton Hotel in Baghdad. By this time I had come to know John Jones a little bit, but I never again saw his airport security man who was constantly having problems out there at the airport.

The Sheraton Hotel is a misnomer—the Sheraton Hotel Corporation will not admit that there is a Sheraton Hotel in Baghdad. Even I, a former Sheraton employee for nine years, was told there is no Sheraton Hotel in Baghdad. The truth is that the Sheraton Hotel Corporation was caught by Saddam in a corporate tangle, which ended up with Saddam taking the hotel away from the parent company. This was the kind of move that Saddam had been making for some time against American corporations that did not give in to Iraqi government extortions.

I quickly saw that no American company would put up the kind of money it took to create a hotel of the sumptuous quality the Sheraton, Baghdad enjoyed. The name Sheraton was all over the hotel despite its nonassociation with the American hotel company.

We did not check in, but went immediately to the eighth floor with our luggage. The eighth floor of the hotel was leased out in its entirety to KBR, as was half of the seventh floor. The offices of KBR were on the eighth floor; the bedrooms for its transitory personnel were on the seventh floor. Russell and I were each given a room on the seventh floor, which were sumptuous by any standards, though the maid service was lacking and chairs were missing. The beds were not really made up, but the single sheet was clean. We knew we were lucky to have a clean, safe place to sleep.

The Sheraton felt at times more like a crazy office park than a hotel. On the fourth floor of the Sheraton, FOX News had their Baghdad HQ. Russell and I thought we should call on our neighbors. The first person we met was an Iraqi "businessman," who was hired by FOX to fix any problems they might run into. His name was Amore, pronounced like the French word for "love." He introduced us to the manager of the FOX HQ. Soon Russell and I had the run of the fourth floor and spent quite a bit of time of the first few days watching FOX News broadcasts to New York.

Their star broadcaster was a former NBC correspondent in Iraq named Dana Lewis. I was very impressed with his delivery on screen, and I introduced myself to him saying I was in Baghdad to write a book, continuing in the tradition of *The Green Berets* and of my last book, *The Hunt for Bin Laden*.

The FOX News group served a fine luncheon and supper at their dining/recreation room, which always had cold soft drinks and a TV set on. But most valuable was their direct line to New York City, which they also let me use on occasion. I hope I never abused the privilege, but when I needed to make a call to the United States the Fox phone was always there.

The other connection I had to home was my satellite phone, which had served me well over Christmas of 2002, when I was in Afghanistan. The satellite phone worked most of the time from the Sheraton Hotel as we stood out on our balcony, overlooking the mosque and the palace. Directly below us was the deserted area where the statue of Saddam Hussein had been pulled down for television viewers around the world to see.

John Jones, a former Green Beret and fellow member of Chapter 38 Special Forces Association (Fort Campbell, Kentucky) was very gracious to me. It was impossible to get secure transportation inside of Baghdad without having some official connection, and John saw to it that we were able to get where we wanted to go in the city. And thus began my odyssey of traveling around Iraq in the midst of counterinsurgency and terrorism. While I was there, five helicopters were shot down. Nevertheless traveling by chopper was the only way to travel around the country. There were convoys taking gasoline and food all the way from Kuwait to Turkey, run by KBR and the military, but with the worries of ambushes and IEDs (improvised explosive devices) and considering the slower pace of convoy travel, we took our chances in the air.

By the time we left, Russell Cummings (retired Special Forces himself) had been offered a job with KBR, which he immediately accepted. In all, our time and travels with KBR showed us yet another side to the war, the search for Saddam, and the massive effort involved in rebuilding a nation.

A Murky Area

As of late October 2003, NGOs (Non-Governmental Organizations) did not have a large presence in Iraq. At most, there were some NGO "Command and Control," or assessment teams, but that was about it. "Private contractors such as KBR are not really considered to be the same entities as NGOs, but this is a murky area to get into," said an officer with the 101st Airborne Division.

The private contractor's involvement in modern warfare has grown exponentially in the last ten years or so. It is now ten times the private involvement during Operation DESERT STORM in 1991, according to Peter W. Singer, a Brookings Institution military analyst. With manpower estimates ranging between ten thousand and twenty thousand people, that would place private contractors in second place behind the United States in terms of the number of people they had contributed to the Coalition.

There were a number of contracting firms with a foothold in Operation IRAQI FREEDOM support. The aerospace giant Northrop Grumman had its own contracting business—Vinnell Corporation, based in Fairfax, Virginia, and operating mainly in the Middle East and Southeast Asia.

MPRI, a division of L-3 Communications, is also based in Virginia—no surprise as Virginia is also home to Langley and "the farm." MPRI has seen action in many African theaters, Bosnia, Eastern Europe, and South America. Among their job postings were: "Public Affairs Trainers" who "provide professional and skill training to Iraqi journalists and broadcasters" and "Military Trainers" who concentrate on developing professional soldiering skills in new Iraqi Army recruits. DynCorp, a division of Computer Sciences Corporation, is also from Virginia. Don't let the innocuous name fool you; these guys don't program computers.

There are quite a few non-American contractors in Iraq. Armor-Group (United States and the United Kingdom) and their subsidiary Defense Systems Ltd. are present in Iraq, as well as many other Middle Eastern countries, African republics, and in South America. Control Risks Group, Ltd., and Sandline International are both from Britain as well. An emphasis is placed on protecting power, oil, and electricity resources, which private contractors do daily. Erinys is a little-known security contractor staffed with former South African Special Forces, who train more than sixty-five hundred Iraqis in how to effectively guard their oil fields.

The largest contractor in Iraq by far is Kellogg, Brown & Root, otherwise known as KBR. KBR is a unit of Halliburton, a huge, politically connected Houston, Texas, conglomerate, once headed by Vice President Dick Cheney. KBR handles every task imaginable: from feeding soldiers to logistics, and rebuilding the nation's infrastructure.

Tivador Toth has been working for KBR for nine years, as director of engineering. He had been in Hungary before the Iraq War. Toth arrived with his KBR team in Kuwait in March 2003 with the first Coalition troops and began the construction of a base camp on a large airfield. KBR takes over logistical functions that can free up U.S. troops for more traditional duties, such as combat. By July he had moved into Iraq, straight to Tikrit.

It is up to the government to determine the amount of money that will be spent on rebuilding Iraq, and liaisons working with companies like KBR determine how these funds will be allocated. Whatever the government decides the cost will be for the particular contract, KBR adds 2 percent to the total, "almost nothing," according to Toth. As for what he thinks the U.S. government will eventually spend in Iraq, he wouldn't wager a guess.

The construction and logistics arm of KBR checks on the availability of the client's (in this case, the U.S. Army) requirements in the local markets to coordinate exactly what they need. Plans, designs, and calculations estimate how much it will cost, a timeline of how long it will take, and how to be the most efficient. The Army decides whether it will accept the estimate—a process that Toth said sometimes took too long.

Manpower is not a problem—private contracting firms have ready access to personnel. They come as advisers, trainers, instructors, and leaders from a multitude of nations, including the United States, Bosnia, and Hungary, or are hired in the indigenous country—in this case Iraq. It is the nonstop, eighteen-hour workdays, from early morning until after midnight, that sap their strength.

The task of rebuilding Iraq and restoring self-sufficiency to its people will not be an easy task, and it simply will not be over in a year or two. And when the Coalition and their private contractors finally do pick up shop and leave, Toth believes that they will leave a vacuum in their wake.

John Jones

John Jones is the chief of Middle Eastern security for KBR. His personal history with warfare and the Special Forces goes back to 1962. After completing Special Forces Training Group in 1963, he served as a junior demolitions expert on a Special Forces "A" in Vietnam in 1964. At twenty years of age, he underwent his "baptism of fire" when the CIDG (Civilian Irregular Defense Group, an Asian mercenary group) platoon he was advising was ambushed by the North Vietnamese Army. He and the platoon "ran" for three days before he could get a helicopter to evacuate the seriously wounded. He kept the walking wounded with him as they managed to fight their way back to his camp, Duc-Co. He was awarded the Bronze Star with "V" device for his actions. Jones's twenty-year career included seven years in conventional airborne units as a platoon sergeant. In 1978 he was in Panama as the senior engineer on a Special Forces "A" team (SCUBA) when the opportunity came to volunteer for Delta Force, a new counterterrorist organization being formed by COL Charlie Beckwith, a Special Forces legend, at Fort Bragg, North Carolina. Jones immediately volunteered for the selection program.

Jones was accepted by the board and began the rigorous Delta Force training. By the time Jones began his Delta training, he had already completed the other Army schools and programs that are considered by professional soldiers to be the most demanding. He questioned what this new training course would offer that he had not already experienced. He soon found out—between keeping up with the high standards of the organization, the intellectual aspect of the training and the peer pressure, it was one of the most demanding courses he had ever completed. Jones learned skills and concepts that would serve him well for the rest of his life.

He also came to respect COL Beckwith well above other officers he had served with during his career and felt that COL Beckwith also respected him. Perhaps Beckwith admired Jones's unconventional "the ends justify the means" approach, while Jones clearly admired the brilliance and ferocity of the Special Forces legend.

Jones was now a master sergeant in the 1st Special Forces Operational Detachment-Delta, or SFOD-D, also known as Delta Force. Among the many missions Jones and Beckwith took part in, the Delta Force mission with particular lasting impact on war planning and on Operation IRAQI FREEDOM was Operation EAGLE CLAW.

EAGLE CLAW

In April 1980, Delta Force was alerted with a potential mission to rescue American hostages held by Iranian militants in Tehran, Iran. COL Beckwith would be the ground commander. The rescue mission would be very complex; members of all four branches of the Armed Forces were involved and the plan included the use of twenty aircraft.

Four MC-130s were to bring the Delta team, the Air Force combat controllers, and the Ranger Company into the staging area/helicopter refueling point outside Tehran, code-named Desert One. Beckwith began planning in earnest, and requested that ten RH-53 helicopters be available for the mission. The Air Force was only able to provide eight birds, their reasoning being that only eight RH-53s could fit onto the deck of an aircraft carrier.

While Delta Force was to perform the actual rescue, a platoon from Charlie Company, 1st BN/75th Ranger Regiment was to provide security for the men and equipment once it landed at Desert Two, the staging area where the hostages would be brought after they were rescued from Tehran. Unfortunately, the mission never made it past Desert One.

The combined rescue force assembled in Egypt on April 21, 1980. Three days later, a fleet of C-141 Starlifters carried the 120-man force to Masirah Island, off the coast of Oman, where they transferred to three MC-130 Combat Talons, accompanied by three fuel-bearing EC-130s.

The Delta Force/Ranger task force landed two hundred miles southeast of Tehran at 2200 hours and waited for the arrival of eight RH-53D "Sea Stallion" helicopters that had lifted off the deck of the aircraft carrier USS *Nimitz*. A twelve-man road watch team, composed primarily of Rangers, was along to secure the site while the helicopters refueled. The team would return to Egypt on one of the Combat Talons.

Before dawn on April 25, SFOD-D was to be flown to a predetermined coordinate by the Sea Stallions, where they were met by CIA assets, who led them to a nearby safe house. The helicopters would remain at their own hide site until the assault on the U.S. embassy compound where the American hostages were held. The plan was to use the helicopters to ferry the hostages to waiting transport.

Beckwith's most important HUMINT ground asset was retired Special Forces legend Dick Meadows, who was in Tehran under the cover of an Irishman. Meadows had conducted the surveillance of the objective, and if the mission had been a "go," he would have taken COL Beckwith on a recon mission prior to the Delta team's insertion.

The task of the Rangers was to secure a landing area for the transports. The Rangers were to fly from Egypt to Manzariyeh, Iran, and secure the airfield there. They would land if possible, or parachute in if enemy resistance was offered.

Once the airfield, which was thirty-five miles south of Tehran, was secure, the Rangers would hold it while C-141s arrived to airlift the hostages and the Delta Force team back to Egypt. The Rangers would then "dry up," or remove all signs of their presence, render the field useless, and be airlifted out themselves.

Taking over and securing a hostile airfield within enemy territory is one of the primary components of the Ranger mission. They were prepared to hold the field as long as necessary if there were not enough transports to take everyone out in one trip. During their training, the Rangers worked out all probable scenarios on a mock-up of the target airfield in Iran.

However, the Rangers did not cross-train with Delta Force, the Air Force flight crews, or the Marine Sea Stallion crews. No one had cross-trained, and there was no dress rehearsal before the green light came on. This would turn out to be an issue for a congressional investigation conducted after the tragedy that soon unfolded.

Two of the helicopters suffered excessive hydraulics malfunctions within four hours of leaving the deck of the *Nimitz* on the Arabian Sea; once grounded, one of the hydraulics repairs was too extensive to be performed on-site. The other six choppers were lagging behind due to bad weather. Having "go/no-go" authority, and refusing to risk leaving anyone behind, COL Beckwith aborted the mission.

After Beckwith's order, one of the Sea Stallions crashed into an EC-130 Hercules while trying to refuel on the ground, creating a huge fireball that engulfed both aircraft. The tip of the Stallion's main rotor had clipped the cockpit area of the EC-130 as it jockeyed into position for refueling. This dangerous refueling practice was known as "hopscotching," and has been largely replaced by air-to-air refueling because of the safety hazards involved. Five Air Force crewmen and three Marine helicopter crewmen perished.

There wasn't enough time to destroy what remained; in the rush to "un-ass the AO" the Sea Stallions were left in place, and the whole scene was under the Iranian military's control by the next day. Moreover, the ground assets were compromised and almost killed. Although planning for a second mission was begun immediately, it was never attempted.

Later, at the congressional investigation, Beckwith was questioned as to why he hadn't gone ahead with the rescue mission, despite the loss of the helicopters.

"I promised the president of the United States that we would not go through with the mission if we lost even one helicopter," Beckwith answered. He had been under direct presidential orders, although that was not known by any of the other commanders at Desert One.

The congressional investigators then questioned Beckwith about the problems with Operation EAGLE CLAW.

Beckwith responded with his own question. "Sir, if you had a professional football team with the line practicing in New York, and the backfield in California, and the first time they met up was the day of the big game, how would you expect them to play?"

This was a turning point in combined special ops missions, and led to the founding of JSOC, the Joint Special Operations Command, less than eight months later. Critical mission failures were directly related to a lack of training, communication, proper rehearsal, and commanders that were unwilling to work with others as part of a joint operation with just one ground commander who has distinct authority over others. The standard Cold War operating procedure of compartmentalization could seriously affect the mission outcome, so JSOC was activated on December 15, 1980, and based at Pope AFB, North Carolina.

Although JSOC's official purpose is to provide a "unified command structure for conducting joint special operations and exercises," numerous reports indicate that JSOC is actually the command responsible for conducting U.S. counterterrorism (CT) operations. According to published reports, JSOC also commands the U.S. military's Special Missions Units (SMUs). SMUs are tasked with conducting CT operations, strike operations, reconnaissance in denied areas, and "special intelligence missions." JSOC's patch is symbolic of the cooperation between the Armed Services, with four swords crossing each other over a globe.

Despite its failure, Desert One brought together some of the greatest minds in special operations, including Dick Meadows, Charlie Beckwith, John Jones, and Pete Schoomaker. Schoomaker was a Delta Force Squadron commander on Operation EAGLE CLAW; after twenty years, GEN Schoomaker was back in the desert sands of the Middle East yet again.

Schoomaker commanded SFOD-D squadrons through three decades (1978–1981 and 1989–1992) on and off, and had a mastery and appreciation for unconventional warfare that few could match.

Schoomaker retired as commander of U.S. Special Operations Command at Ft. Mac Dill AFB in Florida in November 2000, and many felt that his knowledge of Special Warfare was lost forever in the post-9/11 Global War on Terror—a campaign in which such knowledge would be needed the most. Things were about to change, though, as for only the second time in the history of the United States, an officer would be taken from retirement and put back on active duty by a president. The first time was by John F. Kennedy, when he asked retired U.S. Army GEN Maxwell Taylor to serve as the chairman of the Joint Chiefs of Staff in 1962. George W. Bush made his mark on history, and asked Schoomaker to step up to the plate.

On June 17, 2003, President Bush nominated retired GEN Peter J. Schoomaker to be the Army's thirty-fifth chief of staff. The Senate confirmed Schoomaker before he took up his new duties, and on August 2, 2003, GEN Pete Schoomaker replaced GEN Eric Shinseki.

Shinseki had disagreed with Defense Secretary Donald Rumsfeld over the size of the U.S. force in Iraq. Was the war in Iraq turning into another Vietnam? The parallel was increasingly drawn between the two conflicts, as the Coalition's time spent in Iraq mounted.

The most frequent comparison in the special operations community was the similarity of pro-Saddam Iraqi insurgents and the Viet Cong. How do you fight an ideology? The dangers that Coalition forces faced did not meet them on the field of battle, and did not carry a flag or obey the rules of engagement. The skills and lessons learned in Vietnam-era guerrilla warfare could prove to be of great worth in Operation IRAQI FREEDOM.

Schoomaker understood the complexities and nuances of unconventional warfare (UW) and counterterrorism (CT). *De Oppresso Liber,* the motto of Special Forces, was a focus of Operation IRAQI FREEDOM, while "Speed, Surprise, and Violence of Action," the motto of SFOD-D, would also come into play when U.S. forces were able to focus on and strike a definitive enemy force.

The toughest thing to do, then, was to identify the enemy. John Jones, also on the EAGLE CLAW mission, left Delta Force after Beckwith did in 1981. Jones recalled that Beckwith had become a broken man after the incident at Desert One, and lost his shot at becoming a general.

Jones went to Texas after leaving Delta Force. Coincidentally, Texas was home to Halliburton and KBR, though it wasn't until 1999 that Jones joined KBR, finding a perfect niche for his skills. This time with KBR, he went to Baghdad, and Delta-mate Pete Schoomaker was with him (figuratively) as well. As head of Iraq security for KBR, and headquartered in one of Saddam's palaces, Jones works on the security concerns in Iraq.

According to Jones, there are four groups of Saddam loyalists that are of major concern since the defeat of the Iraqi Army. The first group of Saddam supporters is motivated by money or their former positions, which they may have lost and would like to regain. Perhaps they've lost family members supporting Saddam. They are willing to attack Coalition forces, although in Jones's opinion, "they are not willing to commit hari-kari and be suicide bombers. They're willing to do ambushes, but they want to get away and get the money they're being paid by pro-Saddam groups for doing the ambushes."

The second group of Saddam supporters is the Shi'ite Muslims in the south of Iraq, who are funded and supported by the Iranians. The Iranian motivation for this is that they do not want a democracy in the Middle East. An Iraqi democracy could be a model that other countries might want to emulate, which would weaken Iran's monarchy. So, it is to Iran's advantage that the Coalition fail in Iraq.

The third group is comprised of people with purely terrorist motivations, such as Al Qaeda. They will work with Shi'ites, others, or just by themselves. They will pound on U.S. military forces just for the sake of pounding on them, much as they brought down the World Trade Center, showing the world that America was vulnerable.

The fourth group is the Palestinians. The Palestinians are coming into Iraq to draw attention to and further their cause in Palestine. Not one of these four groups of Saddam supporters is concerned with the well-being of the Iraqi people. The Saddam supporters "are all out for themselves," Jones said. Only the Coalition forces are truly concerned with encouraging, protecting, and perpetuating the well-being of the Iraqi people.

According to Jones, "The Coalition forces are here for the right reasons—the Iraqi people. We are willing to hedge our bets, and we are willing to risk our young men and women to make that happen.

"When the U.N. and other organizations stand up and criticize us—the Coalition; the Brits, the Spanish, the Australians, whoever is here trying to make that happen . . . it's so much bullshit, and the American people buy into it. They should stop and really consider what was going on. But we [Americans] buy into the news media's thoughts of why we are doing this. The news media is presenting a negative picture that we're buying into, as we did with Vietnam.

What people don't realize is that Iraq is a pretty big country, about the size of California, eight hundred miles long and three to four hundred miles wide."

Substantial ground to cover and the simple fact that Coalition forces are so outnumbered by Iraqi population give the Coalition only one choice—to win the support of the Iraqi populace. "We have to *win* the peace, not *force* the peace," Jones explained. "This is only my humble opinion," he added.

"Understand the difference between those two? Winning the peace is putting these people to work; getting them money that they can support their families with, so that they're too damn tired at night to pick up a gun and go out and attack the Coalition forces.

"And then when they get their second and third paycheck, and they will have fed their family, their wife is like, 'Hey, Amman, don't fuck this up.' They want to keep this paycheck coming in. That's what we've got to do to win this war, get them to earn money and support their families; something they haven't been able to do in thirty years.

"Iraqis must be convinced to do the right thing. Try rewarding correct behavior and taking away items or choices for bad behavior. There is a lot of commonality between the war in Iraq and the war in Vietnam. There were a lot of lessons learned there that could be applied here. Convoys need to be covered and ambushes need to be stopped before they occur. All of the gasoline that is imported, around a thousand trucks a day, is all being brought in by Coalition forces. A convoy without air cover is a beautiful target to an insurgent."

The New Iraqi Army

Two new military units have been placed on the border between Iraq and Iran to stop the flow of terrorists into the country. New Iraqi Army units are being trained to perform border security. This army is a battalion-sized unit of former Iraqi soldiers. Former Ba'ath Party loyalists are screened before they are allowed to join, but they are accepted if they want the job and are willing to work with Coalition forces.

The screening was accomplished by a combination of HUMINT (Human Intelligence) and cross-checking of names and information in counterintelligence databases. Questions most important in screening include, but are not limited to: Was the candidate a card-carrying member of the Ba'ath Party? Was the candidate involved in the black market or the drug trade? What was the former position the person held, and did they fit into the mold of an extreme Saddam loyalist?

According to a private-sector trainer, most towns in Iraq are "clannish," where everybody knows everybody else's business. This makes it simple in most cases to find out whether a potential recruit was a "good guy or a bad guy."

Part of the funding for the New Iraq Army, border guards, and other projects comes from Saddam Hussein's assets, which were frozen, captured, and "held in escrow," so to speak, after the Coalition invasion, and paid out by the government of Iraq. Money in the Mosul region that used to belong to Saddam has also been put into several hundred schools, playgrounds, youth centers, and a nearby health care facility that treats three hundred people per week.

Letters from Tikrit

The Lion's Den: An Author's Note

At the end of our visit with the 101st Airborne in Mosul, Russell Cummings and I headed down to Tikrit, the home territory of Saddam Hussein. Our Black Hawk helicopter landed at the Ironhorse Drop Zone, which was nothing more than a large concrete circle stuck in the middle of a radius of some two thousand feet or more, and surrounded by the city of Tikrit.

Russell and I had been invited to spend some time in Tikrit as the guest of Mark Vargas and KBR (Kellogg, Brown & Root) at their headquarters in Tikrit, named Camp Speicher after the Navy officer who was shot down in that area during Operation DESERT STORM, and remains Missing in Action. Camp Speicher is a two-square-mile area fenced in and guarded closely by both American and Iraqi guard duty troopers.

The Black Hawk quickly dropped us off and departed to its next destination. With all the shootings in the area we were naturally apprehensive, and the short wait seemed much longer than it actually was. Finally, two welcoming female PAO (Public Affairs Office) officers arrived to collect us in an SUV, which was reputedly armor plated. As I put myself into the front seat of the SUV, I thought of my old friend, COL Nick Rowe, who was in a "hardened" SUV when he was shot dead by a com-

The Ivy Division

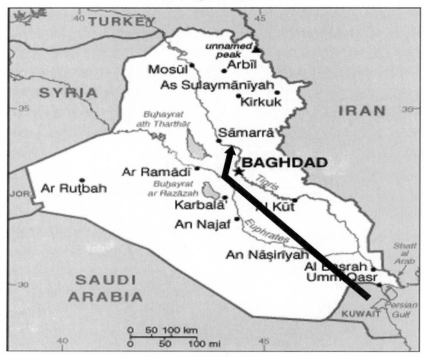

The Fourth Infantry Division (Mechanized) is also known as the Ivy Division. "Ivy" is a play on words for the Roman numeral IV; also, ivy is a symbol of strength and tenacity—this is also the distinctive symbol on the Division's shoulder patch. The 4th ID's Area of Operations was Saddam Hussein's stronghold—the riverside city of Tikrit (located at the end of the arrow). *Courtesy:* CIA World Factbook 2003

munist assassin in the Philippines. I wondered if our SUV had the same degree of hardening as Nick's car, and rather hoped it had more.

This was truly Saddam territory. We could feel it in the air, as we drove through Tikrit on our first-day tour given by the gracious PAOs. After the tour we were taken to our lodging for the first night: the palace known as the "The Ladies Palace," where Saddam's two sons purportedly kept their girlfriends. Like all of Saddam's palaces, it was beautiful and lacked nothing in the area of decorations. It was here that I first noticed that Saddam's initials on walls, corners, and ceilings. (See a photograph of a typical circular initialed emblem in the first photo section.)

Everything was luxurious; marble adorned the walls and floors. All opulent except for one dreadfully lacking area: the latrines. In typical

This shot shows the barren wasteland of sand, stone, and rocks that make up much of the landscape of southern Iraq. The view is toward the outskirts of Baghdad, seen in the distance. *(Courtesy of COL Joseph Anderson, 101st Airborne, 2nd Brigade)*

aken from the vantage point of a room at the Sheraton Hotel in aghdad. Mosques typically provide the only big splash of color Iraqi cities, as in the dome and minaret of the mosque shown ere. *(Courtesy of Russ Cummings)*

Aerial view of a corner of Mosul and the Tigris River *(Courtesy of COL Joseph Anderson, 101st Airborne, 2nd Brigade)*

A typical Mosul street scene with U.S. soldiers on patrol *(Courtesy of COL Joseph Anderson, 101st Airborne, 2nd Brigade)*

View of Baghdad, November 2003 *(Courtesy of Department of Defense and Staff Sgt. Stacy Pearsall)*

An armored personnel carrier convoy from the 101st rolls into Baghdad. *(Courtesy of Bill Angelucci)*

Some soldiers came by sea. *(Courtesy of COL Joseph Anderson, 101st Airborne, 2nd Brigade)*

A HUMMWV convoy *(Courtesy of COL Joseph Anderson, 101st Airborne, 2nd Brigade)*

Troops await helicopter transport to continue their journey into Iraq *(Courtesy of COL Joseph Anderson, 101st Airborne, 2nd Brigade)*

The author looks out of a Black Hawk, a type of helicopter frequently used on the Baghdad-Mosul route. *(Courtesy of Russ Cummings)*

Medallions with Saddam's initials in Arabic were everywhere—on the doors of his palaces, on walls and ceilings, and in the corner tiles of almost every fresco or mosaic in Iraq. *(Courtesy of Russ Cummings)*

Coalition Provisional Authority (CPA) Headquarters hired an Iraqi contractor to remove the first large head of Saddam Hussein from the top of the palace in Baghdad. Saddam's narcissism was omnipresent in Iraq: every main entrance to his palaces had a bust of him. Prior to Operation IRAQI FREEDOM, full statues, busts, billboards, and posters of Saddam were found throughout Iraq. *(Courtesy of the Department of Defense and Staff Sgt. Reynaldo Ramon)*

An upstairs hall in Saddam's palace. Notice the chandelier that runs the length of the ceiling. *(Courtesy of Mark Vargas, CSM (D) Ret., USSF)*

The author sits in Saddam's golden throne in Baghdad's presidential palace. John Jones, head of Baghdad security for KBR, stands at his side. *(Courtesy of Russ Cummings)*

Members of ODA 056, in the vicinity of Mosul airfield. Note the Soviet-era ZSU AA machine gun being towed by their Land Rover. *(Courtesy of U.S. Special Forces, 10th Group)*

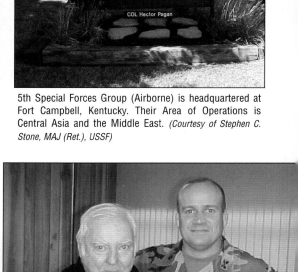

5th Special Forces Group (Airborne) is headquartered at Fort Campbell, Kentucky. Their Area of Operations is Central Asia and the Middle East. *(Courtesy of Stephen C. Stone, MAJ (Ret.), USSF)*

The northern Iraq town of Ayn Sifni, seen through a spotting scope from a hilltop Observation Post 2, north of the town, before the attack. *(Courtesy of U.S. Special Forces, 10th Group)*

Surveillance photo of an Iraqi bunker in the vicinity of Ayn Sifni. *(Courtesy of U.S. Special Forces, 10th Group)*

The author interviews LTC Haas, a Special Forces battalion commander with the 5th Special Forces Group (Airborne). *(Courtesy of Stephen C. Stone, MAJ (Ret.), USSF)*

The Tikrit palace, destroyed in 1991, rebuilt in 1995, and bombed in Operation IRAQI FREEDOM. One of Saddam's favorite palaces, and in his hometown, it is now a command post for the 4th Infantry Division. *(Courtesy of Mark Vargas, CSM (D) Ret., USSF)*

he Iraqi National Training Camp is located on an island, which is art of the Tikrit palace compound. Here, ex–Special Forces nstructors train Iraqi police, Civil Defense Corps, and border uards, so that Iraq can be self-sufficient after the war. *(Courtesy f Mark Vargas, CSM (D) Ret., USSF)*

Once a grand, ornate hall in Hussein's Tikrit palace, this room now serves as a place for American soldiers to pump iron during "down time." *(Courtesy of Russ Cummings)*

At Camp Speicher, named after a downed American aviator who remains missing from the first Gulf War, housing is in the form of cargo containers that hold a bedroom on each end and a bathroom in the middle. *(Courtesy of Mark Vargas, CSM (D) Ret., USSF)*

FOB Ironhorse is the name of 4th ID's base in Tikrit. Photo shows the FOB Ironhorse helicopter pad. Behind the wall in the background is the Detention Center where Saddam was first taken after capture. *(Courtesy of Mark Vargas, CSM (D) Ret., USSF)*

The "broke-down palace" in Mosul: the 101st Airborne had to rebuild the entire interior in the process of taking it as their general headquarters. *(Courtesy of Russ Cummings)*

Mosul's many bridges and other strategic points need constant guard against Iraqi insurgents. *(Courtesy of COL Joseph Anderson, 101st Airborne, 2nd Brigade)*

The 101st relies on choppers for their mobility; Black Hawks, Apaches, and Kiowas are in their arsenal. *(Courtesy of COL Joseph Anderson, 101st Airborne, 2nd Brigade)*

Bruce Willis and The Accelerators perform for the Screaming Eagles on September 25 2003, in Tallifar, near Mosul, on their "Touch of Home" tour. *(Courtesy of COL Joseph Anderson, 101st Airborne, 2nd Brigade, and PFC Thomas Day)*

CSM Jerry Lee Wilson (right) was KIA shortly after this photo was taken; he had reenlisted for the war to be with his longtime friend, Colonel Anderson (middle). Dana Lewis, embedded reporter for NBC and later Fox News, is on the left.
(Courtesy of Bill Angelucci)

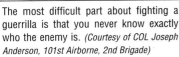

The most difficult part about fighting a guerrilla is that you never know exactly who the enemy is. *(Courtesy of COL Joseph Anderson, 101st Airborne, 2nd Brigade)*

Air Assault outfits such as the 101st rely on their birds to get them in and out of combat faster than any other conventional infantry unit. *(Courtesy of COL Joseph Anderson, 101st Airborne, 2nd Brigade)*

COL Anderson earned the title "Smokin' Joe" for his skill at knocking out his opposition as a champion boxer while a young officer. *(Courtesy of Russ Cummings)*

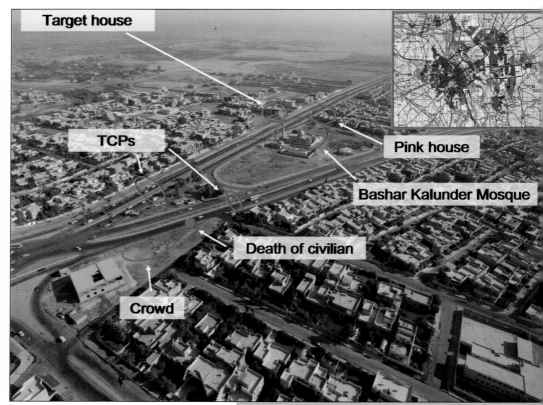

Target house

TCPs

Pink house

Bashar Kalunder Mosque

Death of civilian

Crowd

An aerial photo detailing the major events and locations of the raid on Uday and Qusay in Mosul. *(Courtesy of COL Joseph Anderson, 101st Airborne, 2nd Brigade)*

A soldier from the Strike Brigade's blocking force mans a vehicle-mounted M2HB .50 caliber machine gun. *(Courtesy of COL Joseph Anderson, 101st Airborne, 2nd Brigade)*

Anderson's men came under fire from a sniper located in the upstairs apartment of this pink house across the street from the objective. *(Courtesy of COL Joseph Anderson, 101st Airborne, 2nd Brigade)*

Good reconnaissance is vital to the success of any mission. It could have been the difference between life and death to Task Force 20 when it confronted the Hussein brothers. *(Courtesy of COL Joseph Anderson, 101st Airborne, 2nd Brigade)*

Saddam's sons are shown here postmortem, after the raid.
(Courtesy of COL Gainer, CPIC PRESSDESK)

A Kiowa gunship circles over the target area to provide close air support for Task Force 20 and Colonel Anderson's blocking force from the 101st.
(Courtesy of COL Joseph Anderson, 101st Airborne, 2nd Brigade)

Volleys of wire-guided TOW missiles were used when the Hussein brothers made their last stand and continued to return fire on the assault force. *(Courtesy of COL Joseph Anderson, 101st Airborne, 2nd Brigade)*

Colonel "Smokin' Joe" Anderson calls for support fire from Kiowa gunships after Task Force 20's assault force is beaten back by a torrent of gunfire from the holed-up fugitives. *(Courtesy of COL Joseph Anderson, 101st Airborne, 2nd Brigade)*

Improvised Explosive Devices, or IEDs, claim the lives of Coalition solders in Iraq nearly every day. *(Courtesy of Mark Vargas, CSM (D) Ret., USSF)*

IEDs are found in many forms, such as this makeshift mortar that fires rocks, metal (nuts, bolts, etc.), or glass from a tube or pipe packed with gunpowder taken from dismantled artillery shells. *(Courtesy of Mark Vargas, CSM (D) Ret., USSF)*

IEDs can be made from almost anything, but key components are wiring, a firing device, a primary explosive (blasting cap), a secondary explosive (gunpowder), and projectiles for fragmentation. From a distance, IEDs like this one are indistinguishable from roadside debris. *(Courtesy of Mark Vargas, CSM (D) Ret., USSF)*

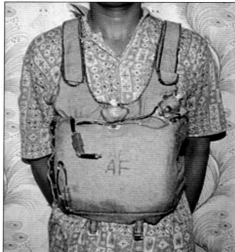

Suicide bomber vests like this one were found stockpiled in many locations, even mosques, during the war. *(Courtesy of Mark Vargas, CSM (D) Ret., USSF)*

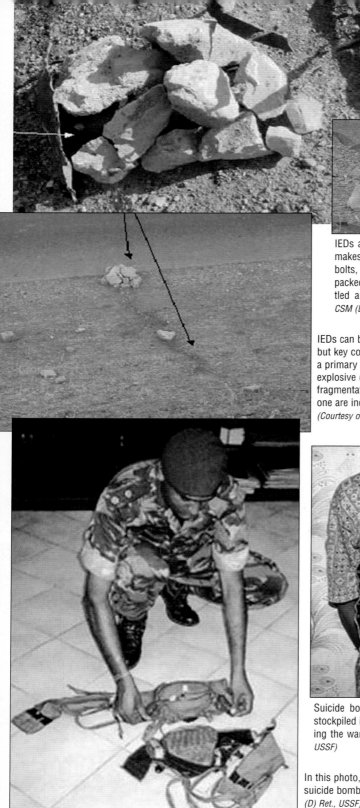

In this photo, a soldier inspects components of a suicide bomber getup. *(Courtesy of Mark Vargas, CSM (D) Ret., USSF)*

A HUMMWV still smoking after it was destroyed by an IED *(Courtesy of an anonymous source)*

IEDs such as remote-detonated, improvised mortars caused the damage to this truck. Note the force of the fragmentary projectiles. *(Courtesy of Russ Cummings)*

X-LARGE
STRIKE FACE
E WITH CARE

Body armor on the ground after a deadly IED attack against a HUMMWV. Flak jackets can be inadequate against IEDs; their failure points to a need for high-tech body armor to protect U.S. troops. *(Courtesy of an anonymous source)*

An M1A2 Abrams main battle tank was totally destroyed after running over a large IED. *(Courtesy of an anonymous source)*

A close-up side view of the damage done by IEDs. *(Courtesy of an anonymous source)*

RPGs, mortar, and artillery rounds, are a common find in the war-torn country of Iraq. RPG-7 launchers like these shown here have been responsible for over 50 deaths in attacks on U.S. helicopters since November 2003. *(Courtesy of COL Joseph Anderson, 101st Airborne, 2nd Brigade)*

Thousands of buried caches such as these dot the Iraqi landscape; more are found every day. U.S. troops are never exactly sure what they will find on these raids. *(Courtesy of COL Joseph Anderson, 101st Airborne, 2nd Brigade)*

A soldier in MOPP Level 4 protective gear carefully examines a barrel that could contain BIO/CHEM components. The suspect barrels and chemical stash were at OBJ Murray, south of Karbala. As it turned out, it was a combination of a pesticide plant and PLO training camp, and not the "smoking gun." *(Courtesy of COL Joseph Anderson, 101st Airborne, 2nd Brigade)*

Many of the weapons were hidden underground, where they remain hidden and a steady supply for the insurgents, until good HUMINT or a metal detector reveals them. *(Courtesy of COL Joseph Anderson, 101st Airborne, 2nd Brigade)*

It's a daunting task to try and eliminate the countless weapons caches in Iraq. Caches were placed in schools, amusement parks, and clinics. *(Courtesy of COL Joseph Anderson, 101st Airborne, 2nd Brigade)*

Soldiers of the 1st Brigade, 1st Battalion, 327th Infantry Regiment, Bravo Company, during inventory on weapons found in a local Iraqi's backyard in Thalatat, Iraq. *(Courtesy of the Department of Defense and Spc. Jesse Artis)*

The weapons of choice: AK-47 and AKS-74 assault rifles, SKS battle rifles, and RPK and RPD machine guns, all Soviet-bloc assault weapons left over from the Iraqi Army. *(Courtesy of COL Joseph Anderson, 101st Airborne, 2nd Brigade)*

Weapons found in a Baghdad amusement park *(Courtesy of Bill Angelucci)*

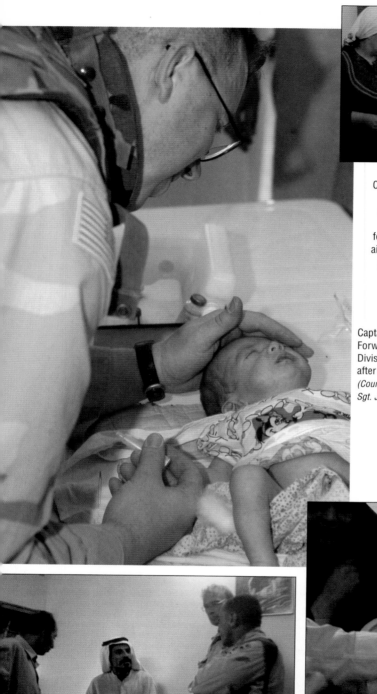

Children always touch the hearts of Coalition servicemen. High death rates among Iraqi children are frequently due to a lack of sanitary facilities and proper medical care. The Coalition forces have strong outreach programs aimed at improving health care in Iraq.
(Courtesy of COL Joseph Anderson, 101st Airborne, 2nd Brigade)

Captain Elden Rand with the 64th Forward Support Battalion, 4th Infantry Division, comforts an infant boy in Tikrit, after giving him immunization shots.
(Courtesy of the Department of Defense and Sgt. Jack Morse, U.S. Army)

On a night mission that the author went on, Army medics tended to an Iraqi boy with an injured hand.
(Courtesy of Russ Cummings)

U.S. Army medics are the most highly trained in the world. Everyone is helped, even the enemy—a shock to many Iraqis. These medics have gone out at night to Iraqi homes—on their own time and at great risk—to tend to those who are sick and wounded.
(Courtesy of Russ Cummings)

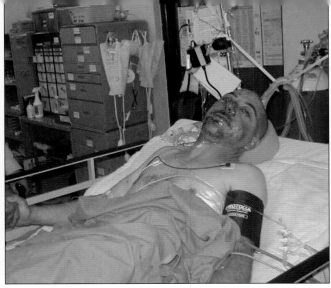

Colonel Smith, 3rd Brigade Commander, 82nd Airborne, points to a map in an interview with the author. *(Courtesy of Russ Cummings)*

Another casualty of Iraqi insurgency, shown here as the author visits the hospital in Iraq. This soldier survived a deadly helicopter crash. *(Courtesy of Russ Cummings)*

The author stands with CW2 Fisher, one of the skilled doctors who treat the wounded in Operation IRAQI FREEDOM. *(Courtesy of Russ Cummings)*

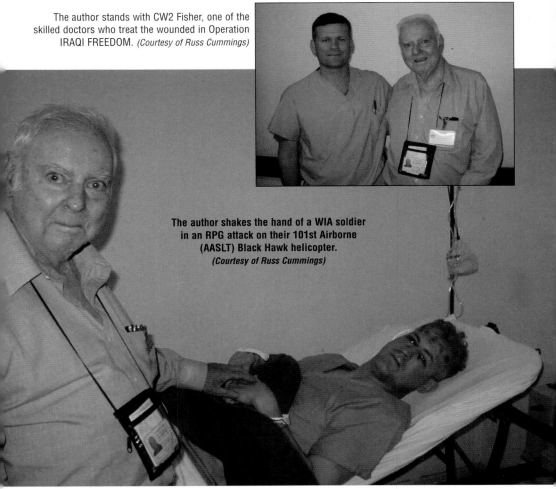

The author shakes the hand of a WIA soldier in an RPG attack on their 101st Airborne (AASLT) Black Hawk helicopter.
(Courtesy of Russ Cummings)

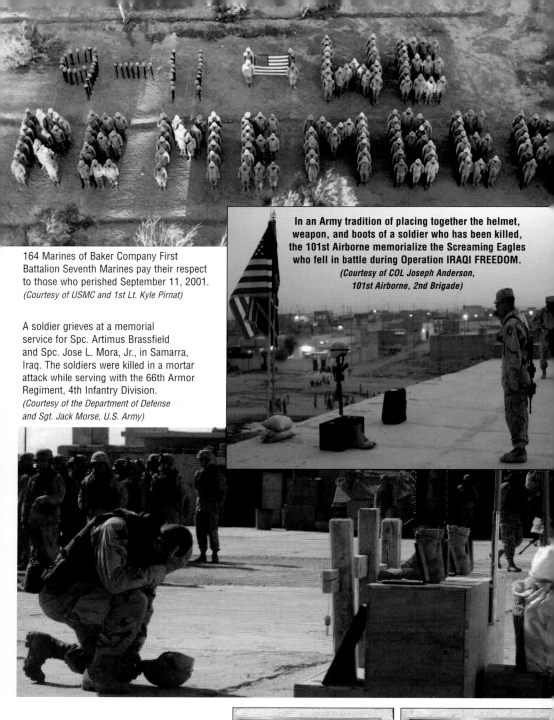

164 Marines of Baker Company First Battalion Seventh Marines pay their respect to those who perished September 11, 2001.
(Courtesy of USMC and 1st Lt. Kyle Pirnat)

A soldier grieves at a memorial service for Spc. Artimus Brassfield and Spc. Jose L. Mora, Jr., in Samarra, Iraq. The soldiers were killed in a mortar attack while serving with the 66th Armor Regiment, 4th Infantry Division.
(Courtesy of the Department of Defense and Sgt. Jack Morse, U.S. Army)

In an Army tradition of placing together the helmet, weapon, and boots of a soldier who has been killed, the 101st Airborne memorialize the Screaming Eagles who fell in battle during Operation IRAQI FREEDOM.
(Courtesy of COL Joseph Anderson, 101st Airborne, 2nd Brigade)

Green Berets MSG Kevin Morehead and SFC Bill Bennett served with valor in Afghanistan; they gave the ultimate sacrifice when they were Killed in Action in Iraq. Memorial plaques honoring the soldiers were placed at Gabriel Field, Headquarters, 5th Special Forces Group (A).
(Courtesy of Stephen C. Stone, MAJ (Ret.), USSF)

MSG KEVIN N. MOREHEAD
ODA 585, B CO., 3 BN, 5th SFG (A)
KIA
12 SEPTEMBER 2003 VIC AR-RAMADI IRAQ
OPERATION IRAQI FREEDOM

SFC WILLIAM M. BENNETT
ODA 595, C CO., 3 BN, 5th SFG (A)
KIA
12 SEPTEMBER 2003 VIC AR-RAMADI IRAQ
OPERATION IRAQI FREEDOM

Middle Eastern fashion, the toilets consisted of a hole in the marble floor—the architectural term for toilets of this type being "Asian" toilets. I was very glad I only had to spend one night there as, at the age of seventy-eight, squatting over a hole in the floor left much to be desired!

Mark Vargas is an old friend from the 5th Special Forces Group at Fort Campbell, Kentucky. The last time I had seen him prior to my visit to Iraq had been during my book tour for *The Hunt for Bin Laden*, in March 2003, when we had dinner together after a Chapter 38 meeting at Fort Campbell, Kentucky. Mark, with twinkling brown eyes, a wide warm smile, dark hair, and a walrus mustache, is a man of six foot five inches of solid muscle.

Mark went out of his way to show us the layout of the KBR camp. They had their own heliport and many amenities, but what amazed me the most within the camp's enclosure was the makeshift nine-hole golf course, built by a 4th ID medical unit.

Through a contract with the Army Material Command, KBR is tasked to provide logistical service and support to the 4th Infantry Division base camps. This support encompasses Forward Operating Bases Speicher (Tikrit North), Ironhorse (Tikrit Palace), Warhorse (Baqubah), Packhorse (Tikrit South), Bayonet (Kirkuk), Lancer (Bayji), Pacesetter (Samarra), Lion Base (North Balad), and Kirkush.

To ensure that the U.S. military receives effective, efficient, and timely support, KBR employees live and work side by side with the U.S. military at all 4th ID camps. Support for the 4th ID includes operations and maintenance for dining facilities, refuse service, housing, housing operations and maintenance, latrine and shower services, laundry services, heavy equipment support, horizontal and vertical lift services, and morale welfare and recreation services. At Camp Speicher convoys are formed, stocked with supplies of clothes, food, and gasoline for the military, and sent to places like Mosul in the north or Baghdad, one hundred miles farther south with many hours of driving through notorious "ambush alleys." Some of these alleys were as long as seven miles and were under constant surveillance by the enemy.

In the late afternoon of our final day at Camp Speicher, Russell Cummings and I went out with a group of 4th ID medical personnel to take what medicine was available and offer assistance, supplies, and equipment to the local people. Russell had been a medic and a captain in the Green Berets. He helped give medical assistance to a woman with a broken leg and to other locals including children who had cuts, bumps, and other wounds that otherwise wouldn't have been taken care of.

There was typically a great reluctance to "officially" use any medical people or supplies from the U.S. government, unless, as sometimes happened, a local citizen was shot by American forces or hurt by American construction or military action. What we witnessed was one of many strictly volunteer efforts by the medically trained Americans.

An Arabic-speaking lieutenant colonel and an Egyptian-American officer who were with us spent much of the time talking to the people we visited. Later, I discovered that the lieutenant colonel who had been conversing with the locals held a meeting back at Camp Speicher. It transpired that the locals had known Saddam's family and his closest associates for many years. Some of them, apparently, had almost daily contact with family members who were in Mosul to the north, which was also a seat of Saddam's personal power. The lieutenant colonel and the Egyptian-American officer seemed to have drawn information from many of the people they had been treating. It turned out that I had been witnessing a HUMINT (Human Intelligence) effort to find out where Saddam might be hidden. This proved to me, once again, the value of compassionate services to the local population who, to a significant extent, contributed to the capture of Saddam Hussein as well as many of his supporters.

During my time in Tikrit, I spent time with both KBR and members of the 4th ID stationed there. LTC Steve Russell was the commander of Task Force 1-22 INF, a battalion of the 4th ID. The 4th ID was a relative latecomer to the war in Iraq. Units such as the Special Forces and the Screaming Eagles had seemingly fought most of the fight and captured much of the battlefield glory. As time would tell, however, the 4th ID would, with the capture of Saddam Hussein, become an icon in their own right.

During the course of my interviews, I found that LTC Russell had kept a moving chronicle of the 4th ID's efforts in Iraq. The excerpts that follow are from descriptive letters written by LTC Russell, spanning from June 20th to Christmas, 2003. They outline the missions, problems, and uncertainty facing soldiers tasked with fighting a war against pro-Saddam insurgents in the Ba'athist stronghold of Tikrit, Iraq. Tikrit had always been Saddam's "home," and it was near here that he was finally captured.

I came into possession of the letters when LTC Russell said good-bye, as we left Tikrit. He handed Cummings and me a wealth of information on his unit and their purpose in Iraq. "I hope everything we've done for you here will be of some assistance in your new book," I recall the young and energetic lieutenant colonel saying. Only when I had arrived back home, and put the floppy disk that LTC Russell gave me into my computer, did I realize that his letters would be such a monumental credit to himself, his troops, and the United States of America.

Not long before, Chris Thompson, my project co-coordinator, heard a radio interview with the father of a soldier killed in Iraq. The father had expressed his dismay with the lack of detail from the Department of Defense when they told him that his son had been killed in action. No other insight into the matter was given, other than he had a certain amount of time to alert the rest of the family before the news was released to the press. The father did not want the first word of his son's demise to be heard by anyone in the family on the television, so he braced himself and began making phone calls before the story and his son's name aired.

Wondering how his son had spent his last moments on earth, the father came across some rather grisly footage on an Al-Jazeera Web site, in which his son's humvee, which had been ambushed by insurgents, was shown in blazing color. The father lamented the fact that the only bit of closure he had received was not from the Army, but from Arab television.

As we delved into LTC Russell's letters, we realized that much of what the letters contained were what the families of fallen soldiers needed for closure. We preferred they get it from their unit commander rather than from Al-Jazeera. LTC Russell wrote (about his letters), "I also have been thinking that the letters have become something more than just my personal assessments. Perhaps they can be used to tell our great soldiers' stories as we as a nation try to assimilate all that this last year has entailed. I have only meant them to convey what we have lived here and to serve the memory of those we have lost." In his own voice, LTC Russell brings the stories to life. They have been gently altered for the purposes of protecting the lieutenant colonel's family and privacy, allowing a bit of literary license for context, but without altering the facts, details, or overall content and voice.

The Widow's Tears

Her heart has stopped; she cannot breathe
At the letter she never wanted to receive

She all but crumbled to the floor
At the minister and officers at her door

The officer says "I'm sorry, Ma'am"
As he hands her the telegram

The world now no longer makes any sense
With the delivery from the Department of Defense

Sympathy on their faces clearly shows
But none of them knowing the pain she knows

Wanting it all to be but a bad dream
She clutches her heart, an anguished scream

Her head in her hand and starts to cry
All the while wondering "Why?"

Facing an Army wife's worst fears
Shedding now the Widow's tears

—Katie Morris (2003)

Saddam's Hometown

[LTC Steve Russell]

June 20, 2003

As most of you know, our soldiers operate in the city and surrounding villages of Tikrit, Iraq. The Tikrit area was the birthplace and home-town of Saddam Hussein. Needless to say, this has made it an inter-esting place to operate, as there are many "die-hard" loyalists to the old regime. Most are not, and there are even some who are welcoming our soldiers because they fear the local population will kill them for living privileged lives under Saddam.

Our operations target hostile forces trying to prevent the efforts of U.S. soldiers and the Iraqi local government and police. The local government is making great progress here. I cannot speak for the rest of Iraq, but if Tikrit is any indication, these people are well on their way to self-government. We have made great strides in working to-gether and they continue to provide us valuable information on the ac-tivities of hostile elements within our sector.

This phase of the war in my mind seems to be one of insurgency. The Iraqi Army had no formal surrender and the soldiers were not formally processed anywhere. Instead the Iraqi soldiers simply dis-solved into a hundred cities, towns, and villages. Most want simply to get on with their lives. A small minority appears to cling to the past. These are the ones that are attacking our soldiers. In the last few weeks, we have engaged them and recently we have hurt their local command and control structure in such a way as they cannot quickly recover.

RPG War

The first week of June saw our soldiers attacked in a series of small arms and RPG raids. The hostile elements were not afraid to engage our forces. On the 4th of June, hostile elements attacked a section of our B Company Bradleys (Bradley Fighting Vehicles) attached to 3-66 AR. Our Infantry avoided the initial strike but as they came around the village, they were ambushed from the rear. An RPG penetrated the rear ramp door of the lead Bradley.

Providentially, the penetrator warhead on the RPG had miraculously threaded the fire team of Infantry in the vehicle—missing them all. The warhead hit some electronic equipment near the turret wall and exploded. Although the five men suffered flash burns and shrapnel wounds, their body armor and Kevlar helmets saved their lives, and all escaped without severe life or limb injury. All are recovering well and a couple have now returned to duty.

On the night of June 5, a Bradley from the same company hit an antitank mine on the front left side of the vehicle. The blast ripped a hole through the driver's compartment and sent the front drive sprocket, a couple of road wheels, and the hull access covers flying. The resulting laceration in the hull was almost big enough for me to climb through.

The driver, a young private, endured the shock of the blast, instantly suffering two broken legs and a broken arm. His body armor and equipment saved him from more severe injuries. This brave young man kept his head and immediately hit the fuel shutoff valve and reached behind him to drop the ramp door, allowing his fellow Infantrymen to escape from the vehicle. His comrades came to his aid, as he was trapped in the vehicle. He is now recovering well from his wounds.

That same night, our C Company also had a Bradley hit by an RPG. The cone of the warhead hit a case of water, causing the warhead to malfunction. Miraculously, the warhead did not explode and we were able to render the explosive safe. Our men suffered no injuries. Our men also acted quickly on a mortar that was fired on U.S. forces, which we subsequently captured with fifteen rounds of ammunition. The soldiers continue to behave with amazing discipline and our nation should be very proud of them.

On the night of the 5th to 6th of June, hostile elements struck our civil-military coordination building. This is where local Iraqis come to work out issues with U.S. forces in our area. A volley of RPGs ripped the stale night air after plunging into the walled compound. Soldiers reacted immediately as hostile small arms fire peppered the compound. Our men gained a position behind walls, Hesco Bastions (concrete barriers brought in by Army Engineers), and windows as they returned fire. The initial volley wounded four of our men, but they continued to fight the assailants who had positioned themselves on the rooftops of homes across the main highway.

An MP from our task force a few buildings down at the Iraqi police station opened up with .50 cal fire on the rooftops. His suppressive fire allowed the men at the other building to deploy a Bradley at the enemy element. An enemy element from a different direction then opened up on the MP with an RPG, severely wounding the young soldier. Our Bradley opened up with machine gun and 25mm fire along the rooftops, effectively deciding the contest.

All firing at this point ceased. The brave MP had emptied a can of .50 cal ammunition before falling unconscious from his wounds. We were able to evacuate and stabilize him at our aid station. He later died from his wounds and loss of blood. Our other soldiers suffered mostly shrapnel wounds. The enemy paid dearly. While we did not realize it at the time, we wounded at least four and were later able to capture four others involved in the attack along with 2 × RPG launchers. Information on other enemy wounded or killed remains unknown, although reports from locals say we caused a great deal of damage to him.

The Big Stick

From this point, we acted quickly. The curfew was strictly enforced in Tikrit—a city of approximately seventy-five thousand. Those caught out after curfew were rounded up in the local soccer stadium, where we employed them as a trash detail the next morning to help keep Tikrit beautiful (an optimistic task at best). The effect was immediate, as the locals had no desire for such work and the streets were eerily empty during subsequent nights.

We then focused our efforts to grab the initiative like a stick and beat the enemy with it. For the last week, we have had great cooperation from the local government and police. Our own efforts have focused on hostile activities. Using multiple, simultaneous raids, we have captured a number of important individuals that led us to bigger fish. By now you all have heard that High Value Target (HVT) #4 [Abid Hamid Mahmud al-Tikriti, Presidential Secretary and cousin to Saddam] was captured here in Tikrit on the night of June 16. Our men performed superbly and worked in cooperation with Special Forces.

We also spoiled an attack on our market, and our flash checkpoints from C Company captured fourteen armed men with AK-47s in the space of an hour and a half. Information from raids and pressure on people we detained led us to the info for HVT #4's capture and culminated this week with the raids on the Hadooshi farm on the night of the 17th. The Hadooshis were believed to be personal bodyguards of Saddam Hussein. It was here TF 1-22 Infantry seized AK-47s, night vision and surveillance equipment, sniper weapons, global position equipment, and large amounts of ammunition—not your typical farm implements.

But the biggest catch of all at the farm was $8,303,000 in U.S. cash and another $1 million worth of Iraqi currency. We also found an estimated $2 million worth of jewelry that belonged to Sajida Khairallah Telfah, better known as the wife of Saddam Hussein and mother of Uday and Qusay.

I had never seen such cash or treasure in my life. It simply boggles the mind. Our men performed magnificently and our recon platoon leader, 1LT (First Lieutenant) Chris Morris, ensured our great success with his quick actions at the farm. He decided to take the farm with his scouts even though we intended to maneuver additional force there. The activity at the farm called for immediate action, however, and the element of surprise and the discipline of our men carried the day.

CPT Mark Stouffer's A Company also struck gold with a captured top-ranking Republican Guard officer and also one of Saddam's bodyguards. The noose is tightening. Now the enemy is scattered and on the run. The next morning after these operations, our men captured a man at a checkpoint attempting to flee with $800,000 U.S. cash in a gym bag. C Company, 3-66 AR has been a big help as well with our flash checkpoints.

Local authorities report we have hurt the subversive elements severely. Even the Muslim Imams have expressed an appreciation for our efforts. But our work is far from being over. The hostile elements remain and attempt to strike back with indirect-fire attacks or attacks on our convoys. We remain vigilant.

The men have good morale and are flushed with the recent successes. We are living well for the most part, billeted as we are in former palace compounds. The weather remains oppressive and all we generally do is soak our uniforms with our own sweat in the 115-degree heat. But we are eating well and have generally good hygiene. Our equipment is holding up relatively well, given the operations and environment. The robust Bradleys and body armor have earned the absolute respect of our men as they have repeatedly shown that they will save lives.

July 3, 2003

Wanted to drop another note to let you all know how things are going with the "Regulars" of TF 1-22 Infantry.

The pace of operations since my last update on 20 June has been brisk. Our A Company along with a platoon from C Company flew by CH-47 (Chinook helicopter) in support of operations along the Syrian border.

Our task force was given about forty-five minutes notice from alert to liftoff. The men operated out of rucksacks for about five days and performed superbly. The heat there was oppressive like the rest of the country, but there was a little greener vegetation and the temperatures were actually quite cool to the men at night.

When our battalion reassembled, we operated in farmland vicinity of the Tigris River. The Bradley Fighting Vehicle smashed through the gate, removing wrought iron, concrete, and mortar in a cloud of dust and was quickly followed by our Infantry shuffling down the ramp of the vehicle to secure the area. I must admit it was a wonderful thing and something we never get to do in training.

Fedayeen Funk

The health of the men has remained good but the "Fedayeen Funk" personally struck me one morning. Dizziness, vomiting, and diarrhea combined to overwhelm me for about a twenty-four-hour period. Fortunately, the battalion has an ample roster of talent and they allowed me the rest I needed. Our men see bouts of this type on occasion and the soldiers have coined several entertaining terms to describe the maladies: "Saddam's revenge," "The two-cheek sneak," and as already mentioned, the "Fedayeen Funk." Fortunately, our medics and docs attack these with medications that "shock and awe" the viruses into submission within a day.

We had the privilege to brief Administrator Bremer and Acting Secretary Brownlee recently and they were very complimentary of our soldiers and the success of our operations. We maintain the initiative and refuse to hunker down. Some BBC reporters interviewed me recently with a story already written and they needed the sound bites to support it. But we could not agree with their estimation that operations had somehow turned for the worse for us in Tikrit. I explained to them that the acts of violence we had seen represented the actions of a desperate and losing foe.

Our cooperation with the locals continues to improve and the Iraqi government and police officials have joined our forces in their own future. I cannot speak for all of Iraq, but we have the upper hand in Tikrit and make it a heavy hand only for those who do not comply.

The command sergeant major and I went to Mosul to visit part of our A Company troops attached to the 101st Airborne there. The town is on the site of the ancient city of Ninevah. Its hills, taller trees, and greenery were a pleasant contrast to our area of operations. The men there are doing well and are making the best of the situation there.

They are not as heavily engaged there and generally are performing duties guarding the airfield.

Our C Company will change commanders soon as CPT Randy Taylor departs to be a comptroller and CPT Brad Boyd takes over the fighting soldiers of "Cold Steel." We also sent home our first group of soldiers released by the Army's removal of *stop loss* and *stop move* policies. Our strength remains robust and I was very happy to send these men home after their great service to our nation. They can be very proud of their accomplishments.

We continue the fight as if we are here until the job is done, and I am convinced we will get the big boys eventually. We have already gotten #4 and continue to erode the support base of people harboring them. The fact that they remain on the run and uncoordinated gives me great satisfaction.

We see the concern in the American press and the angst from the people at home but what we truly need is for the nation to continue to stand behind us. Every reason that brought us here is still as valid as it was in March. If not us, then who? Who will step up for these 26 million people? Our resolve remains clear.

Creatures of Combat

1st Battalion, 22nd Infantry, Tikrit, Iraq—July 26, 2003
"Regulars, by God!"

Long hot days have greeted us but not necessarily in the morning. Our men conduct operations at all hours and the average soldier is active sixteen to twenty hours a day. Sometimes we get more rest but nothing can be scheduled. Our operations drive our activities and soldiers get snatches of rest when they can. They need not be told.

The sun bores into our vehicles, our clothing, and eventually us, compensated by our profuse sweating that soaks our uniforms literally from shoulder blades to kneecaps. Our equipment absorbs even more sweat as it pinches and encases us like an exoskeleton, transforming us into stinky, sour, salty, and drenched creatures of combat.

We have become accustomed to it now but we are comforted by the hope that we are now past the summer solstice and daily lose seven minutes of daylight, which will gradually result in cooler temperatures. When we shed our equipment, we attempt to dry out, and this being accomplished, our uniforms take on the appearance of stiff and badly starched fatigues, with a map of salt stains lining the shores of where the sweat had advanced in our clothing.

The sun also bores into the metal of our weapons and sometimes our rifles are so hot to the touch that we must wear gloves to remain comfortable. But the sun does not penetrate or lessen our morale or our ability. We are able to fight under these conditions as our enemy has learned to his own detriment.

The day after my last update—July 3rd—soldiers from our B Company were greeted with a fireworks display of a different kind. A Bradley Fighting Vehicle was on patrol with a tank section on a dusty street. The platoon sergeant in the vehicle noticed that a tire was in the road and, this being unusual, told the driver not to drive over it. The driver—who had placed his armor plated vest on the floor below him that morning on a gut feel and wore a vehicle vest in addition to it— veered to the right. When he did, a violent explosion erupted through the vehicle.

The engine in the front of the vehicle lurched cock-eyed as the hull-access cover on top sailed through the air, followed closely by the entire transmission of the vehicle. As the transmission completed its trajectory, road wheels, sprockets, and associated smaller hatches, accompanied it. The platoon sergeant's helmet was blown from his head and immediately consumed in flames, although his head was miraculously untouched.

Inside, the driver felt a searing heat, smelled the Halon fire extinguishers blow, which consumed the flames, had his feet and legs bounced upward by his armored vest, and felt a sharp pain to the back of his neck and left-hand fingers.

The soldiers in the back were consumed in a concussive shock wave of blast and heat that was extinguished as quickly as it had lashed at them. One soldier's glasses were blown from his face, while another was nearly knocked out but he somehow maintained consciousness. The platoon sergeant felt sharp nerve endings and blood on one of his legs.

After the one second of time that encompassed this, the men immediately reacted. The driver, despite his wounds, was able to pull himself free, exit his station, and help the others get out. All exited the vehicle, covered by the tanks in trail. The men could not imagine having been inside the vehicle that they were now viewing. For two of the men, this was the second time they had suffered a mine explosion while in a Bradley.

Now full of adrenaline, they accounted for themselves and equipment and realized that God had spared them from what should have been certain maiming or death. They were able to secure themselves, evacuate the wounded, and recover the destroyed vehicle. Of the eight men aboard, all have since returned to duty but one. He is expected to fully recover. We remain "Regulars, by God."

"Pepsi" War

In the next couple of days that followed, our positions were probed with a series of "pinprick" attacks, producing little but damage to the enemy. In an act of desperation, assailants made improvised bombs from Pepsi cans filled with gunpowder from artillery shells and packed with improvised fragmentation such as glass or gravel. The top was then sealed with tar and an improvised fuse added. The attackers would sneak up at night on our positions behind walls and then attempt to fling the bombs at our troops. The flying, sizzling cans hit the pavement, giving the appearance of a cigarette flicked by a smoker into the street that then rolled a small distance. The ensuing flash and bang caused little damage and our soldiers in most cases captured the stupid manufacturers of these beverage bombs.

After a couple of days of "Pepsi" war, a more serious attempt at injury to our soldiers in C Company was thwarted by their alertness and swift action on July 7. Two men on a motorcycle followed the first sergeant's convoy that was rotating troops from a position. The assailants intended to ride up to the trail vehicle and shoot a soldier point-blank with a pistol, as had been done earlier in Baghdad. The men, having had scraps with punks on motorcycles before, carefully watched the riders.

As they approached their turnoff, the first sergeant decided to make the turn but to use the vehicles as an instant barricade on the road. The tactic caught the punks completely by surprise. The cyclists braked sharply and tried to jump their bike across the median to escape the soldier blockade. The soldiers fired warning shots. The passenger attempted a feeble aim with a 9mm Beretta pistol. The soldiers' next shots showed no mercy. The men volleyed rounds in the distance, hitting the armed man in the leg. The driver gave up but his passenger still attempted resistance, only to be shot in the jaw by SPC (Specialist) Uribe's M-16A2 assault rifle. That ended the engagement. Both men were captured and the wounded man struggles to this day with tubes stuck in every opening of his body.

The following day, our entire battalion ventured out on a fifty-kilometer raid of a house belonging to Saddam Hussein's first cousin. Our Recon Platoon, along with the attached Brigade Reconnaissance Troop, scouted the initial objective area and provided an inner cordon. A Company with attached engineers provided the assault forces while C Company provided an outer cordon, reinforced by some tanks from C Company, 3-66 AR attached to our task force. C Company also moved along the Tigris River in RB-15 Zodiac rubber boats to affect a cordon of the riverbank at the target house.

The cousin—much to our disappointment—did not occupy the house, but he had been there recently. We discovered this only after a grand entrance provided by the "Gators" of A Company. Unable to gain access to the single entryway in the back of the plush house, the men—armed with a ten-pound sledgehammer—wailed on a system of sturdy antitheft bars that covered the door to the kitchen and all of the windows.

After four minutes of sweaty work, the soldiers compensated their futility with a door charge of C-4 explosives, using the "P-for-Plenty" method of measurement. The resulting blast effectively remodeled the kitchen with a nice open-air view to the bluffs on the Tigris. It also rearranged the dishes in the cabinets—as well as the cabinets—and provided for permanent open windows in all of the rooms on the ground floor.

A continued search of the house revealed important documents and photographs and small amounts of explosives. Hidden in the yard was a cache of RPG launchers, ammunition, a machine gun, and several Kalashnikov rifles. Our mission complete in a couple of hours, we picked up our "Regular" navy from the Tigris and then moved with the entire task force back to Tikrit.

"Graffiti" War

Back in Tikrit, we began the "Graffiti" war with the enemy. We wanted to counter an array of absurd and poorly written slogans that prophesied the return of Saddam and death to Americans or those who work with Americans. A silhouette of Saddam's head often accompanied these slogans. Our initial actions were simply to paint bayonets stuck in the Saddam heads, some even adorned with blood spurts or an eyeball popping out. We also added the financial news that a $25 million reward awaited those who brought him in dead or alive.

Seeing that we began to stir a hornet's nest of sorts, we upgraded our information campaign—thanks to SPC Haggerty—with neat stencils and Arabic writing attesting to the same theme as before. We will not allow the enemy to win even the slightest advantage—not even graffiti.

To keep the enemy from returning to his venomous themes on the wall, we target them, sending sniper bullets nearby as a warning. We also have wrapped concertina wire around one major sign along the main street and placed magnesium trip flares within the wire—so if they pull the wire away to alter our handiwork, they get the scare of their lives. Since our graffiti campaign started, we are beginning to see more and more people just cleaning all of it off their walls or replacing it with paintings or professional signs.

Curiosity Killed the Cat

By the 12th of July we saw a couple of Iraqis who work with us being targeted by hostile forces. The attacks came more as threat vs. action but some improvised explosives were thrown at people's farms. In one case, a Pepsi bomb sizzled on a sparkly arc into a man's courtyard and rolled to a stop. His curious cat spotted it and immediately pounced after it, paw raised for action, just as it detonated. I guess the old saying is true after all.

Constant movement and action from our task force characterized the days that followed. We planned, assembled, raided, exploited, reassembled, and set up again for the next operation. An area to the east of the Tigris, known for its love of mortars and a willingness to use them, was the initial focus of our operations.

As our soldiers moved through the farms and fields on a wide area, we noticed the little things that cause us to look closely at an area. Before too long, the farms and fields yielded a bounty of a different kind. Soldiers with minesweepers and shovels soon harvested rifles, weapons, and rocket-propelled grenade launchers with their evil projectiles. Farmers claiming their innocence could not explain the weapons or their lack of leathery hands and feet that betrayed their true profession. Now they are unemployed.

Our operations continued with our mechanized Infantry delivered to their objectives in Bradleys, trucks, V-hulled boats, and helicopters. We remain versatile and the impact on the morale of the soldiers is manifestly positive—many of them having never used these methods before at Ft. Hood or in their careers. But I see them as Infantry and will employ them by the best means to get the mission accomplished. And accomplish it they do.

The impact on the enemy has been measurable and we continue to hurt him. He must learn that he cannot sustain his operations, be as flexible, match his will against ours, or defeat our forces. Further, he clearly lacks the popular support of his own population. What a reminder of how we must maintain the support of our citizens at home and, with God's help, nothing will alter the certain outcome.

But the enemy did attempt to strike back, and characteristically, in a most cowardly way. Not only does he hide behind his women and children, engaging us from multifamily dwellings, he also attempts to kill those who cooperate with us—including those who are older and indefensible.

One such target was a man who worked with our forces since our arrival. He was the one who owned the curious cat. On the 14th, he was visiting his son's auto-parts shop in Tikrit. A group of four men came into the shop and began to threaten and argue with the fifty-five-year-old man. Weapons were soon exposed. The man pulled a pistol and fired at the attackers to ward them off.

He quickly emptied his pistol, and being out of ammo, was surrounded and shot once point-blank in the head and twice in the chest. His two sons came running to his aid, one with an AK-47, which he promptly emptied into the man that had just killed his father. He then used the rifle to club another man senseless. His older brother—armed with a hammer—nailed away at the head of another man. The engagement effectively was over and some of them got away. Nothing could bring back the father.

Two days before he died, this man gave us information about a village to the north of Tikrit. We used it to target a series of selected farms and maneuvered our forces by tank, Bradley, truck, scout humvee, and even boats in the Tigris River, as the village abutted its banks. Within four hours, our men had unearthed over 250 AK-47 rifles, 56 crates of Composition 4 (C-4 plastic explosives) each weighing fifty pounds, 8 crates of blasting caps for the explosive (25,000 in all), surveillance equipment, and a variety of military goods and wares. The men felt proud to at least discover something to honor his death, although we were all very saddened by the loss of this poor, older, honest, and decent man. Their numbers are too few in this god-forsaken place to lose even one.

But one more we did lose—a local national translator. He was a simpleminded and humble man in his forties who had a knack for the bottle and one night drifted away from his dwelling. When his body was discovered floating in the Tigris River, having lodged in our military float bridge, we noticed signs of struggle and a severe beating. No doubt he was rolled into the river to finish the attack on his life.

Saddam's Anniversary

The enemy did attempt attacks on us as well in his grandiose return on the much-vaunted 17th of July—the day Saddam came to power and a former holiday in the old regime. Every Iraqi believed that Saddam's loyalists might return and defeat the Americans on this anniversary.

We first learned of the enemy's activity in Tikrit when he spread rumors that the U.S. forces had imposed a curfew banning all movement on the day of the 17th. We noticed on the evening of the 16th that many of the shops were closing early. We asked the locals why and soon learned of the rumor.

We immediately countered with bullhorns and translators telling the people that the 17th was a normal day and they could move freely as they were now a free people. The cheers and applause that greeted these messages could be readily heard above the bullhorns. That the message got out was obvious when the city was teeming with normal activity on the 17th.

That evening, however, the enemy attempted to be teeming himself. At 2350 hours on the 17th, I moved about the city in my humvee convoy with a five-ton truck to collect curfew violators for a ready labor force to clean off graffiti. As we cruised around southern Tikrit near the Women's College, also known as "RPG Alley," we once again confirmed why we gave it this label. Making a right turn, we heard the *whoosh* and *bang* of RPGs, fired by attackers who did not anticipate our change of direction. The sound an RPG makes upon contact is best described as sounding like a Dumpster dropped from a fifty-story building. The volley struck in a prong with the left fork heading near an observation post atop the Women's College and the right fork just barely missing our vehicles because we turned right instead of heading straight.

We immediately jumped the median of the multilane street and headed the unarmored vehicles back into the enemy. Our men deployed out to the *crack* of what sounded like pistol shots from a roof. Angered at this point at the enemy's cowardice, we moved forward and taunted him, shouting expletives for him to be drawn out.

Gaining the defilade of a low and crudely laid block wall, we coordinated with an element of the MPs to move to the east and provide a cordon on the backstreets. This accomplished, we began to see our Recon Platoon humvees move up on our left as we moved north along the two alleys. As we met in the crossbar of an "H" of streets, we once again taunted the enemy. This time he obliged.

Gunfire erupted in a series of automatic weapons bursts. The first crashed near our feet sending newly chipped gravel in all directions accompanied by that clearly recognizable sharp *crack* of bullets aimed at you. As we returned fire in the direction of the attackers on a roof of a small building in the top half of the "H," a second burst from a rooftop on the upper-right leg of the "H" peppered the scout trucks. A third burst that appeared to come from a submachine gun at the same location splashed over the middle scout truck.

The gunner mounted in the cupola of his humvee uncontrollably corkscrewed out of the vehicle with the shout, "I'm hit!" and collapsed into the street. "Q-Beam" white lights soon fingered the rooftop, revealing an attacker. As a sergeant tried to get to the aid of his buddy, we acquired the man on the rooftop. At the same time as a medic dashed around a humvee and grabbed our wounded man by the nylon strap sewn in the back of his armored vest, we engaged with more small arms and Mark-19 grenades. The wounded soldier was dragged to safety while the *thump, thump, thump* of three grenades from the Mark-19 grenade launcher signaled the deadly arc of fire-power that soon ended the engagement.

The report rang out that our man was OK. A 9mm bullet had grazed above his right eye, creating an eleven-stitch cut, and then lodged in the back of his Kevlar helmet. This accounted for his spinning to the ground. As the medic checked him, he told the soldier he was OK, placed a bandage on him, and handed the man his rifle back. Through oaths and epithets our wounded man assured all of us he wanted to find the man who shot him. He recovers now with swellings, that if he were back home, might be mistaken as the result of a very bad barroom fight.

Our men continued to search the area for the man we surely must have hit, and found evidence of positions. We determined his number to be two or three men. True to form, his "miss-and-run" tactics produced little and he gained sanctuary among the multitude of innocent families lining the streets. For our part, we took great satisfaction in driving him off but our bloodlust was up and we wanted evidence to satisfy it. It would soon come in the form of a black mourning "martyr" banner appearing with one name and the same date on a mosque nearby, calling on those to honor him as he died attacking the Americans.

Scroll forward a couple more hours. Now the terrain changes to a dusty farm village to the south of Tikrit. A Company patrolled through the streets checking for anything abnormal. Flying rocket-propelled grenades certainly qualified. The men brought their Bradley section into action but the assailants fled to a house. The "Gators" of A Company quickly recovered from the near misses of RPGs and then brought their force to bear on the house.

Infantry spilled out the back of the vehicles, joining others that were brought up in a truck. The house was empty of attackers—but not his weapons. The cowards fled, leaving an RPG launcher and three rockets. Patrols went to police up the attackers the next day.

Scroll forward another hour, but this time the scene switches to northern Tikrit to the "Cobras" of C Company. A skinny man on a motorcycle cruises down the four-lane road with an even skinnier weapon. The silhouette reveals it to be an RPG launcher strapped to his back. Still a good distance from the "Birthday Palace," but close enough to be deemed hostile, fusillades of fire greet the man, causing him to turn wildly and escape down a side alley. He is quickly absorbed into the city and into the night. His attack and no doubt his pride were thwarted but unfortunately we did not get him.

The enemy's boastful claims of Saddam's return on the 17th of July never materialized. Instead, the view that the Iraqis had here when they opened their windows on the morning of the 18th was of their own police, government officials, and American forces providing for their security. They seemed to accept it. They also seemed to acknowledge that Saddam would not return.

Even his image on the Farouk Palace gate was blown from its mount on the morning of the 18th, providing a powerful visual to those that observed it. The huge bronze statue that sat atop a fifty-foot-high arched gate was soon laced with explosives. The metallic body of Saddam holding a banner and sitting astride a charging horse flanked by rockets soon trotted down the parapet, stumbled, then crashed with a finality symbolic of Saddam's former regime.

When the dust settled, the people seemed to settle with it. They have been somewhat calmer and assured since, realizing that all the fearful talk of Saddam returning was just talk. The evening of the 18th was calm—except for a volley of mortar rounds fired into an insignificant patch of sand near C Company, 3-66 AR—the "Cougars."

A More Developed Enemy

Now that we are in the post "return" period, the people seem to cooperate more but we also see a more developed enemy. Take the evening of the 19th for example. An observation post (OP) providing security and warning to C Company noticed a two-man team in all black, long-sleeved clothing and black veils stealthily scale a wall and begin to work toward a corner near the entrance. They each carried loaded RPG launchers. The OP soldiers took aim and let out an accurate burst. The first bullet literally struck two inches from an attacker's head, when it penetrated the rear flange of the weapon, causing him to lose control of his RPG.

Startled by the shot, he also prematurely squeezed the trigger and fired his RPG grenade wildly into the street. The second attacker also pulled the trigger of his weapon, sending a deadly blast into the compound wall but fifteen meters from where he intended it to go. A metallic, echoed boom—followed by a shower of gypsum-starved concrete—blended with the sharp chatter of American rifle fire.

The badly shattered enemy fled over the low wall he was pinned against and into even darker shadows. A quick reaction of men assembled inside the compound. A Bradley Fighting Vehicle, not waiting for the gate to be opened for sake of time, crashed through it and flattened it to the ground. Other forces began to cordon approximately four blocks of the city along a two-street axis. The enemy fled on foot, ditching a grenade and other items that would mark him as hostile. The soldiers weaved through city blocks, unable to find those whose attack had been thwarted once again.

The next morning, a command-detonated explosive hidden in a pothole erupted into a humvee of a passing element using the main supply route in our area. Three soldiers were wounded but fortunately, they were very near one of our surgical hospitals. The "Cougars" quickly assisted them in their tanks and provided medical assistance and thankfully the men were not seriously injured. Sifting through the debris, the men noticed parts of a cell phone used to detonate the device. Also visible were parts of a mortar tube, apparently packed with C-4 and used in a very unconventional manner.

The Regulars used our own mortars, but in a more conventional way the next day. Finally given permission for counter battery fire, the "Thunder" soldiers of our mortar platoon registered 120mm rounds, sending earth and stubble skyward from abandoned fields. In the last several days, we have fired numerous rounds to counter the enemy's indirect-fire attacks. Since we began this, we have seen little more activity. This is the first firing of "regular" mortars since Vietnam and the men are very proud to carry on the traditions of our veterans before us.

A Strange Mood

The evening of the 22nd, a strange mood descended over the city. Every eye is glued to the television sets as the breaking news of Uday and Qusay Hussein's deaths jolts like an electric shock. The city is eerily quiet but not without danger.

At approximately 2250 hours, another familiar "Dumpster crash" is heard signaling an RPG attack as we head south in our command group convoy. We head north along the main highway that bisects the town and see a pall of smoke. Local men gesture from balconies with general directions deduced from their pointing fingers. A quick patrol from our men loops around the block but finds nothing. The target was a photo shop wedged into a corner. Maybe the assailant didn't get his film on time.

On the 23rd, we saw the enemy become very active. Perhaps the news of Uday and Qusay's deaths ignited hatred and anger. Regardless of what sparked the evening events, the enemy would soon pay dearly.

At about 2130, our C Company reported stopping a car that had sped at a high rate of speed with 25 million dinars (about $15,000 U.S.). Being an unusual sum, the men called to ask what to do. We took my translator to the scene to decipher the situation and learned that the Iraqi males in the car had made a legitimate business transaction on the sale of some property and were afraid of being robbed, so they hurried to their house. Deducing this after verifying it with documents, we let them go and proceeded south in the city. The C Company patrol then collapsed their checkpoint and prepared to leave.

As they left the T-intersection, a crash of RPG rounds accompanied with small arms fire thundered about them. No damage was caused to our men in the Bradleys. The attackers fled to points south as quickly as they had fired. Hearing the explosions near the location we had just left, my convoy cut to the east a couple of blocks down and then headed north in complete blackout with our night vision toward where we thought the attack might have come from.

A white Nissan pickup truck fishtails around a corner. My safety instinctively flips to fire on my M-4 carbine. My driver, SPC Hoeffer, veers left to block the pickup. Weapons are visible. Four men in the truck. Looks of surprise flash from underneath all-black Arab head-dress. Hoeffer rams the vehicle.

The enemy is startled by the impact. I'm on my feet charging the vehicle, shattering the windshield with rifle fire. The second vehicle in my group now rounds the corner, seeing enemy fire sail through the air, but it is unnoticed by the two of us. Hoeffer cuts down the man exiting the passenger side of the truck. The enemy driver never made it out after my opening burst.

I shift to the two men in the back. Hoeffer and I have them in an "L" with no place for them to go. Blurs of clothing, AK-47s, and ear-splitting sound. I squeeze my tactical flashlight on my weapon and fire heavily into the man in the back and then at the other man as he attempts to take cover on the other side of the vehicle. Hoeffer denies him refuge with his rifle and he becomes still in a wadded-up heap by the right-rear wheel—AK-47 nearby. Our other soldiers in the trail vehicles come up to support but the enemy lay in heaps. A Fedayeen cell is destroyed.

Simultaneously, rifle fire erupts to the east along the main street of the city. A blue car and an ambulance move cautiously down the road. Two men exit the ambulance with AK-47s and get into the car. We have waited a long time for this one. Snipers engage. The blue car races as glass shards fly from its rear windshield. The ambulance driver cannot maneuver. Spider-webbed circles the size of half-dollars sequentially dot the driver's side of the windshield.

The vehicle stops. A man struggles out of the vehicle, badly in-jured, and collapses on the street. Unidentified fire arcs toward the soldiers. A confused "friendly" force from a completely different unit on the main street—also a main supply route—mistakes our men for the enemy. Our men keep their heads and attempt to gain their atten-tion, shouting that they are American forces. No avail.

Our three men remain disciplined despite the automatic grenades that impact their location. Our recon element rockets toward the loca-tion and forcefully disengages the confused element. Three Regulars are wounded but, thankfully, the wounds are shrapnel wounds to the flesh only. Two are returned to duty, another will return shortly.

Pumped with adrenaline as we search for the four men from the pickup, I take this latest development hard. Our ambushes have been extremely successful, now darkened by the careless actions of well-meaning but non-Infantry soldiers. We continue the search and find Indian currency and French cigarettes. What does it mean? Three AK-47s, two RPG launchers with rounds prepped and ready, two hand grenades, an M-79 40mm grenade launcher with six rounds, and several magazines of small arms ammunition are pulled from the truck and the dead. Armed to the teeth, the enemy clearly intended on more attempts to kill Americans.

Three points of the city are secured. The enemy's attack is defeated at each point with heavy price exacted from him. We learned later that the four in the truck were the sons of bodyguards of Saddam Hussein or sons of his relatives.

The next day, another cell attempts a daylight attack on C Company's compound in an open field abutting to the east. The engagement begins with sporadic rifle fire. Perhaps the enemy attempted to draw us out. He is obliged but not in the manner he expects. Bradleys in an "Overwatch" position wail on a now-ubiquitous white Nissan truck. A man struggles and flees the burning vehicle, only to be shot sideways through the lungs by a soldier's rifle fire.

RPGs launch and crash from a northern side street. Additional C Company force is brought to bear and is engaged from the south. Small arms, 25mm chain guns, and machine guns *crack* and *thump* in swift reply. The contest ends. Another cell is destroyed with one enemy killed, two wounded, and one surrendering. Those from the harboring houses are detained. C Company is unscathed.

The damage to the enemy is manifest. His anger and carelessness continue to cost him in deficits he cannot repay. The city takes on an apprehensive calm. So continue the gurgling gasps of a dying regime. Their lifeblood now draining, it is only a matter of time. Meanwhile a new Iraq is born.

Hot!

August 24, 2003
"Regulars, by God!" "Deeds, not Words."

We finally won the battle to get e-mail. It took a lot of effort, but now the soldiers can at least drop a note every few days with better turn-around on news to their families. We set up three terminals for the soldiers to use in the battalion headquarters and the companies rotate on a schedule.

Beginning the 27th of July, CSM Martinez and I made the rounds to the companies to award the Combat Infantry Streamer to each Infantry Company guidon (unit flag). It is a great honor to the units and one of which they are very proud. Also during these visits, we took the opportunity to talk to the soldiers about their concerns. These ranged from the need for certain items of mission-essential equipment, to small comfort items to help them relax when they are not on patrols, to how to better communicate with their families. We have been able to improve in all of these areas. We fought to get the newer body armor vests for all of our soldiers and won, though not without exertion. Now all our soldiers are better protected.

After coming back on the 27th from Bayji (north of Tikrit) where B Company is, we had activity that quickly reminded us that we have much work to do even while feeling proud of our accomplishments. Someone placed a bomb in front of a house in central Tikrit. The blast blew open the gate and damaged the wall of the courtyard. The Iraqi family there asked our soldiers to help them move to relatives that night as it was after curfew. My operations officer, MAJ Brian Luke, obliged and as the family was escorted a few blocks to the east, one of our soldiers noticed a shovel leaning against a wall.

SPC Garcia began to look at the dirt and the shovel. Within minutes, 44 antitank mines, 20 lbs. of C-4 explosives and 200 lbs. of propellant were unearthed. More digging: 9 grenades, 4 mine initiators, an AK-47, and 30 60mm mortar rounds soon followed. This same building had been cleared not a few days before.

As this developed, a burst of gunfire erupted to the south in an arc across the main highway toward the governor's building. A Company soldiers soon enveloped an area of two warehouses. The soldiers entered the first and spotted five men, one armed with an SKS rifle. The Iraqi man immediately dropped it when he saw the Americans and our men quickly deduced that these men were just food guards.

They continued on to the next warehouse. A man stood in the shadows as the soldiers approached. SPC Morgan entered with his fire team and shouted at the man to come forward in English and Arabic. The man darted into the shed instead, and appeared a second time with an AK-47. SPC Morgan aimed his rifle at the man and killed what turned out to be the assailant that had attacked the governor's building. An enemy and lots of deadly mines and explosives were now in our hands.

We continued to thin the ranks of those attacking our men the last week of July and we also received detailed information as to the location of an important bodyguard of Saddam Hussein. This particular man was often seen in photos with Saddam and his family. The locals also knew him as a vicious murderer.

In a lightning raid, the Recon Platoon and A Company secured three houses in residential Tikrit. We were looking specifically for three men; two were bodyguards and one an organizer for the former regime. Within forty-five minutes, we had all three men. The raid made national news and the men were extremely valuable to our efforts.

The main target—Saddam's personal bodyguard—didn't give up without a fight. Our scouts found him upstairs, emboldened with liquor, attempting to grab a Sterling Submachine Gun. Butt strokes and quick action prevented his death. He swung at the men but soon found himself being dragged down the stairs, his head hitting each step. Subdued and in his courtyard, with slight bleeding to the forehead, bulbs flashed from the several media present. The news quickly spread in Tikrit to the elation of all, who now saw this former cutthroat of Saddam brought into our custody.

The 30th and 31st became eerily quiet. This was perhaps the first time in weeks that nothing happened—no gunfire, no attacks, nothing.

Our raids continued with success. On the 1st of August, we bagged three more men—all with ties to Saddam. While I cannot specify the ties, I can say they were involved with the personal family duties and staff. Now each raid seemed to feed upon the other, with encouraging results.

The Candy Box

Discouraging news shortly followed. We learned from a frantic local sheik that same evening that the bodies of Uday and Qusay Hussein were to be delivered to his village the next day and then buried in the local cemetery. Not pleased at the news—as this village also has our men in it—we worked all evening to confirm this. We were told to do nothing. The corpses were to be turned over to the Red Crescent after being flown to our city. We were instructed to provide no escort or involvement.

We watched at a distance as three corpses (the third being Mustafa—Qusay's fourteen-year-old son killed while firing an AK-47 under a bed) were laid into the dirt. Arrogant men, some veiled, surrounded the graves in pathetic prayerful worship over these murdering lifeless forms. They piled dirt mounds above their sunken corpses and then secured an Iraqi flag to each mound with dirt clods along the edges. The funeral passed uneventfully. But a candy box in the middle of the main highway in town would shatter the quiet of the previous two days.

The enemy launched an attack in the early evening using improvised explosives. The first was nearly identical to the second except in result. Each bomb appeared to be a box (one candy, the other Kleenex) packed with C-4 explosives and nuts and bolts serving as projectiles. How they were detonated remains unknown.

Our Recon Platoon traveled up the main highway through the city center. Congestion by the telephone exchange offices narrowed the lanes to one. A median, elevated with planters, served as a directional backstop for the candy box concealed among so much other trash in this unsanitary country. The first scout passed by but the second seemed to disappear in a concussive mass of flame and smoke. Glass flew everywhere from the telephone exchange building. Policemen inside were knocked off their feet. Windows from a taxi full of kids blew into the youths as the pavement took on an appearance of an unfinished mosaic of glass.

Our soldiers in the third humvee quickly dismounted to see if they could assist but the truck was not there. Its driver, his eye bleeding and his arm filled with fragmentation, threw the vehicle into low gear and nursed the humvee with four flat tires out of the blast zone. The soldier in the backseat took searing heat and fragmentation to the neck and left arm. His left eardrum registered no sound.

Men yelled to each other as the staff sergeant—unscathed in the front-right seat—assessed his men in the vehicle. The gunner up top could be seen bleeding from the face and neck. But all were moving and so was the vehicle. The scouts continued their wobbly ride toward our compound. The perforated vehicle went through the gate. The men cleared their weapons with bloody hands and then made their way with assistance to the aid station. Two have returned to duty and the third will need more time for his ear to heal but will recover.

The second bomb detonated approximately twenty minutes later and about two miles north along the same road. Military Police vehicles, similar in appearance to our scout vehicles, became the unintended target. No major damage occurred in the mistimed blast except a few headlamps and cosmetic damage to the fiberglass hood of a single vehicle.

After talking to my wounded scouts and seeing that they were going to be OK, we continued on with our combat patrols. That night I headed south along the highway to the burial village and located the new graves of Saddam's sons. Flushed with the emotion of having three more of my men wounded, and having drunk two quarts of water, I paid my respects on the graves of Uday and Qusay Hussein.

We spent the day of the 3rd of August planning for a simultaneous raid on each side of the river. We were looking for two individuals who have been organizing attacks on our soldiers. Our intelligence was good and we found the locations of the farms and a house in the northern suburb. The targeted men were not there, although their families were. We found important photos, information, and documents. The raid proved successful however as the next morning one of the two men sought came to the civil-military relations office to complain about the raid on his undamaged house. We took him to our complaint department where he has remained ever since.

Our combat patrols continued in the city with ambushes laid out for an elusive enemy. Assailants with RPGs fired on a C Company patrol near the Women's College but hit nothing. A Kellogg, Brown & Root worker driving north of Tikrit did hit a mine, however, and lost his life in the ensuing blast. It was a terrible tragedy that illustrates the dangers in the use of contractors on the battlefield.

On the night of the 5th, our men saw a small group walk across the main street in town with an RPG launcher and AK-47s. Seeing no clear shot, they waited. Soon a man appeared around a corner with an RPG at the ready. Our men fired first, wounding the man in the leg. He shrieked in pain and then calm settled over the alleyways.

The next night, the 6th, we captured the head of a Fedayeen cell in a hotel raid covered by a full complement of media. We detained thirty-nine individuals (we released thirty-eight) but among them was our man. Two of his new recruits fled the following day but we caught them motoring south toward Baghdad based on a tip from the locals. Later, a merchant brought us their RPG launcher with three rockets. He said he saw them hide it earlier and brought it to us once he learned we had captured them. We continue to see the Iraqi support increase along with each success.

But the arms still flow into the city. Locals had told us so and the merchants from the market complained to the governor and police about it. They said that the weapons were being used to attack them and the Americans. We decided to set daylight ambushes on the Friday market to curb the flow.

At 0730 on Friday the 8th, we finally confirmed that the complaints were true. Our snipers noticed two men in a red car pull into the field surrounded by the market shops along the streets. The field is also used as a "flea market" where anyone can vend his wares or produce. These two men decided to vend weapons. They laid out wheat sacks filled with AK-47 magazines and grenade launcher attachments. Next, they set up various other small arms items on the now empty sacks. Finally, they pulled an AK-47 out of the trunk. The men reported it but wanted to be sure these were weapons dealers. After small devices and electronic switches for bomb making and then more AK-47s appeared, the men engaged.

The sharp *crack* of a sniper rifle drew little attention at first. A vendor selling crackers not ten feet from the arms traders took little notice, thinking the men were testing the weapons. But then he noticed that one man holding a weapon jerked and suddenly dropped it, his arm bleeding profusely. The driver of the red car, unaware of what was happening, watched as one of two other men present handled weapons. The man turned around with an AK-47 seeking the direction of the fire. A round ripped through him. He ran forward, weapon in hand. Another round found its target. Then he slumped to the ground.

The driver ran frantically to the car, attempting to flee. Our sniper squad leader gauged the approximate location of the driver through the hood—the car was facing away from him—and fired. The round perforated the hood and then hit the man in the head. He stumbled out of the car and died. The last armed man stood little chance. A round through his leg cut him down and he dropped the weapon. The engagement was now over.

The Recon Platoon then rushed to the site. A sea of confusion billowed among the locals. A clear path parted around the arms dealers as the crowd receded from the site. A bystander had already stolen one of the AK-47s but everything else was still there when the scouts arrived. Soon soldiers from A Company cordoned the market. We secured the scene. The two wounded were transported to the Tikrit hospital. Iraqi police appeared and assisted in crowd control and body recovery. The press arrived and we gave a full account of our ambush.

Not waiting for the details, the French AFP media went to the hospital and found two boys from a village about thirty kilometers across the river that had been injured by an unexploded shell of some kind in an unrelated incident. Assuming that the boys were somehow connected to our actions against the enemy, they flashed pictures around the world stating that we had wounded the boys with grenades at the market.

Fortunately, the rest of the media not only have higher standards, but also reported the facts. Some (not many) in the media asked me why we did not give the arms dealers any warning. I stated that they became combatants as soon as they produced weapons and that no such warning had ever been afforded my men. Our actions sent shock waves through the town and effectively curtailed illegal arms trade in the city. The governor thanked us for our actions as well as the mayor. The police chief stated that the two men we killed from the red car were known thugs that smuggled weapons from a major military complex on the outskirts of Baghdad. They would show samples, fill orders, and arrange deliveries. What is certain is that we see no more weapons traded openly in Tikrit.

The enemy, not able to take us on directly, began to focus more on explosive devices and land mines in his attempts to strike at us. Over the next week we discovered some of these before they could be used and each week we discover some new attempt before it strikes. We are thankful for the prayers that make this possible.

West of Tikrit, an unfortunate driver in a truck lost his leg when he and a fellow soldier supporting the engineer battalion ran over an antitank mine laid along the edge of a road. And to the south of us, an artilleryman lost his life in a similar episode. Our snipers and patrols continue to shoot at suspected devices as before while locals have helped us in intercepting several others. We remain vigilant. It is in our best interest.

On the 11th of August, we successfully raided three more objectives and netted two former Republican Guard officers—one a division commander and the other a corps level chief of staff. The third objective netted us a leader of Fedayeen militia. By the 13th we had seen small enemy attempts to harass or strike back at us. On a secondary market street, CPT Boyd's convoy narrowly escaped harm as assailants rolled a volley of RPGs down the street like some game of tenpins. The rockets *whooshed,* skipped, and scraped along the pavement, but made no contact for them to explode. The enemy attackers had fired from several hundred meters away in the middle of a street and then fled.

The Farms

Our actions continued to have momentum. By mid-month, two men wanted by our forces—one who worked for Saddam's family— turned themselves in to us and on the same day we received weapons from helpful Tikriti merchants with keen eyes. Even so, the young and the stupid continue to step forward. In a suburb to our south, attackers launched a volley of RPGs at A Company soldiers in yet another classic "miss-and-run" attack. Our "Gators" responded so quickly that the enemy was forced to flee for his life and abandoned his rocket launchers in the street. The attackers melded into the local population before they could be caught. Hence, we continue to work with the locals, the sheiks, and plan more raids.

One benefit of our dialogue with the sheiks has been the recruitment of reliable militia that we are now training. Tapping into some previous experience I had on a much grander scale when I served in Afghanistan, forming the plans for the Afghan National Army, we moved out with a modest training program that is producing a good-quality small element to assist the local government and our forces. Through the great work of 1LT Deel and SGM Castro, and with the assistance of a couple of former drill sergeants in each company, we move forward to train Iraqis in martial and civil arts that will help them stabilize their own town.

As to the continued raid planning, our efforts to find a bomb maker paid off when we raided a house on the 17th as a part of a wider operation. We found plastic explosives, electronic switches and devices, fragmentation pellets, blasting caps, a few weapons. While raiding this house, alert soldiers outside began to root around the fields across the street and found three grenades and a 60mm mortar system with seven rounds of ammunition. All in all, it was a very productive week.

The enemy continues to adapt his tactics to counter ours. His only cowardly refuge has been to hide among the population and among legitimate emergency services. On the night of the 18th our soldiers at a temporary checkpoint searched an ambulance that was bringing back an older man from the hospital. Seeing this, someone in a white car placed an explosive on a side street and ignited the fuse. A Company soldiers reacted to the blast to the west. The ambulance drove north to get out of danger and as it did, the white car pulled alongside the Red Crescent vehicle and sent a burst of gunfire toward another unit's outpost. The outpost responded, seeing the fire come from what appeared to be the ambulance.

Also seeing the fire exchanged between the outpost and the ambulance, our snipers engaged the ambulance as it sped north, the victim of a cruel crossfire. The white car, fully masked in its movements, then dashed down a dark alley and made good its escape. The ambulance shuddered to a stop.

The driver, fearing for his life, got out of the front seat to escape the bullet exchange. He nearly made it but for one round that hit his ankle. Another aid man was cut by glass from the windshield. The older man in transport took a round to the shoulder and the thigh. The police and our forces quickly arrived along the dark street. The police took the seriously wounded victim to the hospital where he was stabilized.

The ambulance then began its journey northward toward a police checkpoint, met by both police and our scouts. After much confusion, we determined what had happened and treated the man with the ankle wound. We took him to better care to remove the bullet. We also handed over the ambulance back to the emergency workers. The Iraqis helped us piece together the confusing puzzle and, while frightened and initially angered, became more angered at the fact that the attackers would once again use innocent people as shields.

Some of the cowardly activity is planned on local farms. Some of the people talk. Some of the farms get found and raided. Such was the case with one farm that we had raided before—the one where we found the eight and a half million U.S. dollars, and Sajida Hussein's jewelry. Seems they continue to plan and fund there.

We acted quickly on the intelligence that a planning meeting was occurring at the farm. Confirmed sightings of two particular individuals on our hit list caused us to go in quick and bristling. We surrounded the farm with reconnaissance troops to set the cordon and then A Company rolled up to the compound gate and flattened it with the momentum of a Bradley Fighting Vehicle.

The Bradley continued forward as occupants of the two large farm complexes scrambled. Soldiers poured through the gap and more soldiers spilled out the back of the Bradley. Fingers of light danced around each corner and flashed around each window and room. Back alleys were cleared, aqueducts jumped, orchards searched. Men and women are questioned. The targeted individuals had left three hours before. But they leave knowing they are hunted men who must live like the rats they are. And they know that no rat hole is safe.

The next day, the 20th, we got an emergency request for help from another unit working in our area. While coordinating information on a market street, armed attackers masked within the population open up a deadly burst of gunfire. The soldiers' translator falls dead with a torso wound. A soldier collapses with a serious thigh wound and another is also hit in his extremities and severely wounded. The soldiers return fire. The enemy's damage done, he flees, unable to be pursued by this small wounded band.

Men from our C Company rush to the scene. Shocked and bloody men are lifted into vehicles, accompanied by their angry and equally shocked peers. Our soldiers cordon the area, conduct a wide search, and gather little from the locals who have either closed their shops in typical fear or claimed they saw nothing. The men's lives are saved by a medical evacuation. A translator, an American citizen, will speak no more. Vigilance, vigilance, vigilance. My burden is that every soldier of mine goes home—and with a pair of legs.

One such sparing occurred on the 22nd of August. A tip from a distraught local warned us of a plan to attack the Tigris Bridge. He stated that the attack would occur within an hour and would be with RPGs, small arms, and mortars using a water-services truck as a mask. Our response was immediate. A section of M1 Abrams tanks changed the scenery of the bridge and our checkpoint there. The enemy did materialize at a distance and launched a single pathetic 82mm mortar round, impacting just across the near bank of the river at dusk. The scenery of his own attack also changed; he missed and now ran.

An hour later, our Recon Platoon headed south along the main highway. They approached a decorative gate incongruently guarding a wadi that funnels the waste by-product of Tikrit into the Tigris River. Our men affectionately know this depression as the "Stink Wadi." That night it exuded more than just odor. A volley of RPGs raced across in a flash from the south bank of the wadi. Small arms accompanied the volley.

The scouts' weapons erupted in a converging arc that raked and then secondarily exploded on the bank. Unable to get to the scene quickly by the nature of the wadi, distance, and terrain, the men could not determine the damage they inflicted. But they blew up something. When searched later, the area was vacant, revealing little information.

The revelation of information took on a different form in Tikrit the following morning. Our C Company posted security along the main street of the city near the telephone exchange offices. Bradley Fighting Vehicles and tough soldiers mixed with the squat, dilapidated structures of the city. A small crowd gathered at a new café in town—an Internet café. Words are exchanged, cameras roll and snap, a pair of scissors is lifted off a pillow as the owner and I cut a ribbon at the entrance.

While thrilled, it all seems so foreign to me given the context of the previous days. For a brief moment these small trappings of normal life—of normal pursuits and daily living—awaken me. As I leave the café an old woman is nearly struck by a car and a bicycle as she attempts to cross the busy street. Our soldiers step into the four lanes of traffic and she is escorted across the thoroughfare. As we pull out in our vehicles, we cradle our weapons, begin to watch rooftops, examine every trash pile, and check each alley. A sea of people is scanned quickly—what is in their arms, what are their facial expressions, do they make unusual movement? We pull away and reenter our world.

"Duck, Duck, Goose"

The farmlands along the Tigris River lay rich with vegetation. Palm trees stand as sentinels row on row, aligned and supported by murky irrigation ditches. Fields adjacent to the groves produce wheat. Varieties of trees sag under the weight of pomegranates, apples, and citrus. An occasional farm surfaces amid the boundless orchards and fields. The farm occupants—subsistence farmers who work for middle-aged men whose girths are expanded by too much lamb—tend the crops.

They also plant a bounty of a different kind. Hidden between irrigated ditches lay pits that contain everything from mortars, rocket-propelled grenades, artillery rockets, grenades, and machine guns. As important as it is to find these things, the desire to find those planting them is tenfold by comparison.

We targeted two such sowers of discord south of the village of Owja—the birthplace of Saddam Hussein, outside of Tikrit. They were siblings, with the now-familiar string of tongue-tying names that also convey the names of their fathers, grandfathers, tribe, and birthplace. Our soldiers worked hard to locate these brothers because they were among a group of five spawns that had attacked our forces with RPGs.

We arrested the first brother in Owja. Now we had the location of their family farm along the Tigris. Our forces moved in and cut off egress routes, in coordination with Special Operations Forces and attack aviation. By dusk we had surrounded the brothers' farm. The remaining brother began to run into the nearby fields. The helicopters spotted him. Soon we closed in on him and found him hunkered down in a field—his war now over.

Others continued in their belligerence, however. On August 26, an informant came to our forces telling us of a farm southwest of Owja that had weapons and self-proclaimed Fedayeen fighters. Given that we had experienced attacks along the main highway nearby, this seemed plausible.

I ordered our Recon Platoon to scout out the area and see what they could find. Two sections of scouts approached the farms just after dusk. They turned off the main highway and were soon greeted with a hail of gunfire from AK-47 rifles. The scouts immediately returned fire, sending the assailants deep into their own farmhouse. Rifles *cracked,* .50 caliber machine guns *thudded*, and 40mm MK-19 grenade launchers *thumped* in a warlike symphony of gunfire. The projectiles smacked the modest farm. Two individuals were briefly spotted running out the back and into an irrigation ditch immediately behind.

1LT Chris Morris called in the contact and stated he was maneuvering on the houses but needed additional force to affect a proper cordon. He said he still had visual contact with the attackers. CPT Mark Stouffer's A Company responded with a quick reaction force. Soon the area was cordoned with Bradleys, Infantry, and scout humvees. The four attackers were captured—amazingly unharmed although terrified—in the initial farmhouse and the one connected by the irrigation ditch behind it. None of our men were wounded. The enemy was detained and all of his weapons captured.

As this drama played out south of Tikrit, another unfolded within the heart of it. Repeated roadside bomb attacks along 40th and 60th Streets plagued the modest homes and businesses there. For three months we had fought battles along these alleys. While most of the attackers had been ambushed or subdued, the explosives threat continued. Just the night before, when my command convoy had turned onto 60th Street, a young adult Iraqi male in all black sitting on a curb suddenly bolted for a side street. Alerted by this, we gave chase for two blocks but he had disappeared over the many walled housing compounds. He appeared unarmed but could have been a scout or a bomb initiator. We queried the locals about him but none claimed to know him.

Now a night later, not far from this same area, C Company had a rifle squad patrolling the side streets between 40th and 60th. At about
0300—well after curfew—the night air was shattered by the distinct
sound of an AK-47. The patrol alerted toward the sound of the gunfire. As they neared the area, an Iraqi man ran at full gallop around the
corner where the gunfire occurred. SPC Haines, on point, raised his
rifle and fired into the man. A round caught the Iraqi square in the
head, carrying away a portion of his face. The sprinter stumbled to
the ground, losing his sandals in the awkward momentum, already
dead before he fell.

I immediately recognized him as the same man in black we encountered the night before. A few men were somewhat taken aback as
FSG (First Sergeant) Evans, CPT Boyd, and I rolled him over in his
own fluids so we could search him. Some had still not seen death
close and personal before. In his pockets were batteries of the type
used to initiate roadside bombs. His war was over now.

At the end of August, information came our way via a well-
established network of sheiks. Developing this network was no small
task. By custom, sheiks can be appointed to represent several families
or can represent thousands. How do you determine who represents
forty people vs. forty thousand?

When we arrived, every man claimed he was the sheik that the
Americans should deal with and as such, he was also entitled to special privileges, badges, weapons, cars, and even women should we
have them—whatever we can provide. They in turn would "guarantee" everything from security, support with the Coalition, promises of
uranium, "vital" information, and even Saddam—should they see
him, of course. So our challenge was how to separate these men of
grandiose importance from the real sheiks that clearly commanded
the respect from the locals.

The solution seemed simple enough: create a meeting of sheiks on
a weekly basis and make it open to all. Those who would attend
would probably be supportive somewhat or they would not come.
Secondly, those who would sit on the front row would probably be the
"real" sheiks. And so it was. Within a few weeks, we had identified

those to whom everyone seemed to defer. By the end of August, we had solidified a "Council of Sheiks," with ten representatives from the controlling tribes that represented about two hundred thousand people in our region.

One of these sheiks had been very cooperative with us already. Although secretive—Iraqi Arabs seem to revel in the thrill of private liaisons and somewhat theatrical trappings—he provided us with important breakthroughs regarding those resisting our efforts. Now he wanted a private dinner meeting east of the Tigris on one of his tenant farms. I have come to call these rendezvous "lamb grabs"—the slaughtered goat or lamb consumed for dinner by being pulled from the bone with bare hands. While the information provided that late evening in August was noteworthy, I will remember the dinner more for the kids.

The tenant farmers had a solitary mud house where they housed their four families and twenty kids. Unlike other "lamb grabs" we had attended, the wives and children were necessarily present. This allowed for some wonderful interaction among our soldiers. The laughter of the kids as they ran like kittens, chasing our weapons' laser lights was a lift. Soon, my men were teaching them all sorts of games. By far the most enjoyable was the American favorite where the children are tapped on the head while in a circle, and dubbed a various waterfowl. One titling causes the child to have to run after the name caller—"Duck, Duck, Goose" had come to Iraq.

Criminals, Convoys, and Catwalks

While my men and I enjoyed this out-of-place respite near the foothills of the Jabal Hamrin Ridge east of the Tigris, our C Company soldiers on patrol spotted a white car in downtown Tikrit with bullet holes in it. They immediately stopped it and subdued four males with three AK-47 rifles. To the north of the city, near the village of Mazhem, C Company, 3-66 Armor soldiers began the opening round of what became the "battle for the ammunition supply points."

On the night of 28 August, the "Cougars" found fourteen people living inside a bunker bloated with munitions. The bunkers are roughly the size of gymnasiums. The outer walls are double, forming a catacomb around the structure and also allowing the criminals to hide in the nooks and crannies in complete darkness. Our men must clear them much like we would a tunnel, with the same associated risks.

The enemy hired looters, brought in from Samarra for about two dollars a day. They had an entire operation going with 57mm anti-aircraft shells. First, they removed the rounds from the boxes. Next they took a hammer and cracked the rounds' seals with the brass cases—an indicator of their intelligence. (Of course, all of this works best while smoking.) Then they emptied the powder pellets into bags, stacked the brass, and bagged the warheads. The warheads are the type most commonly used for roadside improvised explosives. The propellant is used to make other types of bombs, and the brass is melted down into ingots and sold. All of the proceeds go to support-ing your local terrorist.

We knew of the operations, but did not have enough manpower to cover all the areas. Consequently, the improvised-explosives war manifested itself significantly in our area—partly because we were killing the enemy in the direct firefights in the city and partly because they could salvage munitions without much risk from our patrols.

I assigned the task of ending this operation to CPT Jon Cecalupo's C Company, 3-66 Armor. Although this was not a tank mission, we needed the manpower. Jon, the son and brother of an Infantryman, aggressively put his talents into the mission and established a series of ambushes with his dismounted tank crews.

Each night for a month, a "cat and mouse" war developed. The looters would come into the perimeter—most of the time armed—and set up shop for the night. In about thirty days, CPT Cecalupo's men had engaged scores of the enemy. They had killed 5, wounded 65, and captured over 100. For every night of bloodshed, a new day of the same awaited them.

Concerned, I met individually with the tank men doing the grisly work of separating the stupid and the lawless from the living. What I found was yet another example of how professional and dedicated our soldiers are. The men assured me that they fully understood the mission. They told me that for every bomb material supplier they killed, captured, or maimed, then one less bomb would be on the road. They were right. At the end of a month's hard labor, the battle of the ammunition supply point was won. But the bomb war continued to be waged in the streets and supply routes of Tikrit and its villages.

On August 29, we patrolled the streets of Tikrit much like any other night. Long shadows fingered out and then dissipated in the pale streetlight while the dogs roamed wild in packs. At about 2330, when we turned onto 40th Street, one pack assaulted us in an impressive wedge formation, with all dogs barking in support. They came to within five feet of our vehicles. While we were admiring them for their aggressiveness, a violent explosion silenced the barks and our thoughts. What was it? An acrid smoke filled the air behind us. The dogs made a disorderly retreat in full scamper.

The trail vehicles seemed OK. We immediately turned the vehicles around, covered both double lanes of traffic and headed south back toward the enemy. Once we arrived, we jumped from the vehicles and sought to engage the attackers. We shouted taunts at the enemy and attested with oaths and epithets to their incompetence. But none answered our challenge.

On the west-side curb at the corner were the signs of the explosion. A vegetable oil tin packed with what we determined to be ten blocks of TNT and a hand grenade was the basis of the bomb. Clearly legible on a piece of the metal were the words, "A Gift from Sweden." The bomb did not have the forcefulness it could have due to the poor wiring of the explosives. The grenade and two blocks of TNT detonated but the other eight scattered in the blast radius. Our dispersion and tactics had lessened the effects of that blast.

A curious man unrelated to the incident observed us with amusement from the balcony above his restaurant. Seeing this, red rifle lasers soon lined up on this man's dress and he, like the dogs, beat a hasty retreat. The attacker could be one of several thousand people hidden in nearby houses and apartments. We resumed our patrol.

August 30 dawned with another bomb on the streets. C Company Infantrymen discovered this one—two sticks of C-4 hooked to batteries and tied to a bottle of diesel fuel. Our soldiers called the explosives experts who detonated it. Not far from the bomb, later in the afternoon, a C Company patrol dodged a volley of RPGs that missed wildly. One crashed into an Iraqi house, badly wounding a two-year-old child. Our soldiers immediately responded and saved the girl's life. She was stabilized and taken to the local hospital.

As this unfolded, we received a tip about a weapons cache of RPG launchers on a farm. We went to the house of the supposed farm owner. He was not there but a relative was. We told him there would be no trouble if he took us to the farm and pointed out the weapons. He complied.

We already had his brother in jail and he said he wanted no trouble with us. He would help. He did. After a ten-minute countryside journey, the man walked us to a deep irrigation ditch and pointed to a pile of cut hay at the bottom. As we pulled six sacks of weapons out, we realized that we stood little chance of ever finding these weapons without informants. We returned to our headquarters with twenty-six RPG launchers.

The next few days brought an attack on the governor's building, and more roadside bombs. September 2 was particularly noteworthy. It started with a discovery on the northern highway bypass. Several large-caliber artillery shells were "daisy-chained" together along the guardrails. We disarmed them before they could be put to use. C Company patrols discovered two more bombs in northern Tikrit and detonated both of them. At the southern highway bypass, a patrol from 299th Engineers discovered yet another one.

As long shadows signaled the end of the day a convoy, from our support company that was bringing supplies and soldiers returning from emergency leave, approached only a few kilometers from this bomb. No matter. Another one awaited.

A tire in the road instantly became a brownish cloud of sand, flame, and shrapnel. In the lead humvee, the officer in charge felt a sharp pain to his right knee and arm. An A Company sergeant sitting in the back was thrown sideways and into the middle of the humvee by the force, and suffered neck lacerations.

The cargo truck behind it collected a spattering of shrapnel that cut into tires, metal—and flesh. A specialist from our support company felt a deadening pain to his face and head and shoulder. Blood poured from the gums where several of his teeth had been. Another soldier facing the back took slicing shrapnel through his left foot.

Amazingly, no one was gravely injured. The soldiers gathered their wounded comrades and rushed them to one of our aid stations a few kilometers up the highway. We arrived and secured the area, equipment, and damaged vehicles. Big hunks of artillery shrapnel lay embedded in the asphalt. The tire was nothing more than an array of belted cords and loose rubber that had bounced in all directions. With our casualties and equipment secure, we quickly recovered everything from the scene. There will never be dancing Iraqis on our equipment. We will kill every one of them who tries.

On September 3, we had success against these bombers and others. An informant tipped our soldiers about a bomb maker in Tikrit. We planned a raid that resulted in the capture of C-4, propellants, sealants, clocks, timers, switches, wire, grenades, and rifles. Two individuals were also captured. Later that evening, six to nine mortar rounds impacted near the Tigris Bridge access road. All fell harmlessly into an empty lot. We received reports about the location of the attackers east of the river. Not being our sector, we alerted the Brigade Reconnaissance Troop commanded by CPT Des Bailey. But they were several kilometers north of the activity at that moment, so we decided to cross the river and go to the location in support of the troop's efforts. As we closed near the troop, their convoy came under RPG and small arms fire about four hundred meters to our front. They returned fire with .50 cal machine guns, grenade launchers, and rifle fire. The brush caught fire as a second outburst occurred. We lent support with Bradleys and Infantry.

The next morning, a bloody sandal was found in a concrete aqueduct. The charred area around the attackers' launch point attested to the one-sidedness of the fight. None of our soldiers in either attack were wounded.

By the 5th of September, we found ourselves guarding Tikrit and its environs in a most unusual way. We received instructions to ensure no attacks came for a four-hour window. No bangs, no booms, no fuss. A tall order but one we clearly understood.

The Secretary of Defense would be in Tikrit and it would be complicated if Mr. Rumsfeld appeared announcing the success of Iraqi security forces and clearly visible signs of progress to the backdrop of gunfire and bomb blasts. We secured the town without incident.

We also introduced to the Tikriti people our Iraqi Civil Defense Corps on this day. They were amazed. Only a couple of days from graduation, these young men walked proud on the streets of their countrymen. Bystanders looked in amazement. One woman clutched her heart and exclaimed, "Our army! It had returned!"

Our training efforts have been very successful in the Iraqi Civil Defense Corps. Learning from my experience with the Afghan National Army project in the spring of 2002, we put together a program that was far lesser in scale but just as great in importance, given our geography and world attention.

We formed a cadre of officers and sergeants out of hide, led by CPT Jason Deel and SFC (Sergeant First Class) Robert Soden, to conduct the training and to select and hire the new force. We vet the males through the tribal sheiks. Each recruit has to be "guaranteed" by the tribal head in an official document.

Taking advantage of the local customs, we also guarantee that the force will truly be Iraqi because it is solely composed of those men that they choose. To date, we have trained over 350 in our battalion alone and we have had no problems of enemy infiltration. The Iraqi soldiers have proven themselves worthy of their new government and have not been afraid to take risks in our area of operations. We back them fully and conduct operations with them side by side.

Our battle for the streets of Tikrit continued. A sniper team placed near 40th Street to watch over that troubled area had a battle of their own. On September 6th, SPC Cantu and his team moved from a rooftop hideout to cover another location. As they did, three Iraqis engaged them with gunfire and then fled. Not satisfied with the outcome and undaunted by the terrain, Cantu led his team across catwalks and rooftops in the direction he believed the assailants had fled.

Once at the corner, they saw the men congratulating each other and flushed with their imagined heroics. Their victory party was soon shattered by the gunfire of our soldiers. Cantu and his team blasted the men, killing two and wounding the third. The same day C Company, 3-66 Armor continued the battle of the bunkers, killing one and wounding another. The enemy continued to pay a heavy price.

A major concern of ours during this time was how to get at the thugs planning these attacks. We began to place a series of outposts and ambushes in the most likely areas of enemy activity. The locations varied from downtown to suburbs to villages. The labor was not in vain. On the night of the 6th to 7th of September, we raided three suspected locations based on tips, and detained seven thugs and weapons. The night of the 7th, one of our outposts in a northern suburb noticed a group of men with AK-47s coming to an abandoned house for a meeting. We suspected this house all along and had 1LT Mike Isbell's men from C Company posted there, but they were actually looking for a bomber at a house in the opposite direction. Even so, our men opened up on the group, wounding one and capturing five others.

On the 9th of September, a foot patrol from C Company led by SSG (Staff Sergeant) Sanchez, found itself under fire from a white car driving by an alley. The enemy fired RPGs and rifles. Our men immediately returned fire and blasted the car, forcing the enemy to flee. We were unable to locate the thugs thereafter.

We were however able to locate more of those planning their evil deeds. On the night of the 10th we cordoned three businesses along 40th Street. Among the goods in the stores were TNT and C-4 explosives, clocks, mercury for detonators, mortar ammunition, AK-47s, and shotguns—quite a variety for the discriminating shopper.

Toys

Most interesting of all were several radio-controlled cars that were being converted into bombs. The cars themselves were discarded but the bombers were taking the electronic guts from them to attach to blasting caps. Then they would wrap them in C-4 and place them inside a container of some kind for camouflage. The "hobbyists" would then use the remote control (R/C) steering device to initiate the bomb, as a convoy would pass. The range on these devices is about one hundred meters. In a built-up urban environment, that is about the same as one hundred miles in terms of seeing who could initiate the bombs.

To counter some of the threat of this, I took one of the R/C controllers and taped the levers down. The toy cars all operate on essentially the same frequency. We put it on the dash of our humvee, flip it on, and use it as a poor man's anti-explosive device—risky perhaps, but better than exploding bombs through discovery learning.

Since this time, we have received all sorts of good ideas and gadgets to counter the bomb threats. Unfortunately, most of these devices are full of promise and short on delivery. The jamming equipment in "high speed" vehicles also jams our radios—not the best solution.

Other items have been huge white Chevy Suburbans with NASA-like antennae. We might as well paint bull's-eyes as an added touch. These are like going to war in a Winnebago—fine for the movie *Stripes* but not fine in reality.

Elections

Mid-September arrived with promise. The heat still insufferable, our soldiers performed each task magnificently, whether ambushes, patrols, training native levees, or engaging the local officials in democratic processes.

We graduated our first class of Iraqi Civil Defense Corps soldiers and began training the second. We formalized the "Council of

Sheiks" and made the head tribal leaders the representatives rather than open it up to everyone who had a complaint. This allowed us to focus on the best issues. Our mayor began to get his footing and established an effective system of public works. We hired our third municipal police chief—the first was fired, the second was transferred. Our cooperation with the Saladin Government continued to gel.

With this backdrop, MG Ray Odierno tasked all the units to select delegates for each city and province to form representative councils to aid the governors of the three provinces covered by the 4th Infantry Division. Having already engaged many of the sheiks and leaders beforehand, we found an able group of ten sheiks and five professionals from which to choose four representatives for Tikrit. Other cities did the same and then we all came together at the 1st Brigade headquarters for the representative election of thirty-four delegates to serve on the Saladin Province Governing Council.

The big day came on September 13th. I met with our Tikritians in a private room after all were gathered in a general assembly. Iraqi judges were present for each selection and to oversee the ballot count with each battalion commander.

I gave each prospective councilman the floor. The qualifications for why they should be selected varied. One touted his 9th-grade education and character. Others spoke of their law or engineering degrees or were medical doctors. Some had held political office before. My favorite was a tribal head sheik that stated simply, "I am Sheik [so-and-so]." That was the sum of his qualification and he passed the floor to the next individual. He was not elected, but he did get several votes.

On the afternoon of the 18th we were coming back from a visit to B Company in Bayji. Not far to the south, two humvees and a wheeled ambulance were transporting a sick soldier north along Highway 1 to the military hospital. Little did they imagine that before they arrived they would add to their casualty list.

At about 1600 hours, as the lead vehicle neared the spiral arches on Highway 1 south of Owja, a terrific blast shattered the vehicle's windshield, front tires, and side. The humvee belonged to a first sergeant from 1-66 Armor who was leading the convoy. We heard a distant *whump,* and then a radio transmission requesting assistance. The driver lay bleeding but conscious when we arrived. The soldiers there all seemed shaken by the event, which was understandable. The armored battalion's sergeant major arrived shortly after we did.

I remember looking at the young man laid out on the ground. His leg was mauled but not seriously damaged. His mouth and face were covered in blood. He seemed worried and was obviously in pain. The sergeant major and I told him to take a deep breath, relax, and that he was going to be OK. He calmed a bit and then said he needed to spit. He had collected blood in his mouth from what appeared to be some missing teeth.

The men from that unit did a good job putting their convoy back together. They grabbed their casualties and equipment. Fortunately for the wounded soldier, he was traveling with an ambulance and medics so he was going to be fine. I told their men that we would recover their vehicle and remaining gear and to not worry about it. We would get it to them at the brigade aid station.

We did a hasty examination of the area and found the remnants of a Motorola radio bomb. These were not your average bombs. The range on them was several kilometers. As we were in an open expanse of desert along the highway, there was no telling who had initiated the device—except that he was a coward. Several Iraqi cars were also damaged by the blast, although we never learned if any Iraqis had sustained injuries.

We returned to our command post, ate, and then went out on patrol again. We were up in villages to the north that night when we heard some disturbing radio calls from across the river. A section of humvees from the brigade's reconnaissance troop had been caught in an ambush on a levee road. They were responding to reports of an RPG being fired in the area. The lead and trail vehicles came under tremendous fire that killed three soldiers and wounded two others. The remainder of the men fought off the attackers and maintained contact with the enemy.

Soon, the rest of the troop rallied to them and requested medical evacuation support. We immediately responded from our side of the river. I sent C Company with Bradleys and Infantry to support CPT Des Bailey. All of the wounded and killed were brought to our aid station. CPT Brad Boyd supported the cordon of a couple of farms in the area until late afternoon the next day.

Three of the six attackers were captured outright. A total of forty were eventually hauled in and from these all of the attackers were brought to account. Even so, the result could scarcely remove the pain of such loss. The men all belonged to the artillery battalion support- ing our brigade and the troop. Our best comfort lay in taking it back to the enemy.

The next evening, we moved across the river in force with our bat- talion. CPT Mark Stouffer's A Company, CPT Jon Cecalupo's tank company and the S3 and I patrolled the entire swath of land with Bradleys, M1A2 tanks and Infantry from our task force. We contin- ued to support Des Bailey's troop with a section of Bradleys and some mortars for some time after this. In the coming weeks, the peo- ple cried for us to stop operations in the area. CPT Bailey handled them as they deserved to be handled—and captured or killed those equally deserving.

Taps

As LTC Dom Pompelia's and CPT Bailey's units recovered from their loss, we prepared to pay our respects to the fallen. The night before the memorial service—the 20th of September and my mother's birth- day—COL James Hickey called me. He said he had received a Red Cross message. I did not think this unusual, as many of my soldiers had received these unfortunate messages, including me when my grandfather died in July. I was not prepared for the news he gave me. He said that my stepfather had died only a few hours before and that my family had requested my presence. I was stunned. I was accus- tomed to loss on the battlefront but not the home front. I immediately missed him. Just a few days before, I had received one of his letters.

After calling home, I knew my place had to be with my family. I called my commander back and told him I needed to go home for the funeral. He understood and supported me. I told him the battalion would be in good hands with MAJ Mike Rauhut, my executive officer. I left the next day.

While I Was Away

A world away, C Company patrols received fire from the industrial area of the city. The Iraqi Police were also attacked at their main police station. The attacks seemed feeble and the enemy appeared content to "miss-and-run." There were no casualties.

The next day, MAJ Mike Rauhut led the battalion on a magnificent raid into the farmlands south of Owja. Based on an informant's tip, the "Gators" of A Company cordoned the lush, densely vegetated farm. A bountiful harvest of weapons awaited—23 shoulder-fired anti-aircraft missiles, 4 RPG launchers with 115 rocket-propelled grenades, 400 hand grenades, 1 mortar with 39 rounds of ammunition, 51 smoke pots, over 1,000 pounds of C-4 explosives with 1,300 blasting caps. This deadly crop was laid out in our trucks for eventual destruction.

The "Cobras" of C Company had their palace rattled by RPG fire on the 29th of September. An informant on the 30th led our operations officer MAJ Bryan Luke to a cache of sixty rocket-propelled grenades. After weeks of successful raiding, the enemy was severely disrupted. He struck back with more roadside bombs.

On the 1st of October I received a phone call from CPT Matt Weber, our rear detachment commander. He told me there had been an attack with casualties and that MAJ Rauhut was trying to contact me. He got a call through a few minutes later. The news was not good. A sinking feeling washed over me. Here I was, strangely out of place standing in a Texas parking lot while Mike described what happened.

CPT Curt Kuetemeyer's convoy from our support company was traveling north in downtown Tikrit along Highway 1 where it turns into the main street. Passing the soccer stadium, his vehicle approached the Tuz-Tikrit highway turnoff. Suddenly he went deaf and saw a bright flash to his left. The air immediately turned brown with dust and had a sickening sulfur smell. He knew something was terribly wrong. The humvee seemed pilotless. *Hit the brakes!* he thought. Then he thought the brakes must be damaged. He braced for impact.

At a T-intersection in the highway stands the road sign directing a turn off for the city of Tuz. The vehicle crashed the curb, flattened the road sign, and bounced to halt. He could see flames all around him. CPT Kuetemeyer immediately took stock of his soldiers. They were in bad shape. He could see his driver slumped and still seat-belted behind the wheel. The soldier behind her was badly burned and pinned in. The soldier behind CPT Kuetemeyer was in better shape and was also trying to free himself from the vehicle. Despite the shock of the concussion, Curt seemed intact and able to move.

SPC Guckert and FSG Davis in the vehicle behind saw their company commander's vehicle hit by the blast and watched in disbelief. They braced themselves as they entered a brown, flaming fog. They pulled up to the blazing vehicle. FSG Davis yelled for Guckert to pull security and ran to the vehicle. Guckert ordered SPC Bemak to pull security as well and then immediately made a radio transmission for help, her voice calm and in charge. She described the situation and guided life-saving help to the scene, fully aware of her dangerous surroundings. CPT Kuetemeyer and FSG Davis managed to pull the three wounded soldiers from the burning vehicle. They performed an emotional and grisly task, fighting the flames as they attempted to save their comrades in the burning vehicle.

SPC Guckert then informed another convoy that was passing by about the situation. These soldiers pulled security around the vehicles to assist. SPC Guckert joined CPT Kuetemeyer and FSG Davis, encouraging the wounded to hang in there as they rendered aid. Guckert then grabbed her aid bag and began to administer first aid.

CPT Brad Boyd from C Company showed up and provided immediate help with his men. The wounded soldiers were taken by humvee to the battalion aid station. There, our surgeon MAJ Bill Marzullo and our physician's assistants CPT Alex Morales and 2LT Armando Buergette struggled to save CPT Kuetemeyer's driver. She died of her wounds. The other soldiers were treated for serious burns, concussions, lacerations, and broken bones.

Meanwhile, Highway 1 returned to normal after C Company recovered the vehicle. There will never be an opportunity for Iraqis to dance on our equipment. Not in this town. We would kill the whole city first.

On the 3rd of October I boarded a plane in Dallas to return to Tikrit.

Meanwhile, in Tikrit, the soldiers of the 1st Battalion, 22nd Infantry and the 4th Forward Support Battalion gathered at Saddam's "Birthday Palace." The Aggressors of A Company, 4th FSB stood on the asphalt still marked with lines for Saddam's military parades. A chaplain stepped forward and prayed. A Purple Heart and Bronze Star Medal for making the ultimate sacrifice were laid on a pair of boots overshadowed by a lone rifle with a Kevlar helmet planted on top. At a podium, commanders and friends struggled to find words that vocabularies failed to adequately provide. Soldiers stood at attention. Private First Class Analaura Esparza-Gutierrez's name rang out for roll call. She did not answer. Taps resonated in mournful tones. Tears rolled down faces as they remembered her life.

Back to Tikrit

Forty-eight hours later, I was back in Tikrit. The situation had become more intense. Our successful raiding on the members of Saddam's supporting cast would have to be put on hold so we could deal with trigger pullers. The roadside bombs were taking their toll. In our area, the soldiers conducted mounted patrols and sweeps. These were directed patrols for the most part.

The feeling was that the patrols should be armored to lessen the effects of the bombs. I did not agree. While it is true that the effects of the bombs would be lessened, so would our ability to see the bombs on the roads and respond. Soldiers on the ground and wheeled patrols in open vehicles have the best chance of spotting bombs. Additionally, there were demonstrations starting to develop in several cities in Iraq.

Quick responses by our men on October 3rd prevented a demonstration from taking hold and it was rapidly dispersed. My plan now was to prevent them from ever forming. Having been surrounded with fifteen other soldiers by a crowd of five thousand angry people before in the summer of 1999 in Kosovo, I was determined not to have that happen again.

On October 9th and 10th we received intelligence about planned demonstrations. I ordered our forces to flood the suspected area with soldiers, tanks, and Infantry vehicles. It worked. Meanwhile, our scouts silently observed a suspected bomber's house in a suburb to the north. In the evening, this outpost repositioned and received fire from a distance. SSG Shoffner's group was not hit, returned fire, and continued its mission. We then raided several houses in downtown Tikrit tied to bomb makers and bomb layers. Four thugs were captured.

The next night, our training compound for the Iraqi Civil Defense Corps received several mortar rounds. A few crashed the main building but caused no appreciable damage. Saddest loss was the hot water heater that fed the building. C Company, the Iraqi soldiers under our command, and our scouts immediately set out in pursuit. They found and captured three individuals attempting to leave the area from where the strike was launched.

October 12th dawned with the promise of sweltering heat. SSG Charles Darrah of our PSYOPS team left our compound and made it about five hundred meters before a tree on the right side of the road exploded in a downpour of leaves, twigs, concrete, and shrapnel. He and one man received slight wounds but another was more serious. He had nasty leg and arm wounds on one side. He was later evacuated and is recovering well. Another bomb was sighted at the gas station in our northern suburb. An Iraqi fingered two men plotting their evil plans. We found one and captured him. The bomb attack was averted.

Farther north, the "Bears" of B Company patrolled an area on the outskirts of Bayji known by our soldiers as the "projects." The day before they received a cool reception that turned colder when locals began to throw rocks and shake fists. They decided to return to this troubled spot again. 1st Platoon Bradleys, led by a tank commanded by 2LT Erik Aadland from B Company, 3-66 Armor rattled up a trail connecting to a hardball road.

The lead Bradley followed the tank closely and off to the right. The trail Bradley followed to the left. Suddenly the trail vehicle erupted. Smoke and flame shot through the driver and engine compartment. SSG Donald Smith's night vision goggles tethered around his neck disappeared in the blast. The gunner was wounded above his right eye but otherwise OK.

The vehicle abruptly stopped. The soldiers scrambled out of the crew compartment hatch. SSG Smith took account of his men and the other Bradley reported that B14 had struck a mine. The men evacuated the driver out, who was in critical condition. Pulling security, they called for the medevac helicopter on which they eventually loaded him. He was rushed by Black Hawk to the field hospital.

Recovery assets drove forward and towed the vehicle back to 3-66 Armor's compound. As they were doing so, the sparks from grinding metal of blown-off road arms appeared to ignite the fuel in the vehicle. The Bradley began to burn and then its ammunition cooked off. The vehicle was a total loss. The driver never made it either. Another Regular dies. We received the news shortly thereafter and felt at once both angry and sad.

We continued our operations in Tikrit the next day, conducting our bomb sweeps along the main roads and those that connect them. C Company had primary responsibility of the built-up area of the city. In the afternoon, 1st Platoon patrolled with Bradleys and Infantry in the part of the city we call the "chevron" because on the map, it makes a pointed shape at the northern third of the city. 1LT Jason Price was leading a two-vehicle section along the street parallel to the mosque with the soccer field. They turned right, heading east toward Highway 1 and the "Lucky Panda" ice-cream shop continuing to look for bombs along the curbs.

SSG Bordes in the trail Bradley had his turret turned to the rear to provide 360-degree security. He looked forward as the vehicle travels while his gunner, standing up to provide additional eyes for the bomb threat, looked toward the rear. A short distance after they made the turn, SSG Bordes blacked out.

He came to in a daze, realizing something was wrong. He saw his driver was OK after talking to him and could see his gunner standing next to him. He stood back up to make sure he was OK as well, and noticed that he was lying back against the hatch, his helmet gone. The shoe-box-sized Integrated Site Unit (ISU) in front of him was blown apart and pushed against him as well. SSG Michael Bordes called for a medevac and attempted to render what aid he could. No aid could be rendered. His gunner slumped into the turret, already dead.

1LT Price called the medevac and his crews did what they could while also pulling security. The vehicle was hit by an RPG, which penetrated the ISU. We determined that two men had fired a volley of RPGs from a blind corner in the built-up housing area.

As the gunner was the one looking to the rear, he was the only one who could have seen where the shot came from that killed him. CPT Brad Boyd arrived at the scene and they cleared the area looking for the attackers. FSG Michael Evans, SSG Felipe Madrid, and SSG Bordes eased the gunner out of the turret and onto a stretcher. CPT Jason Deel with the Civil Defense troops took him to our battalion aid station.

I received the news coming out of a meeting with local officials and rushed to the scene. There was nothing I could do. The Bradley was not damaged except for its sight and 1st Platoon took it back to the company's compound. I called for a fire truck to wash down the streets. I wanted no visible traces of anything for the enemy to gloat over. We took our losses and cracked down on the city looking for the perpetrators. Locals provided some useful information and a manhunt netted partial results over the next couple of days.

The soldiers of the 1st Battalion, 22nd Infantry and some from 3rd Battalion, 66th Armor gathered at Saddam's "Birthday Palace" on the 15th. The "Bears" of B Company and "Cobras" of C Company stood on that same asphalt used for Saddam's military parades.

A chaplain stepped forward and prayed. Again Purple Hearts and Bronze Star Medals for making the ultimate sacrifice were laid on pairs of boots overshadowed by lone rifles with Kevlar helmets planted on top. At a podium, commanders and friends struggled to find words that vocabularies failed to adequately provide. Soldiers stood at attention.

SPC James Edward Powell's name rang out for roll call in B Company. He did not answer. Neither did SPC Donald Laverne Wheeler Jr. of C Company. Taps resonated in mournful tones. Tears rolled down faces as we remembered their lives, and rifle shots *cracked* in three sharp volleys, interrupting these reflections—a startling reminder of the price of our freedom.

Raids and a Shopping Bag

Two sisters played in front of their house on the 16th of October near one of the city laundry shops in Tikrit. Two women and a man walked along the street about mid-morning. One of the ladies carried a black plastic sack, the kind that is so common among all of the shops and food stands. They conversed a bit and then walked away.

The seven-year-old sister noticed that the lady forgot her sack on the road. She and her twelve-year-old sister went over to pick up the bag and carry it to the lady who forgot it. The seven-year-old made it only a few steps when she was ripped apart by a powerful blast. Her sister was mangled and blinded. She could not walk. She struggled to pull herself to her house, leaving bloody handprints on the concrete and the gate where she lived.

Our soldiers arrived very quickly. The locals were frantic. The parents of the girls wailed in horror and disbelief not knowing what to do. We, the evil Americans, helped an innocent Iraqi girl with life-saving aid. The men evacuated her to the hospital. She survived but is now blind. If only the images of this morning that the men now have imprinted in their minds could be blinded as well. Her sister could only be buried.

LTG Tom Metz, commander of III Corps, paid us a visit on the 17th along with many of the old friends I used to work with at Ft. Hood on the Corps staff last year. We briefed him on our operations and he thanked us for our efforts here, as our division falls under his command at Ft. Hood. It was good to see some familiar faces. MAJ Tim Karcher also was among the group. Our paths have continued to cross since Tim was a lieutenant.

The next several days were fairly calm. We had found more road-side bombs but rendered them harmless—usually by shooting them from a safe distance. We were also able to capture more 60mm mor-tar ammunition and some RPGs, along with another fine citizen of Owja, Saddam's birthplace.

The evening of the 20th, more mortars fell near our C Company, 3-66 Armor's compound. The "Cougars" had several of these indirect-fire attacks. This one was slightly more accurate. The soldier manning the .50 caliber machine gun on top of a storage building at the front gate felt the concussion of the shells and heard the *crack* of each round as it came in—each one getting closer. He turned around to head for cover behind some sandbags. As he did, one round landed in the nook between the gate and the building. The shrapnel caught him in the armpit and leg. Fortunately, his body armor prevented seri-ous injury. He recovered well and has returned to duty.

Intelligence reports had indicated that several of these indirect-fire attacks were organized in a farm village north of the old Republican Guard military complex. The complex was rife with weapons and many made their way into private hands when the army collapsed. We also believed they had connections to Saddam's supporting cast of thugs who harbored him or, at a minimum, supported his efforts. We raided a series of houses on the 22nd and turned up explosives, grenades, an RPG, a heavy machine gun, and other items. While not the mortarmen, they certainly were set upon doing harm. Now they are doing time.

The night of the 23rd, the mortar attackers returned to the "Cougars." This time, the "Cougars" were ready. Seeing the flash of the weapon in the far distance, they engaged a car with two men inside who had placed the tube in the trunk to make their escape. The car fled at high speed. Amazingly, it continued to flee even after several hundred machine gun bullets fired from one of our tanks hit it. We learned later that one of the occupants had been killed. It could not have happened to a nicer guy.

I decided to join the observation posts the next night in the northern suburb where the "Cougars" operate. We set up an independent outpost to add to the effort rather than complicate it. My men and I infiltrated a nearly completed house that overlooked the highway. As we took our assault ladder and balanced the bottom rung on a wall to get to a balcony on the third story of the building, I privately wished I was twenty like the men around me. I made it fine and we set up the observation post without incident.

A family next door conducted their evening routine, oblivious to our presence. While watching the highway and residential area around it, I thought how tough it must be to raise a family here. We saw unusual characters and traffic until the curfew took effect and made notes on this. The night proved quiet, no doubt due to the machine gun marksmanship of our tank company. We left in the early morning darkness.

On October 25, Deputy Secretary of Defense Paul Wolfowitz visited our battalion. He was interested in the success we were having with our Iraqi Civil Defense Corps training. He spent quite awhile with us and was very much at ease. He spoke freely with our troops and did not distance himself as so many visiting officials do. He was impressed with our training. We were already feeling the result of the great work the Iraqi soldiers were doing augmenting security in the city.

Black Hawk Down!

There were other visitors that day. Rotor blades clipped through the air about three hundred feet off the deck. A pair of Black Hawk helicopters not from our division came cruising down the Tigris River mid-afternoon carrying officers visiting their troops. The soldiers in the lead helicopter heard a *crack*. Flames immediately mixed with smoke on the blades. The helicopter started to free-fall.

Only several hundred feet off the ground to begin with, the pilots pointed it as best they could to a field. They simply reacted. The aircraft was unresponsive and burning fast. They managed to land it roughly somehow. The soldiers ran from the blazing craft. The trail helicopter watched in shock at the scene before them and swooped around to pick up the survivors—which miraculously was everyone on board.

Only twenty-five hundred meters to the south, our soldiers saw the aircraft go down from our headquarters. We immediately raced across the river to the craft—now a burning mass of aluminum. CPT Stouffer and CPT Boyd were both in the area with their command convoys and headed there as well.

The other aircraft lifted off with all passengers safe as we approached the scene. I told Brad Boyd to take his soldiers north of the crash site and try to find the possible attackers. Mark Stouffer linked up with the battalion Quick Reaction Force that was from his unit and cordoned the eastern road bisecting the farmland. The chopper was fully gutted by this time, about fifteen minutes after the crash. I ordered the command post to call the local fire department to come and put out the flames.

We found some evidence that an RPG probably knocked down the helicopter but it was hard to be sure. It might have been a surface-to-air missile as well. COL Hickey brought the Brigade Reconnaissance Troop over to secure the site and we searched about one hundred vehicles along the road into the villages.

We found nothing—although informant tips a couple of weeks later led us to some of those responsible. We recovered the wreckage from the farm field and brought it to the 4th Aviation Brigade's airfield, once again firm in our dictum that no Iraqi will ever dance on our equipment in our area of responsibility. The helicopters were from the 101st Airborne Division and were flying around special visitors. Though rattled, they were unharmed.

A Writer's Visit

We received an unusual visitor on the 26th, whose stamina for a seventy-eight-year-old man amazed me. Robin Moore—author of *The Green Berets* and *The French Connection*—paid us a visit to gather interviews and information on a new book he was writing. It was quite a treat to meet and listen to him.

Our normal embedded press also continued to report the work of our great soldiers. We have learned a tremendous amount about how the press operates since we have been here. They are largely very professional, are not afraid of risks, and they file accurate stories for the most part. Even in cases when they are not accurate, it is more a function of inaccurate things given to them rather than speculation on their part.

We have also learned that the editors of their news organizations may never pick up the many good things that they file. A sense of frustration develops even among them when a story they worked gets bumped for the splash headline of "Another Soldier Killed in Iraq Today."

They acknowledge that the public has the right to be informed of our casualties, but the reporters on the ground also concede that it does not convey the true picture when that is all that gets reported. Our raids continued to be covered well but the impacts of them would only be appreciated later.

The evening of October 28 was a sad one. Our intelligence officer, CPT Tim Morrow, was wounded by gunfire while on a patrol in the city focused on leaflet distribution. Fortunately, he is a tough man and we were able to get him to the aid station for life-saving procedures for a gunshot wound through the upper chest. He is now recovering well and is very near being returned to duty with us at this writing. His knowledge of our area and the enemy was hard to replace but we are thankful he is going to recover. CPT Clay Bell has since joined the Regulars to pick up where CPT Morrow left off and is doing a superb job.

As Halloween approached, we were nearly ready to implement a plan we had worked on for some time. Prior to my emergency leave, I told my staff I wanted to solve the problem with Owja—Saddam Hussein's birthplace. This town of about thirty-five hundred people continued to be a thorn in the side. Every time we broke up a former regime cell or captured a funder or planner, they all seemed to have ties to this town. Ultimately, we hoped they would still have ties to Saddam.

I thought through the problem of how to keep the insurgents from "swimming" in the population at large, finding safe harbor to plot their evil deeds. I wanted to scoop up the insurgents into a "fishbowl" to view them better. I remembered studying Napoleon's actions with a census in the Rhineland to root out insurgents and took note of techniques used by the French in Algeria. To counter insurgents in the Rhineland, Napoleon had his men conduct a census of sorts. They would ask at each home who lived there. Then they would ask who lived next door on each side. Then they would go to the next house. If the answers varied, they would focus on the missing names that people did not list but that their neighbors did. It proved effective. In Algiers, the French isolated the Wilayas to prevent insurgents and weapons from passing through. Though both of these efforts were on a much larger scale and were not the same, there were certainly aspects of the operations that we could use for ourselves.

The Census

I told my staff I wanted to fence the entire town and conduct a census. They wondered if I had somehow lost my mind. But without a complete cordon, only the fairly honest people would show up. If the town was locked down, then the only way they could get out was to register.

It was a monumental undertaking but one I felt we could do and still carry out our other missions. The benefits would be several: if the criminal elements stayed, their movements would be known; if they left, they would have to give up their operational support base and would be much more visible and vulnerable to being fingered living in their mud huts on their farms; and if they stayed and changed their ways, that would still have desired effects.

We began the effort at midnight on the 30th. I went to the tribal head sheik in the village and informed him of our actions and what would be required: all males over the age of fifteen must be registered and receive a pass to enter or to leave the town. To get the badge, they had to report to the police station and fill out the information form. Once badged, they could come and go as before but were subject to search at a single entry point into and out of town. All other exits would be closed off. He was shocked but complied fully.

By morning, rolls of concertina wire could be seen scattered along the bordering streets like tossed rings. Soldiers unraveled the wire. The scratch of the serrated steel wire on the concrete signaled the end to normal life in Owja. Soon the scratch gave way to pounding sledges for the reinforcing pickets. We buttressed the effort with about fifty Iraqi men from the local "rent-a-worker" group in town, complete with a paid contractor.

Simultaneously, the intelligence and signal staff readied the computer and camera databases to begin the issuing of badges. Scores of Iraqi men showed up at the police station by 0900. They waited for their badge and, once in hand, were allowed to exit the one remaining open avenue leading to Highway 1. By November 3rd, we had badged twelve hundred Owjite males.

The operation amazed not only the Owjites but the international press as well. They all seemed to be fascinated at the audacity of the move. Many drew comparisons to Gaza or Jerusalem but in reality, that never entered our minds. Nor was it a fair comparison. For one, we had an entire rifle company inside the wire with them. Second, we were not trying to separate one culture from another. Third, the town was not sealed but controlled—they could still come and go provided they had their identification. We did prevent the departure of about three dozen individuals and informed the sheik and tribal town elders that we would question them at a later time—which we did.

The impacts of the fencing of Owja were outstanding. We disrupted the enemy's command and control structure. If he fled, we were able to spot him in the villages. If he stayed, we could monitor his movements. The result had been that over the next several weeks we began to get intelligence and people we had been looking for since June and July.

A momentum and sense of excitement restored our belief that we could knock the supports out of Saddam's protective circle. While we did not know the extent that the cordon would have on the terrorist infrastructure or Saddam, we knew it had to have some kind of impact.

Cat and Mouse

On October 31, C Company found another roadside bomb. They dismantled it before it could be used. Later that evening, several thugs in the northern suburbs fired a 60mm mortar toward the "Cougars'" compound. Nothing was hit but our snipers observed the muzzle flash and were able to acquire the enemy at long range. They managed to get off enough rounds to wound two of the individuals.

Meanwhile, in a village toward the far north of our sector, our Recon Platoon observed several men fire AK-47s in the air. "Cougars" closed on the house and engaged the rooftops with small arms. Meanwhile, supporting Apache helicopters on patrol joined in and lit up the house with 30mm cannons. It turned out that several off-duty police were smoking hash and having a jolly time. They dove into a basement and were found there by our soldiers when we cleared it. It is a miracle they were not killed.

November finally clicked by on the calendar. It opened with a combination of raids that netted some important cell leadership and also with patrols that intercepted several roadside bombs. We began to see many varieties of explosive devices. Doorbell switches became a favorite, followed by keyless locks, toy cars, and in one case a pressure switch. Our sweeps continued to net the majority of them before they could be detonated.

In Owja, the enemy attempted harassing fire and mortar cheap shots—both without effect. Our men returned fire and an elusive hide-and-seek game developed. In the city proper, a black Opel or Toyota sped by and lobbed an RPG at a Charlie Company patrol. The men returned fire but as they did, a large Mercedes truck inadvertently pulled into the line of fire and the attackers escaped down a back alley. Other patrols netted eight mortars with some ammunition while the scouts raided the northern suburbs again—and took into custody the last of a set of brothers we had been pursuing for some time.

By the 4th of November, the Owjites seemed resigned to their new fenced routine. I met with the tribal sheik and the town elders. We had a series of frank and honest discussions about the need for the Bayjat tribe to reconcile with the rest of Iraq. They were concerned about this because they felt that without some reconciliation, they could have no future. They would be forced to fight or die. I told them that one would surely lead to the other and that the reconciliation should be pursued.

I took it up as a topic with the Monday morning sheik council meeting and it provided for some lively discussion. They admitted it was needed but they would not welcome them back simply because they said, "I'm sorry." They asserted that this was not their way. Reconciliation had to come from blood compensation. As I listened to all these men weave their tribal and feudalistic discussions, I was very thankful that I was an American.

That evening, the discussions did not seem to deter a band of thugs who engaged the "Gators" of A Company. Firing from the vicinity from an old air defense bunker, the cutthroats launched an RPG at one of our patrols. They also followed it with rifle fire. Undaunted, the "Gators" gave back in spades. The *thump, thump, thump* of a Bradley's 25mm chain gun preceded the *crack, crack, crack, crack* of 25mm shells impacting the bunker. The soldiers cordoned the area but the thugs were able to beat a retreat from a defiladed position before the cordon was set.

The next night, this cat and mouse game continued in Owja. Our soldiers remained alert as usual. Suddenly, the power cut out and the village became black. This preceded a clattering of small arms fire fired wildly but apparently within the wired village. The soldiers searched the town but the attackers blended into the village population.

The next day, CPT Stouffer shut the only gate into and out of town. The attackers were not found.

November 6th did net one attacker though. On the "chevron" in the northwest part of the city, a C Company ambush observed a man setting up what appeared to be a roadside bomb. He began by tying wire to a lamppost and then proceeded to run it to a location across the road. He did not accomplish this immediately. Each time he saw military vehicles in the distance he would back off and then sit passively on the side of the road to appear as one of so many Iraqi men who squat on the side of the road. Watching the pattern, the "Cobras" clearly viewed his activities and confirmed he was planting a roadside bomb. The soldiers placed him in their sites. What followed next was a given. Their rifles popped into action, and the man dropped on top of his own device. Another Fedayeen dies.

November 7th dawned with somewhat cooler weather, but by midmorning became a very pleasant day. GEN John Abizaid arrived to receive another update from the leadership of the 4th Infantry Division. He and MG Ray Odierno came to the 1st Brigade at about 0900 and all the battalion commanders met with him and our commander, COL Jim Hickey.

I had served with GEN Abizaid before in Kosovo and Germany when he commanded the 1st Infantry Division. The update went well and we had very open and frank discussions with him about the best ways we gathered intelligence. He was very open to our observations. He offered that our leads on Saddam were good and that we needed to have the confidence that everyone develops patterns—Saddam would be no different. He closed with some guidance to all of us as commanders and commented on how he saw the fight continuing.

Informants

While we were meeting, two Black Hawk helicopters headed south along the Tigris River in Cadaseeah. At about 0940 the lead helicopter suddenly burst into flames and nosed toward the river. The aircraft

began to break apart even before it hit the ground. Soldiers from C
Company, 3-66 Armor of our task force saw the craft in flames and
disappear behind the bluffs.

The radio began to crackle. A helicopter was down. It was on fire
and crashed near the river on a sandbar island near the bluffs in
Cadaseeah. The command post received the report from Cougar 5,
1LT Phil Thompson. SSG McClean and SGT Jago of the "Cougars"
got to the scene very quickly. What they saw was traumatic. They
found the bodies of four soldiers—and the partial remains of a fifth.
The helicopter scattered along a straight pattern. The lighter the
pieces, the less they traveled.

The main body of the aircraft tumbled into a ball and burned profusely. 1LT Thompson and CPT Brad Boyd of Charlie Company,
who had heard the radios and arrived shortly thereafter, worked together to do what they could. SGM Cesar Castro had been with the
"Cobras" and followed them as well. The sandbar had bulrushes
about eight to ten feet high. About a quarter of the island was on fire.
The flames continued to spread.

I came out of the meeting at about 1000 hours. My driver and operations sergeant reported the news to me. We raced north to Cadaseeah.
When we arrived, the island was leaping in smoke and flames.

Our first task was to get the fire out. Any recovery of remains could
not be done without that. From what I could see, I could not imagine
any survivors. We drove down to the island. I called for city fire trucks.
My convoy and soldiers with FSG Michael Evans began to stamp out
the flames to try to clear the trail that ran down to the island. CPT Jason Deel and the Iraqi Civil Defense soldiers arrived. I employed them
on the north end of the island to look for wreckage or remains. Our
soldiers focused on the south end that had most of the wreckage.

We contained the flames. CPT Boyd, FSG Evans, SGM Castro,
MAJ Luke, and I set out to find any other soldiers. We had accounted
for five. We had reports of six. Soon, we discovered the sixth soldier
in the body of the aircraft. I will not describe to you what we saw. We
found the soldier's smoldering dog tags and got a name confirmation.
Then we began the grisly work of recovery.

As we worked, several leaders arrived from our unit and the other units involved. We told them we would secure the site, recover the remains and the wreckage. By nightfall, we had accomplished all of this. We took the wreckage to the same spot where we took the helicopter from October 25th's crash. It was an exhausting, tragic day. That night, COL Hickey and I determined to shake up the town. This would not stand. The insurgents had to understand that our Army was more than just humvees.

On the 8th of November, we planned to level several areas where the insurgents had found safe harbor. One was at the very site of the crash. A partially built house sat on the bluffs north of where the helicopter had been attacked. Locals reported that spotters had used a cell phone to signal the attackers from there.

At curfew, we rolled a tank platoon from "Cougars" to Cadaseeah. "Cobras" maneuvered Infantry and Bradleys to a building where we had taken fire from on occasion. The "Gators" deployed south of Owja toward the bunker where we had several fights before. Within an hour, tank rounds, TOW missiles, AT-4s, and machine guns leveled the buildings. U.S. Air Force jets screamed overhead. Bombs sailed across the river at targets designated by COL Hickey. Our mortars and artillery cracked in support.

When morning came, the locals were terrified. They told us they had not been this frightened since April. *Good,* I thought. Tell that to your Fedayeen-supporting, Saddam-loving neighbors. Don't they realize we have the might and resolve of the United States of America at our disposal? Don't they understand that burned in our memories is the investment broker making the best of two horrifying choices as he leaped from the World Trade Center Towers? More importantly, these terrorists were clearly evil. If we could remove them, the innocent Iraqis who had suffered for so long would be better off and could get on with their lives.

Capitalizing on the momentum, we rolled our vehicles into the city. We brought in tanks, Bradleys, and about three hundred Infantry. We did it at the height of the business day. In Cadaseeah, two individuals belonging to one of Saddam's controlling families had a plan of their own. They transported a powerful bomb in a small taxi, intent on some sinister plot. What they had not counted on was the bump in the road they hit on the way out that somehow (providentially, I believe) connected the electrical circuit to the blasting cap. The taxi immediately became a flaming convertible. Eventually the vehicle smoldered out, still occupied by two evil men frozen in their charred poses.

That night, we blasted at previous insurgent mortar locations with our own. One had a cache in it and we saw a secondary explosion when our rounds hit it. In the days that followed, the town became subdued and quiet. We resumed our patrols. Our informant network grew. People began to cooperate whereas before, they would not.

Whatever the correlation, one thing is for certain—we were making progress. We would not win the people of Tikrit over. They generally hate us. We are kind and compassionate to those who work with us, but many detest us here as a general rule. But they do respect power. Some have questioned our forcefulness but we will not win them over by handing out lollipops—not in Tikrit. Too many of my bloodied men bear witness to this. The die-hard Saddam loyalists are the "Beer Hall" crowd of Munich in 1945. They can't believe it is all gone.

Draining the Marshes

Reporters had asked me many times about the status of the hunt for Saddam. I told them he was still a priority but that we would accomplish our other missions whether we caught him or not. Frequently they would ask whether or not I thought he was in the area. I told them I believed he surely could be because his support base was clearly in Tikrit. But rarely would we get an Elvis sighting that was timely. Usually it would be third- or fifth-hand information and almost always, "He was here four days ago." Thanks buddy. That helps.

We were however starting to gather momentum. We knew the four controlling families that we believed surrounded Saddam. The problem was how to get them and once we got them, how to get the big guy. We had some incredible good fortune with a series of raids. The 720th Military Police under LTC Dave Poirier snagged a key member of a set of brothers we had been pursuing all summer. He was not the major player but we believed he would lead us to his other brothers who were major players. We were right.

In the early part of November, this brother began to sing. He gave us key information about his older brothers. One thing led to another. Soon, Special Operations Forces found the key brother we had been seeking since late June. No Iraqi knew it at the time. They found him in a sparse, mud-brick farm well west of Tikrit. When they got him, he dropped his head in resignation. His war was now over as well.

We were once again on the trail. We had been broadly around it in September and October but the increase of trigger-pulling activity among the enemy necessitated our division of labor between the thugs pulling triggers and the thug bosses. Now we had a clear blood trail on the inner circle and an excitement began to build. If we could break the inner circle, we felt it would come down fast. It did. On the 13th of November, we conducted raids with some other forces in Tikrit. Four more men were pulled from the swamp. While lesser players, they were related to some recent attacks and also had some key information.

The locals seemed to reach a peak in discontent—not that they ever loved us. We had oft been criticized in our efforts to win hearts and minds. But how can you win a black heart and a closed mind? The people we were dealing with could not be swayed. They understood power and respected that. Anything else would be a chance to strike back at us. November continued to have numerous roadside bomb attacks but providentially, we had been spared casualties.

Even so, we came back at them with a powerful display of our weaponry. On the 17th of November, our battalion rolled tanks, Bradleys, Infantry, scouts, and Civil Defense Iraqi soldiers into town. I wanted to remind them that our Army was more than just humvees. We had teeth and claws and would use them.

Our teeth and claws sunk into more dark hearts on the 19th with a very successful raid combined with other forces. They took two targets and we took two. The raid resulted in some key figures captured—some related to the attacks on our helicopters. The potential for more information would surely produce more raids. The swamp began to drain. An image of the alligator began to appear below the surface.

While developing more information, we continued an indirect war with the trigger-pulling thugs. Mortars impacted Owja, narrowly missing the A Company "Gators." An SS-30 rocket missed the "Cobras" as it fell short, making a bomb-sized crater in town and blowing gates off of walled compounds and destroying a car. The 10th Cavalry found the launch area on their side of the river and engaged several individuals, killing five. They were from Fallujah.

Indirect attacks were not the only threat. The roadside bombs continued to be the favorite. On the 24th of November, CPT Jon Cecalupo who commands our "Cougars" of C Company, 3-66 Armor was leaving the battalion command post when he made a right turn onto Highway 1. As he did, a powerful blast showered the convoy. But for some reason, the effects were small. The bomb, detonated by a wireless doorbell, had been placed in the opposite lanes. Consequently, the blast blew away from him instead of on him. We were thankful. We did not need another commander to face what CPT Curt Kuetemeyer faced in his command convoy.

A while later, I took my own convoy over to where the attack had occurred. What we found was the result of a clean-burning bomb, probably C-4 explosives. We talked to the local shop owner, who was well liquored. I could tell he was not involved because his own later model BMW was peppered with concrete shrapnel—making him innocent or completely stupid. Both seemed likely. But we were satisfied that they did not know who had executed the attack.

With our convoy that night were a couple of visiting reporters—one from the Pittsburg *Tribune* and the other from NBC News. We discussed the incident briefly and as we did, one of my soldiers, SPC Mike Bressette, said, "Sir, we are standing next to a bomb." I looked at my feet to discover a cinder block capped with cement on the holes.

Protruding from the holes were red, pig-tailed wires connecting the two halves for sympathetic detonation. A sense of mortality immediately washed over me as I said, walking backwards, "Yes we are!"

We backed off and set a cordon. SFC Gil Nail, my operations sergeant who travels in my convoy, set up at what we figured was a safe distance and shot one round of tracer into the device. Immediately it began to burn. Soon, a white-hot jet shot up from the block as if it were a magnesium flare. Suddenly, we heard a medium-sized *pop*— the blasting cap. Thinking it would continue to burn after the blasting cap failed, we continued to keep the area clear and waited while it burned. Suddenly, a violent explosion ripped the night air.

Laughter and banter ensued as a shower of shrapnel and sparks flew over us and provided a nice light show for the evening. "I think it's burned out now, Sir," our men asserted. The reporters watched us in amazement and Kevin Sites from NBC caught it all on film. We resumed our evening patrol.

Ramadan

As the Muslim holiday of Ramadan approached at the end of November, leaders throughout Iraq urged a lifting of curfews in the cities on the condition that no violence would occur or they would be reinstated. Our good will lasted about five minutes.

Shortly after what would have been curfew, automatic weapons fire erupted near the Division main gate. No one was hurt and we were never able to determine from the unit there what had happened. On the 25th, we found more roadside bombs. A big one had an 82mm mortar round with plastic explosives packed around it. They set it in the median of the main highway downtown. We found it and shot it to explosion without incident. Also that evening, some thugs fired an RPG that went skipping down the front road near one of our towers. It failed to explode and no one was harmed.

The next several days were calm. We used the lull to continue our swamp draining by refining some of our intelligence with observation and human sources. In the meantime, we also began to find evidence of weapons caches being brought in for future use. On the 28th we found another SA-7 anti-aircraft missile as well as thirty-five boxes of mortar fuses. We swept the same locations the next day and found over five hundred 120mm mortar rounds still in the boxes. All of these munitions were hidden in the city trash dump on the west side of Tikrit.

December arrived with rains that, no matter how hard it came down, failed to wash away the dust and filth of this land. The nastier weather also made for a reduction in attacks on our forces, but they did not cease. A roadside bomb on the main street in downtown Tikrit heralded the 1st of December. An alert but unarmed security guard watched as a man pulled up in a sedan and waddled to the median carrying a heavy five-liter vegetable oil tin. The car sped off and the man ran into a back alley. The guard called the police who, in turn, called our forces. They flagged down CPT Brad Boyd of C Company while out on patrol. His men shot up the bomb that exploded powerfully in the center of town. No one was harmed and no major damage was done except to the brickwork on the median.

By December 2nd, information continued to flow. A hot tip produced some HOT Missiles—missiles manufactured jointly by the French and Germans. They are wire guided and are similar to our TOW missiles. The cache contained twenty of these and was a relief. Then, the next night we conducted a joint raid in downtown Tikrit. The inner circle network of brothers protecting Saddam was further exposed. Our raid captured another of these brothers. Three more down. More information would follow. Scales, eyeballs, snout, and tail began to break the surface of the murky waters.

As the swamp continued to abate, there was no shortage of unusual happenings. CPT Mitch Carlisle, one of our battle captains in the command post, summed it best: "Every day in Iraq is the strangest day of my life."

The 4th of December was no different. We received a call that a soldier's mother was at the Division gate with an antiwar group and a number of reporters. The soldier was from one of the divisional support units. We were instructed to ignore it. As they were not demonstrating, we did. I began to visualize a weird and imagined exchange in my mind. "MOM! Could you please go home? You are embarrassing me in front of my friends!"

The next several days produced positive results all around. A couple of raids disrupted enemy activity in Owja, Tikrit, and Cadaseeah. We continued to find roadside bombs and disarm or detonate them. In the midst of this, we gave pause on the 6th of December to light a Christmas tree in our headquarters. We sang carols and generally had a good time. We ended by singing "Feliz Navidad," since nearly half of our battalion is Hispanic.

We had another breakthrough on the trigger pullers on the 8th of December. We raided four targets in Cadaseeah that netted eight thugs and explosive-making materials, including several radio-controlled cars. The next day we sucked more water from the swamp. An important tip netted a man long associated with Saddam as the "Gators" of A Company raided a remote Western Desert farmhouse. Simultaneously, Special Operations Forces pulled his brother out of a city to the south. These two men provided additional information to add to the steady stream already flowing from the swamp.

As their intelligence was analyzed, we did not sit idle. We found an important link to mid-level guys and ran it down very quickly. The evening of the 10th ended with two brethren and a variety of nasty weapons. At the time I described it as a "Fedayeen Candy Shop." Any type of attack could have been planned with the variety of weapons found buried in the front yard of a filthy house on the outskirts of Tikrit.

We captured roadside bombs, Pepsi can bombs, RPG launchers with rockets, two different and complete mortar systems (one in the outhouse!), small arms, ammunition, grenades, explosives, and radio-controlled devices for bombs. The upshot of it all was that the occupants denied all knowledge of the find. They said that the Army must have put it there. Oh, we did not think of that! Of course, our own Army issues the Mark 1 Pepsi Bomb. And I would never have seen the mortar system in my own outhouse. Their war is now over.

On December 11th the "Gators" raided a farm based on a tip from a Fedayeen meeting. They captured six men along with small arms, grenades, and ammunition. One case of submachine gun ammunition was actually under the bedding of a baby crib—complete with baby! They left the baby but took the ammunition and the nice PPSH-41 Russian submachine gun to which it belonged. It was dated 1943 and was in museum-quality condition. It now hangs on our wall with other nice finds.

The next day, our soldiers discovered another roadside bomb and blew it up with gunfire. Meanwhile, Special Operations Forces pulled the information of the last couple of weeks from our joint raids and got a jackpot—the inner circle brother we had been tracking all summer. Four down. We began to see the alligator. COL Hickey and others broke the good news to us that evening. The excitement continued to build. That evening, C Company's "Cobras" were on patrol in downtown Tikrit. Two thugs in a black late-model Toyota sedan with right-hand drive dashed down the street on which the men were patrolling. The passenger hung an AK-47 out the window on the left side of the car and fired a burst at the squad. SGT Trujillo brought his rifle into action almost immediately. He fired four rounds at the moving car. All four rounds hit the man with the AK-47 in the head.

The driver, seeing his cousin's head explode, decided to immediately stop and put up his hands. That the soldiers did not kill him before he raised his hands is a testament to the discipline of the men. They showed him quarter but the thug certainly had no doubt about who came out on top as he was shoved to the pavement and subdued. The men pulled the attacker from the vehicle. His bleeding body collapsed onto the street. The men checked him for wounds but all were in the head. There was nothing that could be done. His faint breathing quickly ceased. An idiot dies. His war—and that of his cousin—was now over.

Phone Calls
and
the Capture of Hussein

The morning of the 13th I received a phone call from my commander. I listened as COL Hickey explained the snowball of information now gathering. He told me to alert my soldiers for any contingency and to have a force ready at a moment's notice. He planned to use us and the brigade reconnaissance troop, which he would bring down from the Western Desert. We were going after the alligator.

We had been through the drill many times before. Des Bailey and I had worked together on many a raid in the farmlands east, across the Tigris. Each time, excitement builds because each time could be the catch. Not two days before I had told the press that there was an intensity and excitement about Saddam comparable to our operations in July and August during the well-publicized hunt for him. Sensing my honesty about the matter though no facts were conveyed, several decided to hang around Tikrit despite the urging of their editors. They were not sorry they did.

COL Hickey told me that we could expect something in west Tikrit—that's about what he knew as to the locale. As soon as he had better information, we would act swiftly. By late afternoon the information came. But the location had changed from west Tikrit to east Tikrit and across the Tigris River. We kept a ready force on our side and opposite ad Dawr. COL Hickey proceeded to assemble the forces on the east side for the operation. Special Operations Forces and brigade elements that included LTC Reggie Allen's 1-10 Cavalry, LTC Dom Pompelia's 4-42 Field Artillery with attached engineers (Dom was still on leave and so his exec, MAJ Steve Pitt, would command the artillery soldiers), and CPT Des Bailey's G Troop, 10th Cavalry readied for the operation commencing at 2000 hours.

Our brigade elements provided the cordon while the Special Operations folks hit two farmhouses. In the courtyard of one was the now famous hole from which a haggard Saddam Hussein was pulled. The special ops soldiers pulled him away and then whisked him off to safety. COL Hickey ordered the site to be secured for future exploitation. He called MG Ray Odierno and gave him the good news. While I suspected as much because of the orders we were receiving on the radio, it was not until about 2230 that COL Hickey phoned and broke the good news. "Sid Caesar!" he said. (In the summer time frame, the higher command published "what if" pictures of Saddam if he tried to change his appearance. COL Hickey often joked that one of them looked liked Sid Caesar.)

"Oh, my God!" I said, as I thanked God silently while the boss explained what happened.

"Not a word," he said. "The announcement must be official and it will take some time."

"Roger, Sir. I understand the importance of it."

Contained, self-composed, but about to bust at the seams as I hung up the phone, I kept silent to the men about the news that would change the world. I felt proud and thankful to have been a part of it from the beginning. I could not help but think back to an e-mail that I received from my wife in late October. She said that a man named Dick Dwinnell called her and encouraged her to send me a message. In it, he said that he knew I was a praying man and as a leader one of my missions was to find Hussein. He said that if my staff and I prayed for God to help us find Saddam, He would help us. That next Sunday we did just that. I asked the brigade chaplain, MAJ (CH) Oscar Arauco to lead us. For the next several weeks he continued to lead us until our battalion chaplain, CPT (CH) Tran, returned to us from an illness. And now here I was taking it all in on the evening of the 13th of December.

The next day, the world was abuzz. Rumors and rumblings finally gave way to confirmations. Then the electrifying announcement came from Baghdad. Now we could finally talk about it. That evening when we patrolled the town, it was quiet as a mosque mouse. The city appeared at 2130 the same as if it were 0300. In each flop house, apartment, and home you could see faces lit palely by the television. The regime's war was now over, too!

After the Event

We braced ourselves for the activity sure to follow—especially in Tikrit. We saw a spike in violence after Saddam's spawns were killed in Mosul in July. We didn't have to wait long. While activity was low on the 14th, we did have a couple thugs fire on a C Company patrol south of the "chevron" in town. None of our men were injured although the alleyways and distance prevented maintaining contact with the attackers.

A new type of resistance raised its head on the 15th of December—demonstrations. We had experienced a few attempts at them in late September and early October but broke them up as soon as they tried to assemble. This month was no different. I was meeting with the tribal council of sheiks at about 1000 hours and had gotten through the preliminaries when my operations sergeant came and interrupted our meeting. He whispered that there were several hundred students forming at the tip of the "chevron" and a separate group on the main street. I closed the meeting with apologies and we mounted up our humvees and sped in the direction of the demonstrations.

CPT Brad Boyd had already moved to the "chevron" to contain about five hundred male students. They were marching south along Highway 1 and appeared to be heading toward the second reported group on the main street. CPT Mark Stouffer heard the chatter on the net and readied some of A Company to support.

I took the command convoy and sped north along Highway 1 where it turns into the main street. In the distance we could see a group of about 250 people, mostly women. Brad reported that he had forces closing on the northern group. Looking ahead, I called on my guys to ready the bullhorn. I had learned in Kosovo the value of having a bullhorn that doubled as both siren and loudspeaker. We bounced up sidewalks to get nearer the crowd and then flipped on the blaring siren when we were near the back of the crowd.

The picture that followed reminded me of that *Blues Brothers* scene where they drive the big car into the demonstration on the bridge. Startled women and their flowing black robes scattered in all directions. Cowardly men once at the head of the group suddenly melted into the population at large. Our soldiers grabbed the various Saddam posters and shouted for all of them to clear out or be arrested. Gaining the element of surprise, we bought a bit of time. I called on CPT Stouffer to come to my location to take over traffic control and to keep the main highway open. He was already moving.

Meanwhile, CPT Boyd brought his soldiers around the group and through careful maneuver, herded the group into a dead end. Soon, the scratch of concertina wire could be heard surrounding the trapped troublemakers. His men had already gained moral dominance by heading straight for the angry-faced thug leading the group and then proceeded to subdue him—soundly. Once accomplished, the rest of the crowd scattered but really had no place to go.

After I handed over the downtown situation to Mark Stouffer, we headed up to the "Cobras." Brad had the situation well in hand and the police chief arrived. We were able to work out the situation and turned over the ringleaders to the police. The remainder were given a reprieve, searched, and sent on their way. The groups had one thing in common—certain educators in town organized them all. I intended to take this up with the governor the next day.

That evening we reviewed our procedures for handling crowds. Under Saddam, no demonstrations were allowed. Under the new government, they were not allowed. No matter. We would not allow them, period, and refused to have our supply routes cut off by demonstrators. When December 16th dawned, we anticipated more of the same.

At about 1000 we received reports of another demonstration forming north of town. CPT Boyd filled up his convoy, headed toward the reported location, and called forward one of his elements. Heading north along the "Birthday Palace" boulevard, he spotted a white

Mercedes near one of the drains along the side of the road. The Mercedes masked the drain and then pulled out at a high rate of speed. Sensing danger, CPT Boyd turned to his driver, SPC Miguel Romero, and yelled instructions that were never followed.

A deafening roar combined with concrete, smoke, shards, and concussive blast. FSG Mike Evans, in the second of three vehicles, saw a billowing cloud of smoke engulf the view to his company commander's humvee. The smoke expanded until it reached the other side of the four-lane road. The sound of small arms cracked in the midst.

Hoping that the lead vehicle had passed before the bomb detonated, FSG soon discovered that was not the case. SPC Romero heard his company commander firing at the car. FSG Evans's humvee pulled up to his commander's vehicle. SSG Patrick McDermott was already at his commander's side checking him. He then told SPC Romero to pull the vehicle out of the area across to the other lanes, which he did.

FSG Evans and the other soldiers laid out a base of fire in support of their commander in the direction of the vehicle, but it soon faded into the built-up part of the city. The first sergeant then focused his attention on the soldiers in the lead vehicle. CPT Boyd was OK—a little bloody but OK. He had wounds on his face, arm, and legs.

The doctor sitting behind him was pulled out of the truck and assessed as the worst of the three. He had a nasty face wound as well as arm and leg wounds. The gunner on the .50 cal machine gun took some light shrapnel to the hands, arms, and legs. They immediately pulled out the stretchers and called to alert our aid station. The company Quick Reaction Force arrived in five minutes, pulled security, and recovered the humvee.

SPC Brian Serba along with SPC Broz had already stuck IVs, applied bandages, and administered 5mg of morphine to CPT Boyd and the doc. FSG Evans brought the casualties and convoy to the battalion. I received the news from my XO, MAJ Mike Rauhut. I put on my gear and prayed that they would be OK. I asked God to spare them. We had gone seven weeks without a single casualty and now we had three. After getting my gear together, I ran to the aid station as they arrived.

The scene was familiar. We have been through it many times. The soldiers came into the converted kitchen as field medics held IVs steady. The surgeon and physician assistants went on autopilot, making one hundred quick assessments and giving as many orders on what was needed. The medical platoon soldiers seemed to find everything that was asked for and hand it to them.

I walked up to C Company's wounded doc and comforted him in his pain. He lay on the table knowing what to do, but now he was the patient. I spoke to him to let them take over . . . to take a deep breath . . . that he would be fine. I caressed his head as I spoke to him, not being able to do anything except comfort him and pray. He was in good hands. As I pulled my hand from his head, I could feel his blood on it. I had been through it before. But it is never easy. I feel responsible for them.

CPT Boyd was just as tough on the stretcher as on the street. My challenge with him was to order him to relax. He was cold. But they had to dress his wounds. I told him that the doctors were in charge and to listen to them. We found moments of humor together there . . . in an awkward way . . . the way that only soldiers can understand. It was hard to hold back my emotion but I did. I could tell by their wounds that they were going to be fine. They would be out of the net a bit though.

The docs continued to work them over. As they did another doc entered the aid station. He was a Special Forces medic from the guys on our compound. He said nothing. He simply walked in, snapped on some gloves, and quietly began to work. I don't think that any of us even knew his name but he was one of us—a soldier.

The first sergeant brought his commander out with the others and they placed them on the ambulance. I ordered Brad to put his head down because he kept trying to raise it and the tight fit and his head didn't go well together as they slid him into the slots on the ambulance. The vehicle sped away to the hospital. Media were nearby the whole time. They were not the enemy. They had been on patrols with us and knew the men on the stretchers. But they did the only thing they knew to do. They began to record it. They did it in a dignified way so as not to show the faces of the men on the stretchers. We did not really notice them at the time.

I called the first sergeant and told him to assemble the soldiers from the convoy. I explained to them to channel their emotion. I cautioned them to use it to take it to the enemy, but not to see all people as the enemy. We still had a lot of work to do and these men would return. I did not want to lose more. The men seemed fine. They had already accounted for their equipment and readied for the rest of the day. It was not even noon. I readied my command group as well. I had planned to see the governor. We were going to get at the educators behind the senseless demonstrations. As we readied, a report of a gathering demonstration in downtown crackled over the net. We sped to the location.

As we arrived, we noticed that two of "Cobras'" Bradleys had just pulled up in a herringbone on the northbound lanes in town. The men started spilling out the back and several sergeants began to point to a side street east. Suddenly, a rifle cracked off just as I got out of my vehicle. Then another. On its heels was a good burst from an M240B machine gun. I ran up to the squad and asked what they were shooting at. They said someone in the crowd threw what appeared to be a pipe-like object. Believing it to be a bomb, they fired a burst above the crowd. I told SSG John Minzer to take control of his men. The crowd had already scattered in all directions. Joe Filmore, our translator from San Diego, questioned several of the students nearby. We told them to scatter immediately or be arrested. They wasted no time getting out of there.

We remounted and headed toward the government building. As we passed the shops on the streets, the looks were like daggers. Men spat and narrowed their eyes in sideward glances. Uppity. They were getting Uppity. Fine. I would solve this right now! I already had three casualties this day. I did not want any more.

I put out a net call on the battalion for the commanders to assemble at the "Birthday Palace." I told them to bring everything that could roll and all the Infantry they could spare. Then I called Reg Allen over at 1-10 Cavalry and asked for some attack aviation support for

1400 hours. I told him I was going to do a heavy-handed patrol of the city and clear the streets. I had known Reg since he was a first lieutenant. We had gone to the Armored Officers Advanced Course together. He said I could have anything I needed. He is a good man.

We assembled at the "Birthday Palace" with a large force. I opened an imagery map on the hood of the humvee, and pulled the lead tanks and plastic soldiers from my butt pack on my gear. We talked through a quick concept and then executed it about twenty minutes later. CPT Jon Cecalupo brought the "Cougars'" tanks down the main street. The "Cobras" followed behind and did a herringbone with about eight Bradleys downtown. The ramps fell and our Infantry ran at the sidewalks, immediately clearing the crowds. Reg's aviators swooped overhead at intimidating heights. CPT Mark Stouffer followed with A Company's "Gator" Infantry and Bradleys as well and then CPT Darryl Carter brought up the Iraqi Civil Defense troops. The town immediately became calm. We patrolled in this way for the next several hours, looking for trouble. But no one would give it.

As the soldiers swarmed the city, I called for the PSYOPS truck. We went to the governor and he drafted a tough message to tell his own people. Then he asked if he could go with us to play it around town. I thought it a great idea so he hopped in my humvee and off we went. He sat behind me with a loaded pistol (my kind of governor!) while we drove at idle speed around the city. His bodyguard flanked him and our soldiers watched the shock on the faces as their own governor was telling them to knock it off or his forces would use lethal force and demonstrators would be imprisoned. The wind was out of the sails. We've not had a demonstration attempt in the last week and a half.

That evening I went to the field hospital to see the guys. Brad's gunner was already released back to his unit. He would need some time to recover but could do it from his unit. C Company's doc was moved to Baghdad. He needed some additional care.

I found Brad lying on a hospital bed in the inflated tent hospital. He looked pretty good and seemed to be in good spirits. I told him that I was sending CPT Mitch Carlisle to fill in for him until he could be healed. He told me he did not want to be evacuated further. I told him I would do what I could. While we were talking, a chaplain came in and asked in a low tone if I was the commander of 1-22 Infantry. I told him yes. He said we had another casualty.

The patrol from elements of our B Company cross-attached to the armor battalion in Bayji moved along a route looking for roadside bombs. The lead vehicle faced its turret forward and the trail vehicle faced the turret to the rear. An RPG swooshed on an arc that connected to the turret of the platoon leader's vehicle. The gunner had been leaning up and was looking for bombs when it hit. The rocket hit near the TOW launcher and then the gunner took nearly all of the blast. Only God and his body armor saved him. The platoon leader was also wounded but not critically.

When they brought him into the hospital, all I could do was pray. I begged God to spare his life. The chaplain and I prayed over him. I knew he would have a very long haul. I stayed with him until they took him into surgery. Mike Rauhut and I stood there and reflected on a very tough day. We traveled back to the command post and I knew the day was not over yet. I had to make the phone calls. When I arrived, CSM Martinez had the phone ready . . . but was I. I called the wives of our wounded and answered their questions as best I could.

I felt it would be best to tell them everything about their loved one's condition. While tough for them to hear, I knew they wanted to know. I knew my wife would. So I tried to be honest with them. I would rather have attacked into the Fedayeen than have had to make those calls. At least, this time, I was not calling to explain how their loved one died. You never really know what to say.

I slept soundly that night. By dawn, we patrolled a mostly passive city. The people smiled and some even waved. It was just as if nothing happened. A sense of disgust returned. That day I went to Auja and met with Sheik Mahmood.

We had a good discussion about Auja, the future of the Tikriti people, and the larger issue of how the Sunnis would fit into a new Iraq.

After this visit we continued our patrols and then went back to the palace. I gave CPT Chris Morris, our scout platoon leader, a concept for getting the bomber on the "chevron." I told him I wanted him to plan an operation that would set a trap with observation posts and snipers to last about four days.

The night of the 17th only had one roadside bomb—another cinder block bomb. Hand-drawn on the cement caps was the phrase "Allah Akhbar" ("Allah is powerful," or "God is great"). Anyone wondering about whether or not they hate us should come and fight these thugs. There is no doubt in my mind that they would kill us in our own cities. Instead, we will kill them here.

The next day was calm. The town was actually civil. Chris Morris inserted his scouts for the ambush along the "chevron." The rain fell. The temperature dropped. The enemy stayed inside. I guess the man dresses get a little drafty this time of year. We patrolled our area and checked on the guys out in the rain. Their morale remained good. The week before, I had talked to several of the units. I got all the enlisted together by company and then the sergeants. It was good to hear what was on their minds. We looked forward to Christmas, and I urged the soldiers to stay focused on the mission. Home would be when we set foot there. Not before.

The "Cougars" patrolled on the 19th in Cadaseeah. They saw a Saddam poster on a shop. The men dismounted their tanks and checked it out. A cursory search of the vegetable shop revealed grenades and plastic explosives mixed with the cucumbers and tomatoes. They might as well have hung a sign that said "Idiot Lives Here."

The men searched all the shops in the complex and found another with a garden variety of explosives. As it developed, we sent some Infantry support to them from 1LT Mike Isbell's platoon of "Cobras" and then we ended up arresting two men. We left an observation post on the houses of the shop owners and pulled in two more men over the next two nights. One turned out to be one of the guys who bombed Brad's convoy.

Tidings in Tikrit

A chill is in the air now—mixed with the pall of wood smoke hanging over the city. We were once bathed from head to toe with sweat, but now cover ourselves with items to keep warm and dry. The temperatures here have cooled, but the situation seems to change as often as the weather. The environment in Tikrit at this writing is simmering—not a boil, but simmering.

The last few days have been fairly calm. The roadside bombs have ceased for several days now, since the arrest of the individual in Cadaseeah. We've had sporadic events but nothing out of hand.

The morning of December 23rd, the Fourth Infantry Division had a prayer breakfast. MG Ray Odierno reminded us all that we should be thankful to celebrate it and to remember those who will not be with us this year. Last night we had a wonderful candlelight service at the battalion. LTC (CH) Gil Richardson, the division chaplain, gave the message to our soldiers and we sang Christmas carols.

Today we spent Christmas in Iraq. While away from family we have their love and prayers. While away from our nation we have their gratitude. While away from home we have the bonds of friendship with fellow soldiers. I am thankful to be an American fighting man.

The Ace in the Hole

Homeward Bound: An Author's Note

Russell Cummings and I didn't have any arranged transport to the airport on the day we left Iraq in mid-November. In the early hours of the morning, we took a cab from the hotel with a driver well versed in negotiating an "ambush alley." He was quite good and got us all there in one piece and ready for the next step: a charter flight from Baghdad to Amman, Jordan.

The Air Service Charter was late. It was mid-afternoon when we finally took off from Baghdad in the eighteen-seat Beech Twin. We went up the same way we had come down, in dizzying circles. We followed a "spiral staircase" that rose up from where we lifted off the airfield, and tried to crunch down in our seats as we ascended rapidly from the runway aiming for twenty thousand feet. I did not see any reason why we had to "wind our way up the cone" in this manner, as no shooting was actually going on. Nor had I personally seen any such shooting while in Iraq, although I had witnessed mortar attacks by pro-Saddam insurgents on FOB Ironhorse in Tikrit, and in other locales.

I approached the copilot with the idea of going straight out over the desert. He just laughed. "We wouldn't get a hundred yards out without picking up a couple of these things," he said as he showed me a couple of little brass fragments that I knew to be pieces of flak.

"Where did they come from?" I asked.

The copilot laughed. "The front of the airplane last week," he replied. "We were lucky it didn't cause any serious damage."

So I sweated out the fifteen thousand feet—*only another five thousand feet to go,* I thought.

The air was so thin it almost made me believe there was none there at all. I breathed deeply, but took very little nourishment into my lungs. The combination of thin air and the difficulty I had absorbing enough oxygen made me feel as though I myself was flying without a seatbelt within the interior of the plane. My seventy-eight-year-old parkinsonian body rebelled at the weakness in my legs and arms as we straightened out and headed toward Amman. I wished I were wearing an oxygen mask.

A soldier walking down the aisle pointed directly ahead as the plane changed course heading out over the desert. You could see nothing on the ground—just sand and rock. We knew there were terrorists down there ready to shoot at us, and I rather expected to see flak bursts appearing outside the windows. It reminded me of a similar time, fifty-eight years ago, when I peered down from the front seat in the nose cone of a B-17 bomber, with two .50 caliber machine guns below my feet and nothing to aim at as we evaded the flak from the German gunners below.

As we flew I tried to study the desert below, all the time wondering if terrorists were trying to shoot at us. Our plane was full of civilian Americans, Germans, and Brits who had been in Baghdad for a month helping the Iraqis with their many problems. I daresay we all wondered the same thing as we looked at the landscape below.

I breathed a sigh as we straightened out and gradually descended toward Amman. An air of relief permeated the cabin. The other passengers were now laughing and reaching for their cakes from the food cartons given to us when we boarded the plane.

Russell and I parted company early the following morning—he went on to the United States and I to England for a short break before

heading back to the States. I returned home to Concord, Massachusetts, a few weeks later, and started work on the next portion of this
book.

At that time, I was fairly convinced that Saddam had been killed in
that first raid on Baghdad. "Smokin' Joe" Anderson back in Mosul
had a completely different view—his unit, after all, had killed the two
sons, Uday and Qusay, and he firmly believed their father was still
alive. Anderson certainly wasn't alone in this belief. Many soldiers
and intelligence officers were operating on the same premise. This
was also the opinion of LTC Steve Russell of Task Force 1-22 INF in
Tikrit. They all were working ever harder to close the net. So, of
course, I also considered the possibility that Saddam was still alive,
and that led to the question: *would Saddam be found before or after
my book was complete?*

The Ace in the Hole

"They say you can't do it, but sometimes
it doesn't always work."
—Casey Stengel

It had been two hundred and fifty-four days since Saddam Hussein
was last seen. At times he seemed more a ghost, or a desert mirage,
than a man.

From March 20 on, when the United States initiated the war with a
strike by cruise missiles and bombs on Iraqi "leadership targets," including Saddam, his sons, and key leaders, Saddam was a shadowy
figure. His whereabouts and even whether he was still alive were constantly in question.

Saddam Hussein surfaced briefly on April 4th during an Iraqi television broadcast of two videotapes. Where and when they were made
sparked great debate. Three days after they aired, United States forces
bombed a building in the Mansour district of Baghdad, where sources
had told them Saddam was gathered with his leadership. Saddam sur-

vived again and the Coalition's inability to kill or capture him hampered progress toward a new nation and government. Saddam's loyal Ba'athists continued to intimidate the population, claiming that Saddam was alive and warning he and the Ba'athists would return to power and punish all who cooperated with the new government or with the Coalition.

By the time President George W. Bush formally declared an end to the major military campaign in Iraq on May 1, Saddam and his associates were clearly on the run. Yet the United States seemed no closer to catching this man who was proving to be as elusive and difficult to find as Iraq's alleged weapons of mass destruction. The month of May also brought Paul Bremer to Iraq as the U.S. civil administrator, followed by the twenty-five-member U.S.-backed Iraqi Governing Council's inaugural meeting in July, and the Interim Governing Council appointment of twenty-five ministers in September. But still no Saddam.

Saddam Hussein and the remnants of all he stood for hung like a pall over Iraq. Regardless of the brilliance of the military operations that had ousted him, the speed and precision of Iraq's liberation, and no matter how much President Bush and his allies denied it, success in Iraq was measured by whether or not they got Saddam. The insurgency increased, and U.S. post-conflict casualties mounted, eventually eclipsing the number of lives lost during the declared conflict. Saddam seemed to remain just out of reach, yet close enough to broadcast audio messages to rally his loyalists, while taunting those who cooperated with the American-led occupation. He labeled anyone disloyal to his ousted regime a traitor, and incited Iraqis to murder foreign soldiers and government officials.

It began to appear that Saddam would be another Osama Bin Laden, remaining just out of grasp, the attacks on him always near misses from which he would always, almost miraculously, escape. The United States tried and failed to kill him with laser-guided two-thousand-pound bombs at the war's start. Despite the unprecedented speed with which U.S. forces swept through the country and into Baghdad, he managed to slip away and vanish. A $25 million reward produced nothing. The entire lineup of secret, twenty-first-century, state-of-the-art technology the United States boasted was failing to find him. But survival was nothing new for Saddam. The man who had become known as the Enemy of the Western World had beaten the odds before, and was betting that he could do it again.

Elvis Has Left the Building

The intelligence section for the 1st Brigade Combat Team had received reports about Saddam's whereabouts from the earliest days, after their arrival in Tikrit in mid-April 2003.

While many believed Saddam was constantly on the move between about twenty "spider holes" throughout Iraq, MAJ John S. "Stan" Murphy (1st Brigade, 4th Infantry Division Intelligence Officer [S-2]) and his team didn't completely accept that conclusion. There was little doubt Saddam moved often, but Murphy's team felt strongly that Saddam would remain in the relative safety and protection of the Tikrit area. In addition to Saddam's age, family connections no doubt were playing a significant role in his concealment. His family, tribe, and most of his trusted aides were from the Tikrit region. Perhaps Saddam would move from one location to another in the area, but Murphy believed he would not travel far beyond that. Tikrit had protected him as a young man so it made sense to Murphy that Saddam would do the same at this point in his life.

That didn't alter the fact that there had been a plethora of "Saddam sightings" throughout Iraq between April and December. At the 4th Infantry Division, based north of Baghdad, Saddam became known as "Elvis" because of the number of reported sightings. It got worse after the United States posted a $25 million reward. Reports flooded the Division, some as bizarre as those often published in supermarket tabloids about the King of Rock and Roll. One former general in the Republican Guard, who asked not to be identified, said a friend spotted Saddam praying at his father's grave. Another Iraqi Army officer who had joined the newly reconstituted police force claimed Saddam passed through his checkpoint in Tikrit, giving him three hundred dollars.

Saddam was reported posing as a cab driver, a janitor, and in countless other disguises, frequently said to include a beard and dark glasses. Saddam was also rumored to have a number of body doubles, and to have undergone plastic surgery. None of the reports panned out, but they all consumed vital time and resources nonetheless.

Raiders, Special Operators, and a Man with a Jeep

The task force that had originally set out to find Saddam was replaced by a faster, harder-hitting one with tighter OPSEC (Operational Security): Task Force 121, a joint force of the most elite of each service's Special Operations Forces working in close partnership with Task Force RAIDER, the 4th Infantry Division's Brigade combat team. Task Force RAIDER's commander, COL James Hickey, was the perfect man for the job of hunting down Saddam.

A 1982 graduate of the Virginia Military Institute (VMI), COL Jim Hickey commanded the 4th Infantry Division's 1st Brigade. The Raider Brigade, as it is called, based in Saddam's hometown area of Tikrit, took over the mission to find and capture or kill the deposed dictator. Hickey is all Army, so much so that the Hickey family car is a World War II–era jeep. The Chicago native, one of six children of an Irish-born plumber, wanted all through his youth to attend VMI, admiring its rich military heritage and deep traditions. Since 1839, VMI has produced nine Rhodes Scholars, thirty-eight college and university presidents, a National Football League head coach, three United States senators, numerous U.S. representatives, chief executive officers, explorers, authors, military leaders, actors, an Academy Award-winning producer, civil rights advocates, six Congressional Medal of Honor winners, and the only soldier in history to win the Nobel Peace Prize—General George C. Marshall. The tenacity of VMI's military leaders, such as "Stonewall" Jackson, is legendary. It was the perfect environment for Hickey, who flourished in VMI's military-style education. Hickey was welcomed into the close brotherhood of the military education environment.

Following graduation, Hickey excelled in the Army. He commanded the 2nd Squadron, 3rd Armored Cavalry Regiment at Fort Carson, Colorado, a unit whose history dates back to such engagements as the Battle of Milk Creek in 1879, for which eleven Congressional Medals of Honor were awarded.

In keeping with his alma mater's tradition of the fully rounded citizen-soldier, Hickey engaged in scholarly pursuits, attending Georgetown University as an Army Senior Service College Fellow just before his assignment to Iraq, where he took command of the 1st Brigade on June 13, and was promoted to colonel in one of Saddam's former palaces.

Hickey's top soldier was CSM Lawrence K. Wilson. CSM Wilson entered the Army at Aberdeen, North Carolina, in February 1977. Although he left at the end of his enlistment, the Army remained in his blood, and he reentered in June 1981. Wilson is a soldier's soldier, one who has worked his way through the ranks by taking the hard jobs and serving on the line with his fellow soldiers. Others sought out desks and staff duties, but Wilson worked his way through positions as team leader, squad leader, platoon sergeant, and operations sergeant. He had four assignments as a first sergeant (the top noncommissioned officer in a company) and Engineer Battalion command sergeant major (the top soldier slot in a battalion).

Wilson's quiet professionalism and high standards were an ideal match for Hickey's focused drive and leadership. CSM Wilson turned his soldiers into highly trained professionals while Hickey motivated and led them. Together the two men created and maintained an environment that empowered subordinates. In part it was their innovative approach that eventually led to Saddam's luck running out.

COL Hickey's PSG (Personal Security Guard) was SPC "Joe" (his name is confidential). As one might guess from the need for his pseudonym, "Joe" was many other things, including COL Hickey's Arabic interpreter and aide. This daunting combination of aide, interpreter, and bodyguard to the brigade commander required a true professional. His multilevel skills and abilities were in line with the high standards and innovative, "outside the box" approach adopted by Hickey's group, and which ultimately led them to success.

According to "Joe," his original MOS (Military Occupational Specialty) was 19K (military jargon for a main battle tank crewman). Given his drive and dedication to quiet professionalism, he will be reenlisting for Special Forces training following his deployment with TF RAIDER, after serving under COL Hickey. Joe says that he joined the Army "to be a soldier, nothing more, nothing less." Joe would be there at Hickey's side for everything to follow, and privy to much more than the average E-4 enlisted man.

"Outside the Box"

Task Force RAIDER, together with its Special Operations and interagency partners, shared the same frustrations as their predecessors in tracking down Saddam.

Catching a prey as crafty as Saddam, in his own environment, could not be done by the traditional ways of doing business. Compiling mountains of information, methodically sorting through it all, building the picture piece by piece until it all became clear was not an option. The cultural landscape in Iraq, with its labyrinth of customs, centuries of cultural norms, and family alliances would make such an approach virtually impossible.

Nor would a linear approach be responsive enough to support quick action against Saddam and his supporters as they moved rapidly in the shadows from place to place, narrowly avoiding death or capture. A truly innovative approach was needed, one based on doctrine and experience, but not shackled by it. It needed people who colored outside the lines drawn by the traditionally rigid analysis processes. It needed what many in the military and private sector called "thinking outside the box." It's exactly the kind of thing Donald Rumsfeld wanted from his Department of Defense Transformation Initiative.

That approach is precisely what Rumsfeld and the United States got with Hickey and his Special Operations, conventional force, and interagency team. It was particularly manifest in the unique and eclectic group that were Hickey's S-2 (intelligence) shop under supervision of MAJ "Stan" Murphy.

The Right Team at the Right Time

MAJ Stan Murphy was the son of a fighter pilot who was shot down twice during two tours in Vietnam, ultimately serving a year there as a POW after his second bailout. From childhood, Stan knew he would serve in the military. But he repeatedly put it off, first graduating college and then kicking around in several jobs before enlisting in the Army at the age of twenty-eight. He graduated from OCS (Officer Candidate School) in 1991. An Infantry officer from the get-go, he switched MOS to MI (Military Intelligence) after his promotion to captain. He had attended many of the schools the new job slot had to offer, and knew the schoolbook version of MI front-to-back. However, Murphy had never applied this knowledge to any real-world situations.

Murphy was chosen as the 1st Brigade S-2 on July 1, 2003. He admits feeling in over his head when he started looking at all the information he had to know as well as he knew himself. More than once, he wondered if he could perform his job. The pressure was real and the quarry was elusive. This was light-years more intimidating than a field exercise, and galaxies away from Command and General Staff College (CGSC), from which he had graduated only three weeks before deployment to Iraq.

1LT Angela Ann Santana was attached to MAJ Murphy's S-2 shop from the 4th Infantry Division's 104th Military Intelligence Battalion. She worked the night shift in the Task Force RAIDER Tactical Operations Center as special projects officer and analysis control team leader. In addition to being a proficient officer and skilled analyst, Santana had unique scholarly credentials for a young Army officer. She held both a bachelor of science degree in psychology from Campbell University in North Carolina and a master's degree in counseling from Webster University, in Saint Louis, Missouri.

Like many on Murphy's team, Santana's path to the Army and to the hunt for Saddam took a skewed route. She joined the military in October 1989 as a reservist using the delayed-entrance program. Two days after graduating high school in May 1990, Santana reported to basic training, then completed Advanced Individual Training (AIT)— not as an intelligence analyst, but as a medic, complete with the Army's 91A skill identifier. She then returned to home, school, and occasional reserve training until Saddam Hussein invaded Kuwait later that year.

As was the case with many reserve units, Santana's unit was activated in December 1990 for Operations DESERT SHIELD/DESERT STORM and deployed to Saudi Arabia. There, close to Hafr al-Batin, Santana got her first taste of war and her first experience with the effects of Saddam Hussein's tyranny. She was the youngest soldier in the camp.

As a combat medic during the first Gulf War, Santana administered not only to U.S. soldiers, but to many of the Iraqis who surrendered or were captured. The amiable young soldier spoke often and at length with many of her charges. What she learned appalled her.

The Regular Army Iraqi soldiers treated by Santana lacked basic food, water, or sometimes even shoes. They were trapped as unwilling martyrs to Saddam's dreams of conquest. As Santana saw it, Saddam gave them choices that ended in only death. They could either die fighting the Americans or be killed by Saddam's elite forces for refusing to participate, or for not performing well enough to suit the elite forces.

One defeated and tearful Iraqi soldier told of losing his wife and five children at the hands of Saddam's regime. They were killed for his "crime" of not wanting to join Saddam's Army, of wanting only

OPERATION RED DAWN—THE CAPTURE OF SADDAM HUSSEIN

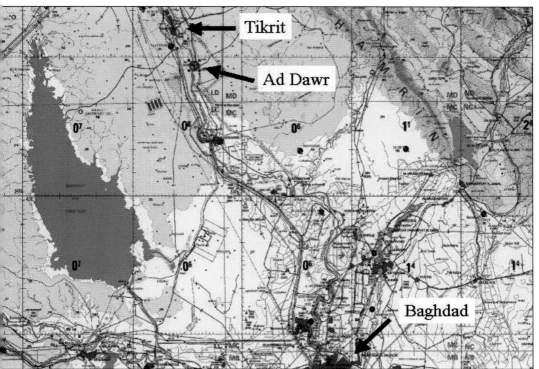

(courtesy of U.S. Army)

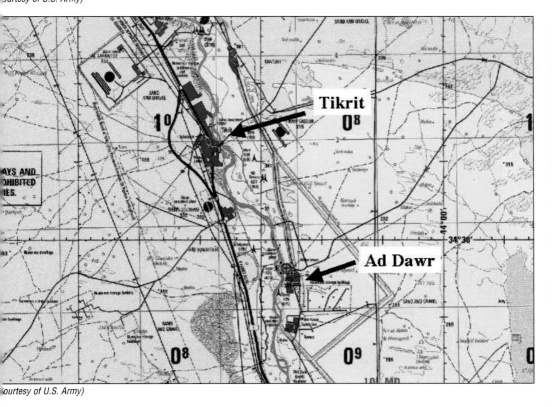

(courtesy of U.S. Army)

THE COMPLEX

Buildings and layout of the farm complex where Saddam had his hideout

Farm House 1

Hut where Saddam was hiding in ground

Tigris River

N

Farm House 2

Hut where Saddam was Found

SADDAM'S HIDEOUT GROUNDS

Army soldiers comb the grounds of Saddam's hideout.

Entrance into Saddam Hiding Place

INSIDE SADDAM'S HIDEOUT (THE ORANGE-PICKER'S BUNKHOUSE)

Saddam was living in a hovel—a bedroom and outdoor kitchen.
This is a far cry from the gilt and luxury of his many palaces.

Kitchen in Hut Where Saddam was Staying

(Courtesy of U.S. Army)

(Courtesy of U.S. Army)

SADDAM'S HIDING PLACE

Soldiers search Saddam's yard where the rug-covered spider hole was located.
Along with weapons, soldiers confiscated $750,000 in U.S. bills.

Saddam's Hiding Place

Hole that Saddam was Found hiding in

(Courtesy of U.S. Army)

(Courtesy of U.S. Army)

Money Found during Saddam's Capture

UNDER THE RUG: THE SPIDER HOLE

Soldiers discover the hole in which Saddam was hiding.

(Courtesy of U.S. Army)

(Courtesy of U.S. Arm

CAUGHT!

Operation RED DAWN is a success.

Saddam is pulled out of the hole by Task Force 121. *(Courtesy of U.S. Army)*

WE GOT HIM!

(Courtesy of U.S. Army)

(Courtesy of U.S. Army)

(Courtesy of U.S. Arm

to care for them and live in peace. The solution to Saddam's recruiters was simple. As the man stood in terror, they executed his wife and children in front of him, then coldly informed him that he no longer had a reason not to give service in Saddam's Army.

When Santana left Iraq after the Gulf War, she was convinced that the best course was to free the Iraqi people and the world from this sadistic and oppressive dictator. She left bereft that he remained in power, never imagining that the course of fate would return her again to finally hunt him.

Like many others, Santana's DESERT STORM experience convinced her that the military was her calling. She returned to the United States to join active duty in October 1993. Only this time, the Army system cast her as an administrative specialist, sent her to executive secretary school, and placed her as an executive secretary for general officers. Santana was back in the military she'd come to love, but she wanted her contribution to be more.

After receiving her master's degree in 2001, Santana was accepted into Officer Candidate School. Santana finally felt she was on a path to give back to the military the knowledge and experience she'd received. Ironically, one of her class exercises in the Military Intelligence Officer Basic Course involved a scenario where Southwest Asia considered courses of action should Saddam be overthrown. As she later stood watch in the Raider Tactical Operations Center and worked feverishly with her fellow soldiers to locate Saddam Hussein, Santana could remember briefing her classmates on the possible reactions of Iraq's neighboring countries if Saddam were ousted, and how the United States would need to intervene to keep them from invading Iraq.

Along the way Angela met and married Special Forces SFC Jose Santana. They were a happy blend of Special Operations and conventional forces, and both dedicated to their choice. The only thing they wanted were the children they'd tried unsuccessfully for more than five years to conceive. The Santanas' assignment to Fort Hood, Texas, offered the opportunity for SFC Santana to take a well-deserved break from the pace of being a Special Operator. They both looked forward to their new locale. Angela Santana arrived at Fort Hood in August 2003, and was assigned to 1-44 ADA BN (Air Defense Artillery Battalion) as their intelligence officer (S-2). Jose Santana arrived in December 2003 and took a position recruiting Special Operations soldiers. The pace of life was just right for starting a family, and as 1LT Santana worked with Division planners on how they would fight a war in Iraq, there was no indication she would be there four months later.

1LT Santana took the opportunity to request her medical records from Fort Bragg and began transitioning from the final stages of fertility testing to fertility treatment. After five years of trying, and in the midst of preparing the 4th Infantry Division for war in Iraq, Angela Santana learned she was pregnant. What should have been the happiest time of her life rapidly became a nightmare. Although her chain of command supported her decision, Santana's transition to the Rear Detachment element (who would remain behind) brought her increasing concern that her fellow soldiers would somehow feel she'd shirked her responsibilities and became pregnant to avoid the war. The stress eventually took its toll and she suffered a miscarriage. Angela Santana deployed less than a month later to join MAJ Murphy's eclectic team in the hunt for Saddam.

Every team needed a consummate technician, and MAJ Murphy's "all-source intelligence technician"—his chief analyst—was CW2 (Chief Warrant Officer 2) Bryan G. Gray. Born and raised in Amarillo, Texas, Gray joined the U.S. Army on January 4, 1989. Like COL Hickey, CSM Wilson, and many of his fellow soldiers, CW2 Gray saw the military as his calling. As long as the recruiter provided him a job that would involve what some might view as the diametrically opposed areas of intelligence and jumping out of perfectly good airplanes, he was satisfied. Gray served his initial enlisted time as an intelligence analyst until being selected for the Army's Warrant Officer program in 1998. He's been an all-source intelligence technician ever since.

Like Task Force RAIDER's top sergeant, CW2 Gray resisted anything that kept him away from soldiers and "the point of the bayonet." While many of his fellow analysts took jobs with comfortable desks, a supply of donuts, air-conditioning, and other amenities, Gray kept himself in the thick of it. He was involved in myriad conventional and Special Operations assignments, including the 6th PSYOPS (Psychological Operations) Battalion of the 4th Psychological Operations Group (Airborne) and the 82nd Airborne Division's 3-73 Armored Battalion, 504th Parachute Infantry Regiment (the Red Devils of World War II fame), all at Fort Bragg, North Carolina. He served with the Army's 2nd Infantry Division Camp Red Cloud Korea and the 10th Mountain Division's 110th Military Intelligence Battalion in Fort Drum, New York, before landing on Saddam's doorstep with Hickey and the rest of the Task Force RAIDER team.

Gray's many assignments had kept him in the thick of America's fight to defend democracy and battle terrorism. He'd matched wits with Saddam and his intelligence forces before in Operations DESERT SHIELD/DESERT STORM, serving in Saudi Arabia, Kuwait, and Iraq. He helped put down and bring to justice men just like Saddam Hussein during Operation UPHOLD DEMOCRACY in Haiti, Operation JOINT ENDEAVOR in Bosnia, and Operation JOINT FORGE in Kosovo. Now Gray was back to further the job he and his fellow soldiers started under President Bush's father—getting Saddam.

One of Murphy's workhorses in the analysis section was Corporal Hal Engstrom. CPL Engstrom was about as far from the "typical soldier" as one can get. From his age at enlistment, to the path that brought him to Task Force RAIDER, just about everything in Engstrom's brief military career to that point was unconventional. He'd earned a bachelor's degree in history and a master's degree in education, and was firmly planted in a career as an educator. He taught English at Cordova Middle School in Phoenix, Arizona. Like most Americans, September 11, 2001, radically changed Hal Engstrom's life.

Engstrom was teaching school when planes, commandeered by radical madmen working under the orders of Osama Bin Laden, struck the World Trade Center and the Pentagon and crashed in Pennsylvania. The implications of such an attack on American soil particularly resonated with this student of history.

On October 19, 2001, at the age of thirty-four, when most men are building a comfortable nest egg and settling into life and family, Engstrom enlisted in the Army. With his educational credentials he could have qualified almost immediately for officer training, but his age put him over the cutoff. Engstrom, not wanting to be kept out of the fight, enlisted in the Army as a private with the hope of eventually applying for warrant officer selection.

When his teaching contract expired, Hal Engstrom went to basic training, followed by intelligence training. Toward the end of his training it began to look like "the system" was working against him. Although it was clear at that point that Iraq was America's next target in the war on terrorism and oppression, Engstrom worried his zeal to join the fight would be dampened by an assignment to an analyst's cubicle in some nondeploying headquarters. It was an assignment many of his fellow soldiers sought, but it was not why Engstrom joined the Army. Rather than sit back and wait to see what the system, with its red tape and endless processes, would spit out for his duty assignment, Engstrom pressed his drill sergeants to help him win an assignment to a unit bound for Iraq and the war against Saddam. Even after winning the assignment he sought, things weren't simple. The orders assigning him to his first unit changed twice, and when he finally ended up in the 4th Infantry Division, he found himself sharing the frustration of his fellow soldiers and commanders by being blocked from entry into Iraq, due to political wrangling with Turkey. He shared the fear that initially plagued many in the 4th ID: they would get to Iraq, but miss the war.

"Everyone," as one soldier put it, "wants to be there when the last round is fired. No one wants to just be there to police up the brass."

Though the path was often frustrating and divergent, Hal Engstrom and his fellow soldiers made it to Iraq and now faced the biggest enemy of all: The Butcher of Baghdad, Saddam Hussein. It was the job of MAJ Murphy's intel team, along with their Special Operations and interagency colleagues, to find the missing pieces and assemble the trail that would lead to Saddam.

Mongo Link

The Iraqi social structure and intricate code of loyalty and silence frustrated American analysts in the same way that Saddam's ability to remain just out of reach frustrated U.S. military commanders. Murphy intuitively knew that he needed to change the paradigm and turn the Iraqi cultural obstacles into weapons in his own arsenal.

First Murphy and his team had to know their enemy. Although Iraq's culture was *not* their enemy, Saddam and his followers were using it as a weapon of sorts. Murphy began reading extensively about Iraq's culture and customs. The more he read the more he understood how difficult and complex their task would be.

His inspiration came from reading the account of an Iraqi father commanded by his tribe to execute his son. The son had informed on two Iraqis later ambushed in an American raid. The tribal ultimatum to the father was simple: kill the son or they would kill the man and his entire family. The father chose to kill his son.

Murphy began to understand the strong tribal traditions. If someone in your network came to your home for sanctuary or aid you were bound by centuries-old tradition to take him or her in. That alone made the number of Saddam's potential hiding places staggering. If Murphy was going to find Saddam he had to break the inner circle of families protecting him. To break the circle he had to understand its constituency. The majority of the reports Task Force RAIDER received reinforced the belief that Saddam was in their area of operations. This made sense. Tikrit is where his family and tribal ties were anchored; they would be the likely ones supporting him with places to stay, vehicles, money, and food. History tends to repeat itself; Tikrit was where he hid and healed after the failed coup attempt in 1959, before fleeing to Syria.

Murphy brought his idea to Hickey and the vision was born. Murphy and his team would find the path; Hickey would follow it. Together they would get their man.

In early July, Murphy started what was to become an immensely complicated intelligence project by putting down four names and a few notes on paper and passing it to Gray, Santana, Engstrom, and the rest of the intelligence section. He gave a simple directive: "Make sense of it." He told them he wanted not only the connections but the relationships. Murphy wanted to know who exactly the "enablers" were. Enablers were deemed to be those trusted members of the former regime who were making things happen, many of whom were not viewed as significant enough by conventional military intelligence thought to make the Most Wanted list. These men, as the analyst's theory went, in turn relied on others below them, the *arbaeen* (or "forty"), a second- or third-tier group. They were Saddam's "errand boys" who did his bidding, cooked for him, amused him, and provided the "yes-man" feedback he craved. MAJ Murphy reasoned that these men were drawn from a close group of five or six trusted families who, when the Coalition stormed into Baghdad, became a secret web of keepers that sheltered and moved Saddam just ahead of Coalition forces.

From the initial list of four names Murphy provided, the team began constructing a picture of the enemy in their area of operations. Over the course of five months the intelligence section mapped a network of Saddam's family, bodyguards, associates, and his most trusted companions. After the brigade had detained most of these individuals over the months, the information became refined, allowing them to focus on individuals who required further targeting and capture. These individuals ran operations for Saddam, reported to him, and would, the team reasoned, eventually lead to his capture.

What began to emerge was an intricate diagram of tribes, families, associates, and contacts unlike anything being drawn or tracked by any other organization. The relationships evolved as the analytic rigor increased and they began understanding their knowledge base of the enemy they faced and how he lived, thought, and operated. Murphy's team shared what they developed. First they brought in other intelligence officers in the Raider Brigade and their subordinate battalions, then higher headquarters, and eventually Special Operations Forces and participating agencies. The ever-expanding group moved beyond just sharing their knowledge; they formed a common understanding. As that understanding grew the gaps requiring critical information became more evident and other agencies operating within the area began helping to fill them in. The intelligence effort grew from a simple outside-the-box initiative by an unlikely combination of soldiers and Special Operations operatives into a combined operation including the assets of the U.S. Defense Intelligence Agency (DIA), the CIA, Special Forces, the 4th Infantry Division, and a Joint Special Operations Task Force (JSOTF)—Task Force 121. The predictions made by the template were increasingly correct.

There were at least twelve raids conducted to capture Saddam throughout Task Force RAIDER's area of operations. Some raid reports indicated they'd missed their man by only a few hours. In November, Task Force RAIDER captured several key Iraqis, which in turn led them to some of Saddam's most trusted individuals in his inner circle.

What started as a simple task to make sense of four names on a sheet of paper turned into a full team effort to reveal an extremely detailed Link Analysis Diagram of the people connected to Saddam. The template of growing information became known as Mongo Link. As the chart gained definition, it listed targets that ranged from "trigger pullers on the ground" to the highest levels of Saddam's most trusted, including those on the card deck of the Most-Wanted Iraqis.

Information from many different sources and means of collection was processed through different intelligence analysts, but ultimately, it all fed to the Mongo Link. One piece of information linked to another, which would link to something that happened on a different day, and so on.

While many U.S. forces and virtually every aspect of the media were preoccupied with finding the "high-value targets" from the top Most-Wanted Iraqis, the trail that led to Saddam was built through lower-level operatives. The relatively low-tech "door kicking," arresting, and interrogation of Saddam's former bodyguards, relatives of people close to him, errand boys, and assorted flunkies began. The detail and number of the links grew downward, ever downward, and increasingly inward to Saddam, in the center of the target.

In the first Gulf War, Saddam claimed to fight "the mother of all battles." In this second round, Hickey planned to knock Saddam out using MAJ Murphy's "mother of all family trees."

The information that shaped this tree became incessant; twenty-four hours a day, seven days a week. Processing it was a daunting, tedious, and often extremely frustrating task. Some days produced huge leaps forward while others left the team feeling like they'd never move another step. But each raid, each report, each piece of information, each detainee, even the attacks against Coalition forces added a little piece to the puzzle. Murphy understood that fighting this type of war was different from fighting a high-intensity, force-on-force war. It required looking at things from a different perspective and looking at the enemy in a different way. It required countless hours of trying to figure out who was who, and how they fit together. They focused on everything from the DIA blacklist (a Defense Intelligence Agency list of enemy persons of interest) to the local trigger pullers in the cities where their battalions operated. Once the Mongo Link took shape, the analysis began to almost feed itself, pointing toward new, better locations to raid and showing linkages more clearly. Murphy continually stressed the link diagram was *a living document*. It became apparent that Murphy's original four individuals played a bigger role in the insurgency than anyone had thought. In September, the template led them to a raid in ad Dawr south of Tikrit, a place they would return to later with better results.

What also emerged as increasingly important was a group of individuals on the link diagram that Hickey referred to tongue-in-cheek one day as the "42-inch waistband club." They were a group of middle-aged, balding financiers and operators with physical builds like bowling pins. They were a direct contrast to the lean twenty-year-old kids who were actually conducting the attacks against Coalition forces. The "42-inch waistband club" occupied key power positions on the diagram and looked to be a critical link to Saddam.

The process was set. All it needed was a catalyst to bring it all together. Hickey, through the efforts of MAJ Murphy's team, believed he knew what, or rather who, that was. They needed the Fat Man.

The Fat Man

The running joke about the "42-inch waistband club" increasingly proved to be the case. Large around the middle, these men never seemed to be the ones who actually got their hands dirty, much like Sidney Greenstreet in *The Maltese Falcon.*

The missing link, the catalyst, was a member of one of five families close to Saddam, a key figure in the insurgency, and one of the individuals who long occupied a space high up on Task Force RAIDER's "wish list." Although they had known all along that he was an important figure in the insurgency, just how important he was became evident as more and more low-level operatives on the list were scooped up. They knew he would possess critical information that might lead to Saddam, so they began tracking him and his family in early July. The more they learned, the more they understood how large a role he played.

Although his and his family's name remains a closely guarded secret, the Fat Man apparently first attracted MAJ Murphy's attention as more than just one of four names on a list drawn up in early July, after troops from the 1st Brigade raided his property in Abou Ajil. Though they missed arresting him by moments, the photographs, documents, and other items they captured connected him to several key allies of the Hussein family. They first believed he was simply a bodyguard for Saddam Hussein, and learned later that he was a senior figure in the Special Security Organization, a force run by Hussein's son, Qusay, and the man ultimately charged with protecting the president himself.

Although more raids snared more operatives, the man who would prove to be the key in finally finding Saddam remained at large. Over three nights during the first week of December, U.S. troops conducted a series of raids in Tikrit, Samarra, and Bayji that netted other suspects and produced more leads. A raid on December 5, in the nearby city of Samarra, yielded $1.9 million in U.S. currency, but not the man himself. They missed him again on December 7 in Bayji. It seemed the Iraqi operative was as elusive as Saddam himself.

After 249 days of searching, many of the Most-Wanted Iraqis were dead or in custody, but there was still no Ace of Spades.

Building Character

COL Jim Hickey didn't sleep much of the night on December 12, 2003. Something kept nagging at him, hanging just out of reach in the shadowy areas of his mind. He had to find Saddam and that's what nagged at Hickey long into the night. Saddam himself seemed to loom out there like the final piece of the puzzle, just out of his mind's reach.

Hickey knew it frustrated his soldiers as well that they had yet to find Saddam. Their frustration bothered him, too. But for the soldiers of TF RAIDER and especially Murphy's group of Saddam hunters, it was Hickey's vision and his quiet confidence that sustained them. He was like John Wayne's Ethan in *The Searchers,* standing with his companion on the cold and snowy plains. After years of frustrated pursuit of two girls kidnapped by Indians, the young man asked Ethan dejectedly if there was even the slightest chance they would ever find their prey. Words similar to Ethan's may have echoed deep in Hickey's mind, giving him the comfort needed to finally drift off to sleep:

> *Seems like he never learns there's such a thing as a critter who'll just keep comin' on. So we'll find 'em in the end, I promise you. We'll find 'em, just as sure as the turnin' of the earth.*

As Hickey fitfully slept and his analysts soldiered on, Special Forces troops in Baghdad were sorting through the latest prizes from their sweep that night. One of them would turn out to be the Fat Man.

Lucky 13

Hickey awoke December 13 remarkably refreshed, and with a strange excitement and renewed confidence burning within him. He couldn't explain the feeling of anticipation.

Murphy, Santana, Gray, Engstrom, and the others were changing shifts, preparing for another cycle of sifting through the relentless search for clues. The humvee and Bradley drivers were working through their daily PMCS (vehicle Preventative Maintenance Checks and Services). It seemed like just another day in Tikrit for them.

Hickey and CSM Wilson made their usual morning rounds, checking soldiers and receiving reports on the status of the task force. SPC "Joe" was preparing to accompany Hickey as usual. "Joe" was surprised at how talkative the normally reserved Hickey was. That strange, positive feeling was becoming infectious. Hickey began to believe his mood was more than the start of a good day, once he got the phone call at 1050 hours. Special Operations Forces had snared Hickey's long-sought-after target: the Fat Man.

Instinctively, Hickey ordered the return of G Troop of the 10th Cavalry Regiment. Although the G Troop had little sleep the night before, something inside Hickey told him they needed to be ready, and ready fast. Murphy and his team also got the word and they prepared for the Fat Man's arrival.

The Source

Once called the Fat Man by Hickey, he's known now only as "the source," a man whose identity and family are a highly guarded secret. Special Operations Forces scooped up the source in a Baghdad raid on December 12, but did not immediately realize he was one of the top names on Murphy and Hickey's list. The source was a senior officer in Hussein's elite Special Security Service (SSS), a key protector of Saddam Hussein, and a charter member of the "42-inch waistband club." He was one of the enablers on Murphy's matrix, perhaps the crucial one who enabled Saddam to continue eluding capture. Saturday morning he arrived by helicopter at Hickey's headquarters, under heavy guard.

Murphy, Gray, and the others watched as the source entered interrogation, and waited restlessly for anything that came out. They knew the next few hours would be crucial. The longer the source took to break, the less chance there was that any information they got from him regarding Saddam's location would be timely. The stakes were higher than ever. Murphy's team knew the source was close to Saddam and they knew he had personal contact with him.

As information slowly trickled out from the interrogation, Murphy and his team compiled and assessed it. All the source initially gave up were several general locations where Saddam might be hiding. He then suggested that Saddam was likely underground, but little was specific. Murphy began to worry. The more time that elapsed, the less likely it was that Special Operations would find Saddam at any location the source might give them.

The interrogators turned up the heat and at 1700 hours, the source cracked, blurting out Saddam's location as ad Dawr. He was hidden in one of two farmhouses on the edge of town. He gave them the names of two men who would be guarding Saddam. Murphy and Hickey knew the area well. Six weeks prior, the 4th ID strung barbed wire around the small farm village of Owja, where Saddam had lived as a boy, questioning or arresting about 60 percent of the village's thousand or so men. It was only five kilometers from the farm where the source said Saddam was hiding.

It all made perfect sense to Murphy and his team. In 1959 ad Dawr was where Saddam hid after his unsuccessful attempt to assassinate the prime minister of Iraq, Abdul Karim Qassim. That time, Saddam escaped by swimming across the Tigris River to exile in Syria, one of the only times he ever left his country.

Once the source gave up the location, Hickey moved quickly to assemble Task Force RAIDER. Special Operations Forces prepared the joint Delta Force, SEAL Team, and Special Operations aviation force. Hickey scrutinized satellite imagery and maps of the area with his staff and Special Operations commandos. Murphy worried that the informant had managed to stall just long enough to ensure Saddam would be gone when the task force arrived, leaving them another *dry hole,* the term often used when raids failed to turn up their elusive prey.

RED DAWN

They called it Operation RED DAWN after the 1984 Patrick Swayze/Charlie Sheen movie of the same title, in which the Soviets invade hometown America via parachute, aided by Central America and Cuba. The film's teenage heroes were called the "Wolverines," the name of their high school football team. The two sites the source gave as Saddam's possible hiding places were designated WOLVERINE 1 and WOLVERINE 2.

The raiding force was a combined 4th ID Task Force consisting of six hundred personnel from TF RAIDER (1st Brigade, 4th ID), specifically: 4-42 Field Artillery Battalion; G Troop, 10th Cavalry Regiment; HQ, 1st BDE, 4th ID; elements from 1st BN, 4th Aviation Regiment; and A Troop, 1st BN, 10th Cavalry Regiment (TF Reserve), together with an elite joint Special Operations Force consisting of air assets and ground elements from 3/10th SFG (A), Delta Force, and Navy SEALs who all formed Task Force 121. The plan was simple: Hickey's force would isolate and control the area while Special Operations Forces went after Saddam.

It was a formidable fighting force, but Hickey was not about to chance a repeat of the raid that killed Saddam's sons, Uday and Qusay. There, U.S. forces found themselves entangled in a four-hour gun battle against three men and a teenage boy who managed to hold back a U.S. force of about two hundred soldiers aided by heavy weaponry and assault helicopters. If Saddam was at ad Dawr, Hickey was going to get him, dead or alive. If Saddam or anyone else chose to put up a fight, Hickey was going to make sure it would be over quickly and the enemy would all be dead.

There was no time for high-tech hardware, fancy briefing slides, complex digital visualization, or lengthy operations orders. Hickey rapidly prepared and distributed a fragmentary order (FRAGO) using photos and sketches. Within an hour of the source cracking, they were ready to move.

Down by the River

If Saddam was in ad Dawr, he could look out at the Tigris at nightfall, and remember swimming that river to freedom years ago. But now he was a tired, haggard, and hunted man lacking both the strength and the desire. Perhaps it was pride that kept him in Iraq, moving from place to place, hiding in taxicabs, holes, and hovels. Perhaps he'd convinced himself the Americans would tire of the chase or that he could elude them as Bin Laden has. Regardless, as night fell on the Tigris, Saddam Hussein prepared for another night in hiding. Soon it would be time to move like before. Whether out of fear, arrogance, or delusion, he stayed where he was that night.

There had been a number of times that the task force had headed out after Saddam. This time, the mood was more than routine prebattle excitement. Hickey's positive feeling that morning had blossomed to full optimism. Murphy and his intelligence team could feel it, too. There was a greater sense of urgency this time, and to the soldiers of TF RAIDER, it seemed that everywhere they looked they could see small Special Operations aircraft, Little Birds, darting across the sky. The task force's Bradley Fighting Vehicles and M1A2 tanks were all moving into position, as were Special Operations white Toyota Hi-Lux pickup trucks and other specialized vehicles.

Hickey and CSM Wilson moved to their vehicles. If things got rough the soldiers knew the command drivers would be in the thick of it, just as they had been before. They could all be counted on when the time came.

Operation RED DAWN was set for 2000 hours. CW2 Gray knew the source was worthy. His gut and his analyst instincts told him this was what they'd all been waiting for. Not wanting to give up a chance to go on the raid, he garnered Murphy's permission for him and CPT Terrell to participate. Gray and Terrell served together in DESERT STORM and they wanted to be together when Saddam was finally brought down. At 1800 hours they put on their battle gear and met Hickey's combat patrol. Gray rode with COL Hickey and Terrell rode with the gun truck. The force departed Raider base and headed out, making final plans as they went. At 1930 hours the task force moved toward the small farm twenty kilometers away, toward a rendezvous with destiny.

"The Institute will be heard from today."

As Hickey headed out on the raid the night of December 13, the ghosts of the many previous raids that failed to snag Saddam no longer haunted him. Although he never smoked, he decided to take along a cigar given to him by a reporter to save for a special occasion. There seemed to be other powers in play that night, and other, more benevolent voices whispered deep in Hickey's mind, giving him a profound calm and confidence. Perhaps it was his subconscious telling him all the pieces finally fit. Perhaps it was his training and battle-space awareness telling him the information was correct. Perhaps it was the voice of VMI's great teacher, mentor, and leader, Stonewall Jackson. If it was the voice of Jackson, perhaps the soft-spoken Southerner repeated prophetic words first spoken in battle one hundred and forty years ago:

"The Institute [VMI] will be heard from today."

Déjà Vu All Over Again

1LT Angela Santana was on duty in the RAIDER Tactical Operations Center (TOC) trying not to be fazed, trying to convince herself this was just another raid, that it was no big deal. It was hard to continually raise her hopes only to be disappointed time after time. Like Murphy, Gray, and the others, she, too, knew the informant was a promising one. As she looked around her she could feel the intensity. Everyone wore headphones in anticipation of a huge firefight like the 101st Airborne had encountered with Saddam's sons. She said a quiet prayer that there would be no casualities and that Saddam would finally be captured. The silence in the room grew deafening as time passed.

As the raiding force moved into the ad Dawr area, it seemed surreal how easily the operation was coming together. Forces were moving into place. It was strange to be moving back down the same roads and into the same areas U.S. troops had searched only a few weeks before without success. It was "déjà vu all over again," as American baseball great Yogi Berra had once put it.

At precisely 2000 hours, the raid began.

WOLVERINE 1 and WOLVERINE 2 were empty. Two more dry holes. Within a five-kilometer radius of WOLVERINE 1 and WOLVERINE 2, Hickey's forces tightened their cordon. The Special Operators moved in on a small mud hut in a compound just north of WOLVERINE 1.

Through their night vision goggles and thermal sights, soldiers of the 4th ID could see Special Operators moving soundlessly through the dark night to the target. Occasionally, the red beams of laser-aiming lights would reflect off trees and leaves, but it was deathly silent, save for the distant hum of OH-58 Little Birds and other Special Operations aircraft waiting for extraction, reinforcement, or attack.

At 2010, with Hickey's troops sealing off the area, Special Operations Forces burst into the hut, a simple construction behind a fence of dried palm leaves. It had been an orange-picker's hut with one room and an open kitchen. They immediately seized one man trying to escape and another man in the hut. As it turned out, one was Saddam's cook; the other was the cook's brother and owner of the property.

Inside, they found that the hut consisted of one room with two beds and a refrigerator containing a can of lemonade, a packet of hot dogs, a can of "Happy Brand" tuna, an opened box of Belgian chocolates, and a tube of ointment. A poster of Noah's Ark hung on the mud-brick wall. There were also two AK-47 assault rifles, various packages of new clothes, and a green footlocker containing $750,000 in American hundred-dollar bills. More telling: an orange-and-white Toyota Corolla taxi was parked outside. Rumors that Saddam had hidden in taxis and even masqueraded as a taxi driver appeared to be true.

Saddam was nowhere to be seen. It looked like yet another dry hole when suddenly, one of the detainees broke away from the Special Operators and ran, telling them Saddam was hiding elsewhere and he would lead them to him. His sudden desire to cooperate and zeal to get them out of there further convinced the operators they were close.

At the command vehicle, CW2 Gray stood next to COL Hickey listening to the radio reports from the Special Operations Forces. Those two individuals were exactly who the source stated would be at the farm. Things were going well.

Reports continued to come in that Special Operations Forces were still searching the area but had not found the tunnels that the source had described Saddam would be hiding in. Hickey calmly told them to take their time. Task Force RAIDER owned that portion of Iraq. He'd hold the cordon all night if necessary.

Another ten minutes went by. Still nothing.

Jackpot

Outside the hut, the two dozen or so Special Operators were preparing to move off and expand their search. Something caught an operator's attention in the darkness of the moonless night, through the unearthly glow of his night vision goggles. The ground just didn't look quite right. The sensation of an odd landscape was nothing unusual under the glow of a night vision device, but it just didn't *feel* right, either.

The closer the operator looked, the more it appeared to be out of place. The bricks and dirt were spread about too uniformly, as if someone were trying to conceal something. A thread of fabric protruded just slightly under the dirt.

Strange.

It was 2030 hours, and the operators brushed away the debris, revealing a Styrofoam plug. True to his training, one of the Special Operators pulled the pin on a hand grenade while his colleagues prepared to pull the plug so he could drop it in. The remaining twenty or so soldiers prepared to fire their weapons if engaged. The plug revealed a hole, the hole revealed a ratty-looking, bearded man. The man raised his hands and announced: "I am Saddam Hussein. I am the president of Iraq, and I am willing to negotiate."

The Task Force 121 commando covering the hole calmly replied, "President Bush sends his regards."

Hickey's radio broke the silence as the Special Operator reported simply, "Sir, we may have the Jackpot."

Hickey waited breathlessly.

Back on the objective, several Special Operators yanked the disheveled, disoriented man to the surface, unavoidably scratching his head in the tight confines of the hole.

The operators quickly removed the 9mm pistol from his belt and checked him for the markings and other features that would preliminarily confirm they had their man. They began to prepare him for transportation with the standard, empty sandbag over his head and flex-cuffs on his hands. As they attempted to secure him, Saddam resisted—trying to shrug off the operators, acting belligerent, and even spitting in one soldier's face. In return, he was treated "just like any other prisoner," and forcefully subdued to the ground where several operators held him down while others trussed him up.

At Hickey's command vehicle, everyone waited in painful silence. The word finally came. Although it was only minutes behind the first call, it seemed like weeks. "Sir, we've got him. Jackpot." Hickey replied simply and unemotionally, "That's great."

Within minutes Saddam was strapped into a Special Operations Little Bird and spirited out of the immediate area. He was later brought to the Baghdad Airport prison that once boasted his name. It happened so fast that by the time Hickey's command vehicle arrived, Saddam was gone.

In the RAIDER TOC (Tactical Operations Center), only a single code word broke the building silence: "Jackpot."

It was as if the entire world suddenly went silent. Murphy looked at LTC Smith, the brigade executive officer, in a long moment of disbelief. LTC Smith said, "We got him. We got him."

The TOC exploded in cheers and "high fives." Hal Engstrom leaned back, put his hands behind his head, and let out a deep sigh of relief.

Hickey, Wilson, "Joe," and CW2 Gray rolled up to the mud hut in Hickey's humvee, parked and dismounted, and walked rapidly toward the hut entrance. On the way, CW2 Gray noticed the orange-and-white-colored taxi parked next to the sheep pen. He turned to Hickey and asked if he'd noticed as well. Hickey gave one of his rare smiles.

CSM Wilson and "Joe" took control of the $750,000 in the green metal box, but not before the command sergeant major rubbed the stacks of bills on his face "just to see how it felt." The Special Operators turned one of the two individuals seized in the raid over to Gray and "Joe," then melted into the darkness from whence they came. Saddam was in custody. Not a single shot had been fired, not a single soldier wounded. It was a capture everyone said couldn't be done.

"Joe" was ordered to transport one of the two detainees to COL Hickey's location. "Joe" and the prisoner struck up a conversation in Arabic as they walked toward the humvee.

"Do you know what you did? Did you know who you were holding? Do you know who your friend was?" "Joe" asked Saddam's trusted lookout, now flex-cuffed and in U.S. custody, as they walked across the orange grove. The detainee began to cry. "I know, I'm stupid," he stammered in Arabic.

"I'm sorry, I never should have taken the money . . . I'm sorry. I made a mistake. . . ." The man kept repeating that he should never have taken the money he was paid to protect High Value Target #1.

"Don't you know who *he* [Saddam] is?" "Joe" again asked the man.

"Yes," the detainee responded. "Yes, I know who he is." The detainee began shouting a stream of expletives directed at Saddam Hussein.

"He's a piece of shit," the prisoner yelled in Arabic. "[Saddam's] a motherfucker . . . I should have never taken the money. . . ."

"Well, it doesn't make a difference now, does it?" "Joe" said, laughing aloud as he led the man by the arm.

We Got Him

When Saddam was first captured he was held in a room with many Special Operators; it was a seemingly casual and rather unreal setting. In Baghdad, Saddam was stripped naked and examined like any other prisoner. As he entered the building on his way to the examination, he passed through a silent gauntlet of Special Operators and the others who brought him in, but who would remain in the shadows, their deeds shrouded in secrecy. Next came a viewing with some of his former aides now in detention, including longtime confidante Tariq Aziz, so they could confirm their former boss's identity. The new Iraqi Governing Council was not only allowed to view Saddam, but to question him.

At about 1515 Sunday afternoon Baghdad time, L. Paul Bremer III, the administrator of the Coalition Provisional Authority in Iraq, strode to the podium and declared: "Ladies and gentlemen, we got him."

In Baghdad and elsewhere, celebratory gunfire broke out as Iraqis took to the streets, many in tears and holding tattered photos of hus-

bands, sons, wives, daughters, and other loved ones lost during The
Butcher of Baghdad's reign of terror.

Eight months after a giant statue of Saddam Hussein was pulled to
the ground in Baghdad in a gesture of celebration, Saddam was finally in custody, dragged from a hole in the ground not far from
where it all began in his youth. The operation was well commanded
by a man who'd been promoted to colonel in one of Saddam's old
palaces just across the river from where he was found.

In his final days of freedom, The Glorious Leader, Direct Descen-
dant of the Prophet, The Lion of Babylon, was reduced to a poor, disheveled has-been living in a mud hut. The lasting image he left on
the Iraqi people is that of a broken, haggard man found living in a
hole.

An American flag at half-mast will fly,
For the American soldier who has died.
Another lay adorned on the coffin made of wood,
Where will lay a soldier who once proudly stood.
Tears of pride and sadness will be shed,
For the American soldier who now is dead.
Fellow soldier will stand to honor his death,
And comfort the family that he has left
Somewhere softly taps will play,
For an American Soldier died today.
—"An American Soldier Died Today"
by Katie Morris

Memorial Funds, Scholarships, and Charities

Operation Family Fund: The Operation ENDURING FREEDOM and Operation IRAQI FREEDOM Family Fund is organized to provide funds, both short term and long term, to families whose loved ones were killed or permanently injured as a result of military action as part of Operations ENDURING FREEDOM and IRAQI FREEDOM.

Operation Family Fund
United States PO Box 837
Ridgecrest, CA 93556

Phone: 760-793-0541
E-mail: support@oeffamilyfund.org
www.oeffamilyfund.org

Fallen Patriot Fund: Established to help families of U.S. military
personnel who were killed or seriously injured during Operation
IRAQI FREEDOM.

Fallen Patriot Fund
c/o Bank of America Private Bank
TX1-492-19-09
P.O. Box 832409
Dallas, TX 75283-2409

Phone: 214-748-3900
E-mail: Info@fallenpatriotfund.org
www.fallenpatriotfund.org

Fallen Heroes Last Wish Foundation: Provides funds to help support and educate the children of American servicemen and -women
lost during Operation IRAQI FREEDOM.

Fallen Heroes Last Wish Foundation
30 West Sola Street
Santa Barbara, CA 93101

Phone: 805-962-7843
Fax: 805-965-6343
Email: fhlwf@ghs.com
www.lastwishfoundation.org

Special Operations Warrior Foundation: The Special Operations Warrior Foundation (SOWF) provides college scholarship grants based on need, along with financial aid and educational counseling to the children of Special Operations personnel who were killed in an operational mission or training accident.

Special Operations Warrior Foundation
P.O. Box 14385
Tampa, FL 33690

Phone: 877-337-7693
Fax: 813-805-0567
E-mail: warrior@specialops.org
www.specialops.org

Mercy Corps: Mercy Corps is working throughout Iraq to assist families affected by years of deteriorating conditions and conflict.
www.mercycorps.org/iraq

Also of Interest

Partners International Foundation: A nonprofit humanitarian organization working in the United States and throughout the world to provide disaster relief and other support. Focuses on women and children.

Partners International Foundation
41 Cedar Hill Road
Newtown, CT 06470
www.partners-international.org

Special Operations Association Colonel George C. Morton Memorial Scholarship: The Special Operations Association grants scholarships to perpetuate the memory of those personnel who served in a Special Operations Unit during the Vietnam War, and who were

Prisoners of War or Missing in Action and who are still unaccounted for in Southeast Asia. The scholarships also honor the late Colonel George C. Morton, an original commander and innovator of Special Operations in Southeast Asia.

Special Operations Association
c/o Alan N. Keller
Chairman, Scholarship Committee
4401 Park Road
Alexandria, VA 22312-1430
www.specialoperations.org

Saddam

Garamone, Jim. "Just Who Is Saddam Hussein?" Armed Forces Press Service, January 22, 2003.

Information from Web site entitled: World History: Saddam Hussein, from: www.worldhistory.com/hussein.htm.

Information from The Iraq Foundation's Web site: Biography of Saddam Hussein: www.iraqfoundation.org/research/bio.html.

Task Force VIKING

Author's 10th SFG interview 1: SGM Strong/MAJ Howard (8SEP03AM).

Author's 10th SFG interview 2: SGM Strong (30JUN–2 JUL03).

Consolidated Journal of ODA 056 (as given to Author).

Task Force VIKING-Concede Nothing Operational Map/Chart.

Raid on Ayn Sifni 060300ZAPR03 Operational Map.

Author's 10th SFG/Rangers interview "A.M./P.M."

The Screaming Eagles

Author's LTC John E. Novalis interview.

Author's MG Petraeus interview.

Author's COL Anderson interview.

"Source Report" that led to "the raid" on Uday and Qusay, courtesy of 101st ABN.

The War Diary of Dana Lewis.

101st ABN "Mosul History" PowerPoint presentation.

Information from: brucewillis.com/notes/journal_detail.cfm?j_id=13.

Information from: www.fas.org/irp/world/iraq/fedayeen/index.htm.

Boyne, Sean. "Inside Iraq's Security Network," *Jane's Intelligence Review, Vol. 9, numbers 7 & 8,* July and August 1997.

Task Force DAGGER

5th SFG (A) Operational Sketch/map (as drawn for Author).

Author's LTC Haas interview.

5th SFG (A) and FL ARNG INF "breaching Iraq" video.

Private Contractors

Author's recollection of his conversation with John Jones, December 2003.

Griswold, Terry, and D. M. Giangreco. *Delta: America's Elite Counterterrorist Force.* Osceola, Wisconsin: MBI, 1992.

Krane, Jim. "U.S. Putting Hired Help on Front Lines." The Associated Press, November 2, 2003.

Author's John Jones/KBR interview.

Author's Tipivar Poph/KBR interview.

Information from www.mpri.com.

Letters from Tikrit

Morris, Katie. "The Widow's Tears," Copyright 2003.

Letters from LTC Russell, 1-22 INF, 4th INF Division.

The Ace in the Hole

By People's Daily Online, "Former Iraqi President Saddam Hussein Arrested."

Thomas, Evan, and Babak Dehghanpisheh, "Inside Red Dawn: Saddam Up Close." Newsweek Online, January 15, 2004.

Chief Warrant Officer 2 Bryan G. Gray, HHC, 1st Brigade Combat Team, 4th ID, All Source Intelligence Technician.

Information from: www.smh.com. "The shame—the desert lion was a kitten," December 16, 2003.

Trice, Calvin R., and Bill McKelway. "A VMI Grad with eyes like 'two deep caves' directed raid that snared Saddam." *Richmond Times Dispatch,* December 16, 2003.

Information from: www.hood.army.mil/4id_1stbde/Raidercsm.htm.

1LT Angela Ann Santana, Alpha Company, 104th Military Intelligence Battalion, 4th Infantry Division attached to 1BCT, S2 (BISE), Position: Analysis Control Team and Common Ground Station Platoon Leader/Intelligence Officer. Transcribed by CPT Alan Roper, 13 Jan 04, Tikrit, Iraq.

Document entitled: "Major Murphy's Response to Narrative Questions."

CNN, Rumsfeld: "In the end, Saddam 'not terribly brave.'" Rumsfeld: "So far Saddam not offering much information." Copyright 2003 CNN, (The Associated Press contributed to this story).

Biographical information, Harold "Hal" Engstrom, Corporal, A Company, 104th MI Battalion (attached to 1st BDE, 4th ID (MI). Position: intelligence analyst. Transcribed by CPT Alan Roper, 13 Jan 04, Tikrit, Iraq.

Loeb, Vernon. "Clan, Family Ties Called Key to Army's Capture of Hussein 'Link Diagrams' Showed Everyone Related by Blood or Tribe." *Washington Post,* Tuesday, December 16, 2003.

On 13 Jan 2004 at 7:53, Alan Roper, CPT, U.S. Army, 1st Brigade, 4th Infantry Division Tikrit, Iraq, wrote.

Sipress, Alan. "Confidant Quickly Became Informant, Pointing the Way." *Washington Post,* Washington Post Foreign Service, December 16, 2003.

McDonnell, Patrick J. "Saddam tried to negotiate during capture." *Los Angeles Times,* 15 January 2004. Accessed online: www.latimes.com.

Thomas, Evan, and Ron Nordland. "How We Got Saddam." *Newsweek,* December 22, 2003.

John Wayne, *The Searchers* (1956).

Los Angeles Times, "Saddam's hunters were set to kill dictator," accessed online on December 21, 2003.

Daniszewski, John, John Hendren, and David Zucchino, "Neighbors now know why sheik looked so edgy; the key was an edgy sheik." *Houston Chronicle,* July 24, 2003. Accessed online: www. latimes.com.

E-mail from Russ Cummings to Author.

Appendix

Morris, Katie. "An American Soldier Died Today," Copyright 2003.

GLOSSARY

10th SFG (A): 10th Special Forces Group, Airborne

1LT: First Lieutenant

2ACR: 2nd Armored Cavalry Regiment

3rd SFG (A): 3rd Special Forces Group, Airborne

5th SFG (A): 5th Special Forces Group, Airborne

A: Airborne

A-10 "Warthog": a slow, low-flying antitank attack aircraft

AA: Air

AAA: Anti-Aircraft Artillery

AASLT: Air Assault

ABN: Airborne

AC-130: "Spectre" gunship, an updated version of the Vietnam-era "Spooky" gunship. The Spectre is armed with chain guns and a 105mm howitzer, and flies at night mainly to provide constant, close air support (CAS) for Special Operations Forces.

ACR: Armored Cavalry Regiment

ADA: Air Defense Artillery

AFB: Air Force Base

AFP: French Media

Al-Jazeera: an Arabic news agency

AIT: Advanced Individual Training

AK-47: the Kalashnikov model 47 assault rifle, probably the most recognizable assault rifle in the world

AN/PRC-126: a lightweight military radio often used in squad operations

AO: Area of Operations

AOB: Area Operating Base

AOR: Area of Responsibility

AP: Associated Press

APC: Armored Personnel Carrier

AR: Armored, can also mean Artillery Radar, or Airborne Recon

ARNG: Army Reserve National Guard

ASP: Ammo Storage Point

A-Team: the twelve-man, basic operating element of the U.S. Army Special Forces

AWACS: Airborne Warning and Control System

B-17: "Flying Fortress" bomber

B-1B: "Lancer"—a multi-role, long-range, heavy bomber

B-2: "Spirit"—Stealth bomber

B-52: "Stratofortress"—high-altitude heavy bomber. Also known as "big ugly fat fellow" (BUFF)

Ba'ath Party: the Arab Socialist Ba'ath Party, the dominant political party in Iraq from 1968–2003

Battery: a group of artillery guns

BBC: British Broadcasting Corporation

BDA: Bomb Damage Assessment

BDE: Brigade

BDU: Battle Dress Uniform

BG: Brigadier General

BIO/CHEM: Biological/Chemical

BIO: Biological Threat

BN: Battalion

Bradley Fighting Vehicle (BFV): a lightly armored fighting vehicle designed to accompany the M1 Abrams tank into battle

Bubbas: military slang term for "guys" or "men"

B-Team: the company-level command and control unit in the U.S. Army Special Forces

BUFF: see B-52

C&C: Command and Control

C-141 Starlifter: a "workhorse" plane used to transport combat forces and equipment over long distances

C-17: Globemaster III—the newest heavy airlift aircraft in the Air Force's inventory

C-4: Explosive

CA: Civil Affairs

CAS: Close Air Support

CAT: Civil Affairs Team

CDR: Commander

CENTCOM: the U.S. Army's Central Command

CG: Commanding General

CGSC: Command and General Staff College

CH: Chaplain

CH-47: "Chinook" twin-rotor transport helicopter

CHEM: Chemical Threat

Chief Warrant Officer: a highly skilled technician who fills positions that are too specialized for broadly trained, branch-qualified commissioned officers

CIA: Central Intelligence Agency

CIDG: Civilian Irregular Defense Group, an Asian mercenary group

CJSOTF-N: Combined Joint Special Operations Task Force-North

CJSOTF-W: Combined Joint Special Operations Task Force-West

COL: Colonel

Combat Infantry Streamer: an award given to infantry units when a specified percentage of their personnel have been awarded the Combat Infantry Badge

Combat Talon: the MC-130 transport plane that normally transports SOF

CPA: Coalition Provisional Authority

CPIC: Coalition Provisional Information Center

CPT: Captain

CRF: Combat Reconnaissance Force

CSM: Command Sergeant Major

CT: counterterrorist, counterterrorism

CW2: Chief Warrant Officer 2

CW4: Chief Warrant Officer 4

Dash 8: a Canadian turboprop airliner with military use in navigation training, coastal surveillance, and passenger transport

Defilade: a fortified position that protects troops against enemy fire coming from multiple directions

Delta Force: U.S. Army Special Forces Operational Detachment unit tasked with counterterrorist operations

Demo: Demolition

De Oppresso Liber: Latin for "To Liberate the Oppressed," the credo of the U.S. Army Special Forces, the Green Berets

DHSK: "Dishka"—Russian heavy machine gun

DIA: the U.S. Defense Intelligence Agency

DOD: the U.S. Department of Defense

Dry hole: a term used to describe the failure of a raid to turn up its intended prey

DZ: Drop Zone

E-3: Private First Class

EC-130: a versatile "Hercules" tactical transport aircraft used for multiple purposes, such as communications and PSYOPS

Embed: embedded reporter

EN: Enemy

EST: Eastern Standard Time

ETD: Estimated Time of Departure

EV: EARLY VICTOR

Exfil: Exfiltration

F/A-18: "Hornet"—a fighter-bomber used by the U.S. Navy and U.S. Air Force

F-14: "Tomcat"—a fighter-bomber used by the U.S. Navy and usually deployed from the decks of aircraft carriers

F-16: "Fighting Falcon"—a fighter/attack aircraft

FA: Field Artillery

Fast-mover: a fixed-wing fighter jet

Fedayeen Saddam: "men of sacrifice," pro-Saddam militia/insurgent group

Flak: the shrapnel from the explosion of an artillery shell

FLARNG: Florida Army Reserve National Guard

Flex-cuffs: single-use nylon restraints designed for civil unrest or crowd control situations

FOB: Forward Operating Base

FRAGO: fragmentary order

FRL: Former Regime Loyalist

FSB: Forward Support Battalion

FSG: First Sergeant

G-Day: beginning of "shock and awe" military campaign

GEN: General

GNP: Gross National Product

GPMG: General Purpose Machine Gun

Guidon: unit flag

Green Berets: the U.S. Army Special Forces

GW2: Gulf War II

GWOT: Global War on Terror

Halon: a halocarbon, used as a fire-extinguishing agent

Hardball: Army slang for asphalt

HAMAS: "Harakat al-Muqawama al-Islamia"—the Islamic Resistance Movement and also a term indicating courage and bravery; operates primarily in the Ghaza district

HDR: Humanitarian Daily Ration

HE: High Explosive

Herringbone formation: a formation created when an armored column turns half of its vehicles (usually odd numbered) to the left and the other half (even) to the right, thus allowing attack from or defense of both flanks

Hesco Bastions: concrete barriers brought in by Army Engineers

Hi-Lux: Four-wheel-drive Toyota truck

HOT: a long-range antitank weapon system that can be operated from a vehicle or helicopter

HQ: Headquarters

HUMINT: human intelligence (sources)

Humvee: High Mobility, Multi-Purpose, Wheeled Vehicle, also known as a "Hummer," and by the acronym HUMMWV or HMMWV—a rugged, four-wheel-drive vehicle that can be set up in numerous configurations including ambulances, "pickup" trucks, communication "rat rigs," and TOW missile launchers

HVT: High-Value Target

HVT #1: Saddam Hussein

HVT #2: Qusay Hussein

HVT #3: Uday Hussein

HVT #4: Abid Hamid Mahmud

ID: Infantry Division

IED: Improvised Explosive Device

INF: infantry, sometimes just IF

Infil: infiltrate, infiltration

Irbil: city in Iraq, also spelled Arbil

ISU: Integrated Site Unit

IV: intravenous

IZ: Enemy Territory

Javelin Weapons System: a man-portable, shoulder-fired, antitank missile system with a range of 2500 meters

JDAM: Joint Direct Attack Munitions

JFACC: Joint Forces Air Component Command

JSOC: Joint Special Operations Command

JSOTF: Joint Special Operations Task Force

KAZ: Kurdish Autonomous Zone

KBR: Kellogg, Brown & Root

KDP: Kurdistan Democratic Party

Kevlar: a protective fabric (proprietary of DuPont Corporation)

KIA: Killed in Action

Kiowa: a light scout/gunship helicopter based on the Bell Jet Ranger

Kurds: indigenous people of northern Iraq/Kurdistan, Eastern Turkey, Syria, and western Iran

Levee(s): Soldier(s). In the context of this book, an Iraqi that the U.S. troops pressed into service for his nation's future; the British used the term during the 1800s

Little Bird: the OH-58 helicopter gunship that usually supports SOF

LOA: Line of Attack

LT: Lieutenant

LTC or LT COL: Lieutenant Colonel

LTG: Lieutenant General

LZ: Landing Zone

M1: Abrams tank

M-16: the standard issue rifle of the U.S. Army, a lightweight weapon that fires a burst of small-caliber bullets with a controlled dispersion pattern

M1A1: Abrams Main Battle Tank

M-203: the 40mm single-shot grenade launcher mounted under the barrel of an M16A2 assault rifle

M-240B: SAW Squad automatic weapon—a 5.56mm light machine gun

M2HB: M2 Heavy Barrel machine gun

M-4: the shortened, heavy-barrel carbine version of an M16A2 used primarily by SOF and vehicle crews

MAC: Military Airlift Command

MAJ: Major

Man-pack: a weapon system small enough to be carried by a person

Mark-19: the M19 40mm belt-fed automatic grenade launcher, which can be fired from a tripod or vehicle mounted

MC-130: the "Combat Talon," the transport plane used primarily by SOF, a variation of the standard C-130 design

Medevac: medical evacuation

MG: Major General

MH-53J: technologically advanced heavy-lift helicopter used primarily by Special Operations Forces; nickname: "Pave Low III"

MI: Military Intelligence

MIB: Military Intelligence Battalion

MK-19: automatic belt-fed 40mm grenade launcher

MO: modus operandi

Mobility ODA: fast-moving, vehicle-mounted, heavy-weapons QRF/recon unit used on an ad hoc basis in the U.S. Army Special Forces

MOPP: Mission-Oriented Protective Posture

MOS: Military Occupational Specialty

MP: Military Police

MSG: Master Sergeant

NASA: National Aeronautics and Space Administration

NATO: North Atlantic Treaty Organization

NBC: Nuclear, Biological, Chemical; also National Broadcasting Company

NCO: Noncommissioned Officer

NGO: Non-Government Organization

NRO: National Reconnaissance Office

NVGs: Night Vision Goggles

OCS: Officer Candidate School

ODA: Operational Detachment Alpha

ODB: Operational Detachment Bravo

OEF/OIF: Operation ENDURING FREEDOM/Operation IRAQI FREEDOM

OH-58 Little Bird: a two-pilot helicopter, used in two variations: a transport/utility model (MH-6) and an attack model (AH-6)

OP: Observation Post

Operation DESERT SHIELD: the initial stage of liberating Kuwait from the control of Iraqi invaders, begun in August 1990 by President George H. W. Bush

Operation DESERT STORM: the offensive action to liberate Kuwait from the control of Iraqi invaders, begun in January 1991

Operation JOINT ENDEAVOR: U.S. peacekeeping effort in the former Yugoslavia, deployed in 1995

Operation JOINT FORGE: a peacekeeping force in Bosnia-Herzegovina that followed the NATO-led Stabilization Force in 1998

Operation JUST CAUSE: U.S.-led action in Panama, which ultimately ousted Manuel Noriega from power

Operation UPHOLD DEMOCRACY: multinational military operation in Haiti in the early 1990s that restored a democratically elected presidency

Operator: short for Special Operator; a slang term to describe SOF personnel

OPS: Operations

OPSEC: Operational Security

Out of hide: taken from existing resources

Overwatch: a system that detects and precisely locates active enemy firings (snipers, direct fire weapons, mortars) in real-time to support ground forces in complex urban terrain

PAO: Public Affairs Officer

Patriot: missile

Pesh: short for Peshmerga

Peshmerga: indigenous group of Kurdish minorities

Pinkies: British term for Land Rovers

PLDC: Primary Leadership Development Course

PMCS: Preventative Maintenance Checks and Services

POW: Prisoner of War

PPSH-41: a Russian submachine gun

PSAB: Prince Sultan Air Base

PSG: Personal Security Guard

PSYOPS: Psychological Operations

PUK: Patriotic Union of Kurdistan

Q-Beam: a laser beam

QRF: Quick Reaction Force

R/C: remote control

Raid: a lightning-fast assault

RB-15: (Zodiac) rubber boat

Recon: reconnaissance

Republican Guard: the elite Iraqi ground forces, tasked originally with regime protection

RH-53: a Sikorsky helicopter

Road arms: suspension components used on BFVs and M1A1 Abrams tanks

Roland: missile system

RPG: rocket-propelled grenade

RPK: light machine gun

RR: Recoilless Rifle

S-2: battalion or brigade intelligence staff officer

S3: battalion or brigade operations staff officer

SA-7: AAA missile

SALUTE: Size, Activity, Location, Unit/Uniform, Time, Equipment

SAM: Surface-to-Air Missile

SAS: Special Air Service

SATCOM: SATellite COMmunications

SAW: Squad Automatic Weapon

Screaming Eagles: moniker of the 101st Airborne Division (AASLT)

SCUD: a long-range, surface-to-surface missile

SCUDNET: system of SCUD missile emplacements

SEAL: (Sea, Air, Land) elite Navy soldier

SF: Special Forces

SFC: Sergeant First Class

SFG: Special Forces Group

SFOD-D: Special Forces Operational Detachment-Delta

SGM: Sergeant Major

Shi'ite: a member of the branch of Islam that regards Ali and his descendants as the legitimate successors to Muhammad and rejects the first three caliphs

SIGINT: Signals Intelligence

SMU: Special Missions Unit

SOAR: Special Operations Aviation Regiment

SOCOM: Special Operations Command

SOF: Special Operations Forces

SOG: Special Operations Group

SOP: Standard Operating Procedure

Sortie: a mission flown by a fighter or bomber

SOSB: Special Operations Support Battalion

SOTF: Special Operations Task Force

SPC: Specialist

Special Operations: operations conducted by specially organized, trained, and equipped military and paramilitary forces to achieve military, political, economic, or informational objectives by unconventional military means in hostile, denied, or politically sensitive areas; also called SO

Special Operator: slang for SOF personnel

Spectre: moniker of the AC-130 gunship

SPF: Security Protection Force

Spider hole: a hole in the earth

SPT: Support

SS-30: rocket

SSG: Staff Sergeant

SSM: Surface-to-Surface Missile

SSS: the Iraqi Special Security Service (also called SSO—Special Security Organization, or the Presidential Affairs Department); or Al Amn al-Khas

Supay: the Kurdish word for "unit"; a Kurdish Supay has from a couple hundred to a couple thousand men

SUV: Sport Utility Vehicle

TAC-P: Tactical Air Control Party

TAI: Targeted Area of Interdiction

Talon: moniker of the MC-130 transport plane

Task Force 7: code name for the British task force in Iraq

Task Force 20: code name for the first U.S. task force that hunted Saddam and other high-value targets

Task Force 121: an elite Special Forces group of Army Delta Force members, Navy SEALs, CIA paramilitary operatives, and other personnel; captured Saddam Hussein

Task Force DAGGER: the code name for CJSOTF-W; this code name was resurrected from the war in Afghanistan, where it was last used

Task Force VIKING: the code name for CJSOTF-N

Team Leader: the soldier in charge of an ODA, often a CPT, sometimes an MSG

Team Sergeant: the highest-ranking NCO on an ODA

TF: Task Force

TF 1AD: Task Force First Armored Division

TF SPT: Task Force Support

TIA: Target Interdiction Area

TIP: Target Interdiction Point

TNT: trinitrotoluene, a yellow crystalline compound used mainly as a high explosive

TOC: Tactical Operations Center

Tornado: all-weather, day and night tactical reconnaissance British plane

TOW: Tube launched, Optically tracked, Wire guided

U.S. SOCOM: United States Special Operations Command

UAE: United Arab Emirates

UN: United Nations

USAF: United States Air Force

USASOC: United States Army Special Operations Command

USMC: United States Marine Corps

USO: United Service Organizations

UW: Unconventional Warfare

Vic: vicinity

VMI: Virginia Military Institute

Wadi: a dry riverbed, Arabic

WIA: Wounded in Action

WMD: Weapons of Mass Destruction

Wolverine 1 and Wolverine 2: the two sites given as Saddam's possible hiding places

XO: Executive Officer

Z: Zulu time (Greenwich Mean Time)

ZSU: a Soviet-bloc anti-aircraft gun, also called "Zeus" (slang term)